THE MAKING OF QUEEN MARY,
UNIVERSITY OF LONDON

The Making of Queen Mary, University of London

Ruth Valentine

Queen Mary
University of London

Published by Queen Mary, University of London
Mile End Road London E1 4NS
www.qmul.ac.uk

Editor: Leigh Money

Copy editing and indexing: Wanda Moore

Typesetting: Bracketpress

Printed and bound by MWL Print Group Ltd

ISBN 978-0-9567899-7-6

First Edition

A note on the author
Ruth Valentine is a writer and a consultant to
not-for-profit organisations. Her publications include
*Hope Costs Nothing: the lives of undocumented migrants
in the UK* (Migrants Resource Centre, 2010); *Asylum,
Hospital, Haven: a history of Horton Hospital* (Riverside
Mental Health Services, 1996) and six volumes of poetry,
the latest *On the Saltmarsh* (Smokestack, 2012).
She lives in Tottenham, North London.

Cover images: (Clockwise from top left) detail of the
Blizard Building, Whitechapel; detail of stained glass
window showing William Harvey, William Harvey Heart
Centre; detail of the tapestry in ArtsTwo; 1930s mural in
the People's Palace.

Foreword

This book is published in the 127th year of the College that is now Queen Mary, University of London. It tells the story of the College's past 27 years, which have seen it grow not only in size and breadth of academic endeavour, but also in stature. The institution which I am privileged to lead in 2012 is confident, innovative and outward-looking.

At the time of writing this book, the environment for English higher education is the most challenging that we have witnessed for a generation. During such a period, it is helpful to remind ourselves of the characteristics and attributes that really define Queen Mary as an institution, so that these can help guide us as we navigate through difficult times.

A natural starting point to achieving this definition is our long and rich history, the latter part of which is so well covered in this publication. The origins of Queen Mary go back 127 years to the founding of the People's Palace, with its remit to provide entertainment and education to the population of the East End of London. Meanwhile, Westfield College had been established elsewhere in the capital, devoted to the provision of higher education to women. Queen Mary and Westfield merged in 1989; a few years later they were joined by the combined medical schools of the London Hospital in Whitechapel and St Bartholomew's Hospital in the City of London.

The thread running through all these antecedent institutions was service to their local communities in the City and East End of London, and community engagement remains an integral part of Queen Mary in the 21st Century. Indeed we continue to lead the sector in this area, a fact exemplified by the recent launch of the Centre for Public Engagement, which will support our staff and students and their work with external partners – businesses, charities, community organisations, government, and the wider public – ensuring that this work achieves a lasting social and economic impact.

Alongside these more obvious activities, one of the most important ways in which we contribute to our local communities is by being a university of the highest distinction, as judged by national and international standards. We can therefore take great pride in our academic achievements, which are encapsulated in our admission to the Russell Group set of leading UK universities in August 2012. This is the perhaps-unique combination that defines Queen Mary – a research-led university that bears comparison with the best in the world and an institution that remains totally committed to its local community.

Whether the environment is benign or challenging, we must continually remind ourselves of our essential character and of our central commitment to students – not only to provide essential skills, to improve employability and earning power, but critically to ensure that they are equipped and motivated to make a greater contribution to UK society or the societies to which they return.

This has been the enduring mission for QM and it will continue to be so, and this clarity of purpose equips us to face a future that will no doubt include presently unforeseen challenges but also major successes. Without complacency but with quiet confidence, I expect to see a continuing rise in the stature, both national and international, of Queen Mary, University of London.

Professor Simon Gaskell, Principal
September 2012

Preface

Queen Mary, University of London (QM) is today one of the largest self-governing colleges of the federal University, and a member of the elite Russell Group of 24 research-led academic institutions. The organisation as we know it was created by the sequential merging of four institutions: Queen Mary College; Westfield College, one of the first women's colleges in the country; St Bartholomew's Hospital Medical College and The London Hospital Medical College. The pre-history of each of these has been told elsewhere.[1] The present volume takes up the story in 1985, shortly before Queen Mary College's merger with Westfield, and brings it up-to-date to 2012. Because the College has had different names over this period, from Queen Mary College to Queen Mary and Westfield College to Queen Mary, University of London, we have chosen to abbreviate it as QM throughout.

Interspersed with the story of the successive mergers and the development of the College as a whole are 'In focus' chapters, which look at examples of particular success and innovation. These include academic subjects as diverse as cancer research and linguistics. There is also an account of the College's infrastructure, including its dramatic new buildings, commissioned from world-class architects; and of QM's local and international connections.

On the basis of the 2008 Research Assessment Exercise (RAE) rating of UK university research, the *Times Higher Education Supplement* scored QM 13th out of all the universities in the UK; the *Guardian* placed it 11th. Nine departments, including Geography, Linguistics, English Language and Literature, Epidemiology and Dentistry, were among the top five in their subject in the country. The College has strong international connections, including a ground-breaking partnership with Beijing University of Posts and Telecommunications (BUPT), with shared teaching and graduation from both institutions. It also has historic links with east London, where it is located; and these have developed to include locally-based research, and intensive work in nearby schools, to enable and encourage students to enter higher education.

The past 27 years have been turbulent for UK universities, with dramatic changes in the political climate in which they function, the expectations of policy-makers, students and society at large, and the ways in which research and teaching are assessed and funded. There never was an ivory tower on the Mile End Road, where QM's main campus is based; but even so, the College has worked hard to increase both access and outreach. This volume chronicles the decisions, influences, alarms and inspirations that have made QM the successful, inclusive institution it now is; and considers the new challenges that are already in view or can be surmised, and how the College prepares itself to address them.

1. Godwin, G. *Queen Mary College: An Adventure in Education* (London: Queen Mary College and The Acorn Press, 1939); Moss, GP and Saville, MV. *From Palace to College: An Illustrated Account of Queen Mary College* (London: Queen Mary, 1985); Sondheimer, J. *Castle Adamant in Hampstead: A History of Westfield College, 1882–1982* (London: Westfield College, 1983); Waddington, K. *Medical Education at St Bartholomew's Hospital, 1123–1995* (London: The Boydell Press, 2003); Clark-Kennedy, AE. *London Pride: The Story of a Voluntary Hospital* (London: Hutchinson Benham, 1979); Fish, SF. *The Dental School of The London Hospital Medical College, 1911–1991* (London: The London Hospital Dental Club and London Hospital Medical College, 1991).

Acknowledgments

This history was begun by Gina Potts, whose extensive interviews with staff past and present enliven particularly the early chapters; some parts of her draft text are incorporated into this version. Lorraine Screene, archivist at QM, has been endlessly helpful, unearthing committee minutes, internal bulletins and ancient photos; the archivists at Barts and The London, respectively Katie Ormerod and Jonathan Evans, have generously contributed to the picture research. Dr Julie Leeming and her colleagues in Planning have produced complex statistics at the drop of a hat. Professors Morag Shiach, Graham Zellick, Brian Colvin, John Charap and Jim Bolton, and Sally Webster provided valuable comments on the book in draft. Gabriella Melis helped analyse the mass of historical material.

Editor Leigh Money has managed this long and complex project with insight and patience, and Professor Philip Ogden, formerly Senior Vice-Principal, has seen it through its development.

QM offers its heartfelt thanks to the many academics and students, past and present, who gave their time and ideas, including the clarification of complex points of their discipline for a non-academic writer.

Contents

Timeline of key dates

1123   St Bartholomew's Hospital founded

1740   The London Hospital founded

1785   The London Hospital Medical College opens

1843   St Bartholomew's Hospital Medical College established

1882   Westfield College founded

1885   Decision to create a People's Palace in the East End. The Drapers' Company provides £20,000 to found the Technical Schools

1887   People's Palace Technical Schools are founded

1896   People's Palace Technical Schools become East London Technical College

1900   St Bartholomew's Hospital Medical College and The London Hospital Medical College become constituent colleges of the University of London

1902   Westfield College admitted as a temporary school of the University of London, made permanent in 1919

1905   East London Technical College becomes East London College

1907   East London College admitted as a school of the University of London

1911   The Dental School at The London Hospital opens

1934   East London College incorporated as Queen Mary College

1939– Wartime evacuations:
1945   Queen Mary College to King's College, Cambridge

      Westfield College to St Peter's Hall, Oxford

      St Bartholomew's pre-clinical students to Queen's College, Cambridge

      The London's pre-clinical students to St Catherine's College, Cambridge

1964   Male students admitted to Westfield College

1968   Association between St Bartholomew's Hospital Medical College and The London Hospital Medical College proposed

1972   The Murray Report on the governance of the University of London published

1984 The Faculty of Science at Westfield College transfers to Queen Mary College

1985 The Jarratt Committee publishes its report on the need for universities to provide evidence of efficiency and accountability for public funds

1988 The Westfield Trust is established to conserve and protect the original objects of the College's Charter, including its religious principles and the education of women.

1989 Merger of Queen Mary College and Westfield College

1990 250th anniversary of The London Hospital, now renamed The Royal London Hospital

1992 Sir Bernard Tomlinson's Report of the Inquiry into the London Health Service published

1992 Merger of Barts and The Royal London Hospitals and their medical and dental schools, which become Barts and The London School of Medicine and Dentistry

1995 Merger of Barts and The London School of Medicine and Dentistry with Queen Mary and Westfield College

2000 The College adopts the working name Queen Mary, University of London, retaining its legal title as Queen Mary and Westfield College

2004 Westfield Student Village (phase 1) opens on the Mile End Campus

2005 The Blizard Building, home to Barts and The London's Blizard Institute of Cell and Molecular Science opens in Whitechapel

2006 The Octagon, the original library of the People's Palace, reopens after refurbishment

2007 The Women@Queen Mary exhibition is staged in the Octagon, marking 125 years of Westfield College and 120 years of Queen Mary College

2008 Queen Mary, University of London is ranked 13th out of 132 UK higher education institutions by the *Times Higher Education Supplement*, following the 2008 RAE

2012 Queen Mary, University of London joins the Russell Group of leading UK universities

Part 1:
The time of mergers

The story so far

The People's Palace, 1891, as depicted by E R Robson, architect.
© Tower Hamlets Local History Library

In 2012, Queen Mary, University of London, with its 16,900 students and 3,800 staff, is a modern, multidisciplinary college of the University of London. In 1985, there was only the small, highly focused establishment known as Queen Mary College, and the three other institutions that were yet to join it: Westfield College, The London Hospital Medical College and St Bartholomew's Hospital Medical College.

Visualise Queen Mary College in 1985. The familiar clock tower, and behind it the main building with its classical portico. To the left, the 1930s People's Palace, with its Eric Gill bas-relief panels of the Muses, depicting Drama, Music and so on, then the long facade of the Engineering Building, followed by the Mathematics Building. To the right, the Physics Department and the small, domed Chaplaincy of St Benet; then commercial buildings, and behind them various open spaces: the Nuevo Beth Chaim Cemetery for Sephardic Jews, with its flat tombstones; grassland; a busy industrial site; the Regent's Canal.

Imagine the students coming out: most of them male, a large proportion of them white, in groups of ones and twos. An ordinary sight for a university of the time, especially one focused on science and engineering, where women were still in the minority.

Queen Mary, University of London, 2012. The 1960s Mathematical Sciences' Building has a dazzling new ground-floor facade. But the most startling change is to the east, between the Queens' Building and the Regent's Canal. With the exception of the Jewish burial ground, the whole site now belongs to the College: a new Library,

elegant teaching and research buildings, cafés, and campus shops; in addition to low-rise student residences of almost 2,000 rooms, with views of the canal and Mile End Park.

Then there are the students. Large numbers of them, emerging from lectures and independent study, from the Students' Union, the cafés and the Library. No longer predominantly male, nor white, nor middle class: this is a student body truly representative of London, the most diverse city in the world, and the East End, its traditional landing-stage. There are young people of African, Afro-Caribbean, Asian, European, South Asian and Chinese origin, and no way – or need at this moment – to know which of them are second- or indeed fifth-generation British, and which have come here to study from overseas.

Nor in 2012 is Mile End the only place where we find QM students. The College has extended westward to Whitechapel, and beyond the East End as far as Charterhouse Square, just north of the ancient walls of the City of London, and Lincoln's Inn Fields. Commercial Law students walk past the Royal Courts of Justice and barristers' chambers; medical students cross from the tranquillity of Charterhouse Square to St Bartholomew's Hospital, the oldest in London. In Whitechapel, researchers work in new purpose-built labs, in the dramatic Alsop-designed Blizard Building; dental students see patients in a walk-in clinic, a hundred yards from the great domed East London Mosque. And any of these students may meet in the evening, back at Mile End, in the Student Village overlooking the narrow-boats and ducks of the Regent's Canal.

Queen Mary, University of London is one of the largest colleges of the federal University of London. It was formed by two mergers: that of Queen Mary College with Westfield College in 1989, and the resulting institution with the previously merged St Bartholomew's Hospital and The London Hospital Medical Colleges in 1995.

The main campus at Mile End was historically the home of Queen Mary College (QMC), and began life as the People's Palace, a philanthropic venture that provided the people of east London with a centre for education, as well as cultural and social activities. A little more detail about each of the four institutions that together make up QM follows.

St Bartholomew's Hospital Medical College
St Bartholomew's Hospital was founded in 1123, by Rahere, jester to King Henry I. Barts, as the Hospital is commonly known, is still on the same site in Smithfield, in the City of London. It has a fascinating history, and its archives illustrate the many developments made in the long history of medicine.

Barts had its first purpose-built lecture theatre constructed in 1791; in 1822 its Governors approved the provision of medical education. Training to date had been informal, based on observation, with little practical engagement. During the 1820s and 1830s teaching provision at Barts expanded. A residential college was opened, and St Bartholomew's Hospital Medical College was formally inaugurated in 1843.

In 1900, Barts became a college of the University of London, in the Faculty of Medicine. Nursing also has a long history at Barts; the Hospital's School of Nursing and Midwifery is now based at City University.

The London Hospital Medical College
The London Hospital in Whitechapel was founded in 1740; until 1748 it was known as The London Infirmary. The Medical College was founded in 1785 by William Blizard (now commemorated in the stunning Blizard Building) and James Maddocks. It was England's first medical school, and offered a pioneering model of medical education, teaching theory as well as clinical skills. The teaching premises were expanded with the new Garrod Building in Turner Street. This was completed in 1898 and is still in use today. Like Barts, in 1900 The London Hospital Medical College became a constituent college of the University of London in the Faculty of Medicine.

Between the two World Wars, medical students at The London studied biology, chemistry and physics for the first MB (the first part of the Bachelor of Medicine) at QM, before going on to sit their second MB at The London.

The Dental School at The London opened in 1911. It grew significantly in the early 1960s, to accommodate expanding student numbers. Read more about the history of the current Institute of Dentistry in chapter 7.

The association between St Bartholomew's Hospital Medical College and The London Hospital Medical College developed as a result of the Royal Commission on Medical Education in 1968: new links were established with Queen Mary College at the same time. The story of the mergers, first between the two medical colleges and then with QM, is told in chapter 6.

Low-relief panels on the outside of the People's Palace by Eric Gill.
They depict Drama, Music, Fellowship, Dance, Sport and Recreation

The London Hospital
Medical College, *c*.1950.
© Royal London Hospital Archives

The front of The Royal London
Hospital in 2011.

5

Westfield College.

Westfield College staff and students, 1904. ©Queen Mary, University of London Archives

Westfield College

Westfield College was founded in 1882 as a residential college, one of a small number of nineteenth-century higher education institutions for women. Its founders shared a vision of 'Higher Christian Education for Women.' They modelled their establishment on the existing women's colleges at Oxford and Cambridge. The chosen site was in Hampstead, and Ann Dudin Brown, one of the founders, provided £10,000 in set-up costs.

From its inception in 1882, the College was officially an examining body, and in 1898 was recognised by the University of London as a teaching body as well. In 1902, it was given temporary admission to the University as a school in the Faculty of Arts. In 1905, a science department was opened, concentrating on botany.

In 1919, the trust deed of the College was changed, to delete the requirement that all members of the College Council should belong to the Church of England. With this alteration, the University of London approved Westfield College as a full member of the University, and agreed to an annual grant. Four members of staff were given the title of University Reader, and in 1925 Caroline Skeel became University Professor of History. (The archive room in the QM Library and a lecture theatre are named after her). By 1929, the College had the full privileges of a school of the University of London, and in 1932 it was granted its Royal Charter.

In 1963, the College agreed to proposals "that men students shall be admitted to the College", which had been debated over a number of years, and the Charter was amended to allow this in 1964. The first intake of over a hundred male students was in 1965. The merger of Westfield and QM is recounted in chapter 3.

Queen Mary College

The East London Technical College, (formerly the People's Palace technical schools), was opened by Queen Victoria at a grand ceremony in 1887, amid much local celebration.

The People's Palace was a philanthropic project initiated by the Beaumont Trust, to provide east Londoners with both education and social activities. The plan reflected a growing awareness of the social and economic conditions of east London, described in 1882 by Walter Besant in his novel *All Sorts and Conditions of Men: An Impossible Story*. Besant imagined a "palace of delights" in the East End, bringing culture and practical education to its "teeming hordes".

The People's Palace was "a place where people of all classes and conditions [could] congregate" and "its Library, its Music, its Pictures, its Lectures, its Literature Classes, and its Technical Schools [would] offer to all the means of thought and knowledge which feed aspiration"[2]. The library was located in the Octagon (still standing), and was heavily used by the local community.

In 1896, the People's Palace technical schools became the East London Technical College, and evening classes prepared students for the University of London and Civil Service entrance exams. From its earliest days, the College had particular strengths in science and engineering. It also taught domestic science, millinery and dressmaking.

In 1902, the College began to award University of London undergraduate degrees, and in 1905 it changed its name to East London College. The College's new aim was to promote higher education in east London, moving away from the locally-focused vocational training of the past. In 1907, East London College formally became a school of the University of London, in the Faculties of Arts, Science and Engineering. Two years later, the College accepted students from The London Hospital Medical College preparing for their first MB.

2. Besant, W. (1882) *All Sorts and Conditions of Men: An Impossible Story*. London, Chatto & Windus.

The leisure activities of the People's Palace continued all through these years, until the 1950s. The Queen's Hall of the People's Palace burnt down in 1931, and the Palace agreed to move from its base, in what is now the Queens' Building, to a new building next door. The old People's Palace rooms were taken over by the College. In 1934, at a ceremony attended by Queen Mary, the College was renamed Queen Mary College. Today the 1930s People's Palace building (acquired by the College in 1953) houses the Skeel Lecture Theatre and the Great Hall, used for concerts and College ceremonies, including – very importantly – graduation.

The first Aeronautical Engineering department in the UK was established at QM as far back as 1907. Given its established strengths in science and engineering, QM kept up with advances in technology, and computer science was taught at Mile End from 1968.

The Drapers' Company and the College
Throughout its existence, QM has been supported by the Drapers' Company. When the Beaumont Trust was planning the People's Palace in 1884, the Drapers' Company agreed to sell the Bancroft's Hospital site in Mile End for its use. The Hospital site had previously been used for a school and almshouse. On 20 May 1885, the Drapers' Court of Assistants granted £20,000 specifically for 'the provision of the technical schools of the People's Palace.'

The Drapers' Company of the City of London was originally a medieval guild for the drapery trade. Early guilds or companies acted as mutual protection societies for their members. The Drapers' Company was probably founded in 1361, and was granted its first Royal Charter in 1364; though an informal association existed as early as 1180. Links with the cloth industry have recently been re-established, with exhibitions, postgraduate and teaching awards and sponsorship, in textile design, conservation and technology. The Drapers' Company today has a range of responsibilities, including the administration of charitable trusts and almshouses. A recent development is the co-sponsorship with QM of the Drapers' Academy

secondary school in Havering, east London: chapter 19 tells this story.

Historically, a member of the Drapers' Company acted as Chair of the QM College Council. Recent members of the College who became members of the Company include Sir Christopher France (Chair of Council, 1995–2003), Dr Colette Bowe (Chair of Council 2003–2009, Professor Graham Zellick (Principal, 1990–1998), Professor Sir Adrian Smith (Principal, 1998–2008), and Professor Philip Ogden (Senior Vice-Principal, 2005–2011). Professor Zellick was Master of the Company in 2009–10.

The Company continues to fund College prizes, lectures and awards. The annual Drapers' Prizes for Developments in Learning and Teaching were established to recognise excellence in these fields. The Drapers' Skills Award is given to students who gain practical skills and experience from an additional module, designed to prepare them for the transition to work.

The College has also introduced an annual Drapers' Lecture on Learning and Teaching, and this has brought in distinguished speakers, including Baroness Estelle Morris, former Secretary of State for Education. The Drapers' Chair of Law was named in recognition of the support the Company has given to the Faculty of Laws.

St Bartholomew's Hospital Henry VIII Gate, 1899.
© St Bartholomew's Hospital Archives

1985

An aerial view of the Mile End campus in 1984.

UK universities in 1985

In the academic year 1984–85, there were 47 universities in the UK, with 290,600 full-time undergraduates, as well as around 5,500 part-time students and 77,490 postgraduates. 29,626 full-time academic staff were paid out of general university funds. The average staff:student ratio was around 1:10, although this varied widely between subjects.

Six years into the radical policies of the Thatcher government, the universities were firmly in its sights. An administration that believed above all in cutting public expenditure was not going to ignore the £1,370.7 million it provided in grant funding. Keith Joseph, Secretary of State for Education, was committed to 'efficiency, economy and standards', and would impose methods for ensuring all three, always within the context of a cut in funding.

By 1985, universities had already felt the impact of these new policies. The University Grants Committee (UGC) had implemented cuts in recurrent grants of as much as 18 per cent for the worst-hit institutions, and reduced the total number of student places (although this was contrary to explicit Government policy). At the same time, the Government had removed all subsidy for overseas students, threatening another source of income. A further UGC decision was to separate out core funding and research funding within the grant, with the aim of 'selectivity': focusing funding on what was seen as the highest quality research. 1985 was the year of the first Research Selectivity Exercise (later the Research Assessment Exercise, or RAE, now known as the Research Excellence Framework or REF), grading research in each university as a basis for funding decisions, and focusing on favoured subjects: engineering, maths, computer science, business studies, physical sciences, and some parts of both biology and medicine.

In 1984, hoping to pre-empt the Government's own scrutiny, the Committee of Vice-Chancellors and Principals (CVCP) set up the Jarratt Committee to examine the efficiency of university governance and management. The Committee recommended a business management model for universities. In May 1985 the Government responded with a Green Paper, widely criticised within the sector, endorsing the Jarratt principles, and characterised by a later writer as:

> notable for its crude espousal of economic instrumentalism, its business-oriented rhetoric, and its refusal to acknowledge the wider cultural role of universities and the special character of academic inquiry. Jarratt ... added to the demoralisation of academic staff following the 1981 cuts.[3]

3. Anderson, R, *British Universities Past and Present* (London: Hambledon, Continuum, 2006).

11

Queen Mary College in 1985
This is the make-up of the College in its centenary year, 1985.

Departmental structure

Faculty	Department
Arts	Classics English French German History Russian Spanish
Social Studies	Social Studies Economics Politics Geography & Earth Science
Laws	Laws Centre for Commercial Law Studies
Science	Chemistry Computer Science Physics Mathematics Biological Sciences
Engineering	Civil Engineering Electrical Engineering Aeronautical Engineering Materials Mechanical Engineering Nuclear Engineering

Students by gender

Students	Men	Women
Undergraduates	2,090	1,089
Postgraduates	444	178
Total	2,534	1,267

Students by domicile

Domicile	%	Numbers (non-EU)
United Kingdom	74.8	
European Union	3.2	
Non-EU *of whom:* Hong Kong USA Malaysia Cyprus Iran	22.0	 222 116 65 55 43

Subjects studied

Faculty	Undergraduates	Postgraduates	Total
Arts	415	71	486
Social Studies	443	120	526
Laws	239	322	359
Science	1,336	213	1,549
Engineering	622	136	758
Associates*	124	—	124
Total	3,179	622	3,801

Staffing

Staff	Posts
Academic	321.5
Academic-related	217.3
Technical	189.3
Clerical & related	156.6
Manual & auxiliary	123.3
Maintenance	43
Other	2
Total	1,053

*Associate students are overseas students who spend time at Queen Mary as part of their degree.

What can we make of all this? Firstly, by today's standards, as well as those of the time, QM was small. In 1981, the average university had 6,390 full-time students; for the political reasons already given, numbers declined slightly over the next few years. In 2010–11, QM had 11,106 undergraduate students and 3,713 postgraduates in the UK, as well as 160 undergraduates and 1,925 postgraduates overseas (of which more later): a 445 per cent increase.

Secondly, there were twice as many male as female students, a high proportion even for that time, when the overall ratio was 60 per cent male: 40 per cent female. In 2010–11 at QM it was 48 per cent male: 52 per cent female. And, in spite of the removal of Government subsidy, the College already attracted a significant proportion of overseas students: a proportion that has hardly changed (25.2 per cent to 25 per cent) though they now come from almost double the number of countries: 122, compared to 67 in 1985.

We can delve further into what was going on. The first ever UGC Research Selectivity Assessment (RSA) rates two departments as outstanding, Laws and Pure Mathematics. Those departments are justifiably proud and delighted. Another seven are above average: Chemistry, Physics, Mathematics (presumably the remainder of the department), Computer Science, Materials, Economics and Russian. And the other sixteen? The 1985 Annual Report declines to tell us; but this result would have had a significant impact on the College's funding.

Then there is the College's teaching. It is interesting to compare the 1984–85 graduation results with the 2010–11 list.

Graduations

Class of first degree	1984–85	% of total	2010–11	% of total
First class honours	87	10	420	16
Upper second hons	246	28	1,192	46
Lower second hons	354	41	713	28
Third class hons/Pass	187	21	247	10
Total	874		2,572	

There is a marked shift upwards in grades. Whether this indicates an improvement in the quality of teaching, or in the overall capability of students, or a shift in assessment methods, is impossible to tell without detailed research. At the very least, it suggests that QM's aspirations for its undergraduates are now considerably higher.

There is a further area of concern: the College's finances. The academic year 1984–85 begins with a deficit of £578,900; and ends a further £100,000 in the red. "Some academics," as Patricia Bettis, the Principal's Secretary at the time, says diplomatically, "are not known for their administrative or managerial skills." If this situation has been acceptable in the past, the Jarratt report and the Green Paper make it clear that there will be changes.

So QM is small, but has aspirations. It also knows that its life rather depends on them. Change is imminent, whether the College wants it or not.

The final chapter of *From Palace to College*, the College history published in the same year (1985) begins: "From the uncertainty that pervaded the years 1967–1984 the foreseeable future offers no relief".[4] The authors have some reason for their pessimism. The University Grants Committee foresees a two per cent drop in funding in real terms for all universities. The 'new blood' scheme, funding new academic posts, and the IT funding stream are both ending, and both have been important to QM. None of this is entirely unexpected; but it will pose significant demands for the College in its centenary year.

4. Moss, GP, & Saville MV, op cit.

Centenary

The College is one hundred years old in 1985, and whatever the pressures, it's going to celebrate. For one thing, it has commissioned two of its staff to write a history of the institution, a lavishly illustrated account of visionary schemes, innovators and implementers, buildings erected and demolished. *From Palace to College* is a statement not only of the connections between events and decisions within and beyond the College, but of a contemporary approach to higher education, with all the challenges it was seen to face. It is, among other things, a quietly campaigning document.

A centenary is, of course, a good opportunity for campaigning, and the College takes full advantage. The Development Trust Centenary Appeal brochure is a glossy document, with the photos and signatures of Sir James Menter, Principal, and Sir Arthur Drew, Chair of the Governing Body, on its first page. The College, they state, needs to grow: "To support this major growth of the College it is essential to construct further academic buildings, to improve the College's cultural, social and sporting facilities and to provide for academic posts & scholarships."[5] Their initial target is £2 million. There is an aerial photograph of the Mile End Road site (see page 10), with the land to the east of existing buildings marked out as already acquired for development. There are also architects' plans and sketches to show how the new site will be used: a computer science and IT building; a home for the Centre for Commercial Law Studies; an expanded Students' Union; the new Library, for which the UGC has agreed funding; student residences, a sports centre, car park and so on. In addition, the Appeal hopes to fund multidisciplinary research and study centres in an impressive range of subjects: biomaterials; computer-aided design education; contemporary Spanish studies; east London studies; electronic materials; health and healthcare; IT; MRI spectroscopy; modern language learning, and the science and technology of measurement. The Drapers' Company, the College's perennial supporter, (see page 8) launches the Appeal fund with a donation of £75,000. By December 1985 the fund has reached £137,467.14.

5. *QMC 1885–1985, Development Trust centenary Appeal.* (1985) London, QM.

The past and the future are accounted for in this rather anxious centenary year; but the present is there for celebration. The papers of the governing body for 1985–86 include a report by Patricia Bettis, who along with her other duties has become Centenary Events Co-ordinator. We learn that two committees have been set up to plan the centenary: one for academic and one for social events. In November, staff and students perform a new rock musical, *The Palace of Delights*, commissioned by the College from its Director of Music (then and now), Alan Wilson. The musical is based on the nineteenth-century novel already mentioned, Walter Besant's *All Sorts and Conditions of Men*, about a young man and woman from privileged backgrounds who plan to set up a Palace of Delight, with entertainments and education, in the East End: the relevance to the eventual QM is evident. 175 invited guests attend the musical's gala performance.

The most formal occasion is the centenary Thanksgiving Service, held at St Michael's Cornhill (the Drapers' Company church) on 9 May 1986, and attended by the Princess Royal, in her capacity as Chancellor of the University of London. Other centenary celebrations include a research fair, showcasing the College's work to guests including George Walden, the Secretary of State for Higher Education (a canny move); a schools' open day attended by over a thousand sixth-formers, and a lecture by Patrick Moore on Halley's Comet (though the Comet itself, even seen through the 12-inch telescope on the Physics Department roof, was found disappointing). A table of the main centenary events is given below. The total cost of the celebrations was £40,986.

Centenary events[6]

Date	Event
28–30 Nov	*The Palace of Delights*, rock musical
14 Feb	Valentine's Day candlelit dinner and ball, with a 1920s theme
5–8 March	*The Matchgirls*, musical by Students' Union Entertainment Society
9–10 April	Research fair
29 April	Lecture by Patrick Moore on Halley's Comet
6 May	Schools' Open Day
9 May	Thanksgiving Service at St Michael's Cornhill
13 May	Lecture by Lord Denning, Master of the Rolls
16 May	Summer concert by QMC Music Society orchestra and choir
Throughout the year	Series of ten lectures on east London Departmental conferences and seminars

In the meantime, of course, the normal activities of the College continue. Dr Judith Chernaik, in the Department of English, has possibly the most visible achievement, having co-founded the Poems on the Underground series, funded by Greater London Arts, the British Council and several publishers. Thousand of rush-hour passengers read, amongst the ads and maps, William Carlos Williams' *This is Just to Say*:

I have eaten
the plums
that were in
the icebox

and which
you were probably
saving
for breakfast

Forgive me:
they were delicious,
so sweet
and so cold.[7]

In the same year, the Faculty of Laws celebrates its own 20th anniversary, with a joint colloquium with the Law Commission, on the subject of law reform. College astrophysicists lead an international consortium that designs and builds one of four instruments to be flown in the European Space Agency's Infrared Space Observatory (ISO). The Observatory, designed for the use of astronomers worldwide, would be launched in ten years' time. The Department of Geography and Earth Science has set up three new research centres, two of them – east London, and Health and Health Care – named in the Appeal (the third is Applied Earth Science). The Computer Centre has piloted the use of 12 workstations in undergraduate classes, and has acquired 40 more.

Departments are moving, even before the building work has started: Engineering shifts its nuclear reactor to 101 Marshgate Lane, Politics moves into the new site by the canal at 357 Mile End Road, Economics expands into the space that Politics has left.

This is QM in 1985: not large; beset by financial problems; with some outstanding work going on; playing to its traditional strengths in science and engineering, but with other departments also flourishing; and facing continued uncertainty because of the politics of the time. We already have hints of the major changes it will undertake over the next 25 years. Meantime other things are happening in the still separate worlds of Westfield College and the medical schools.

6. *QM 100: Queen Mary College Centenary programme of Events.* (1985) London, QM.
7. Williams, WC. *Selected Poems* (Twentieth Century Classics), (London: Penguin, 1990).

The merger with Westfield

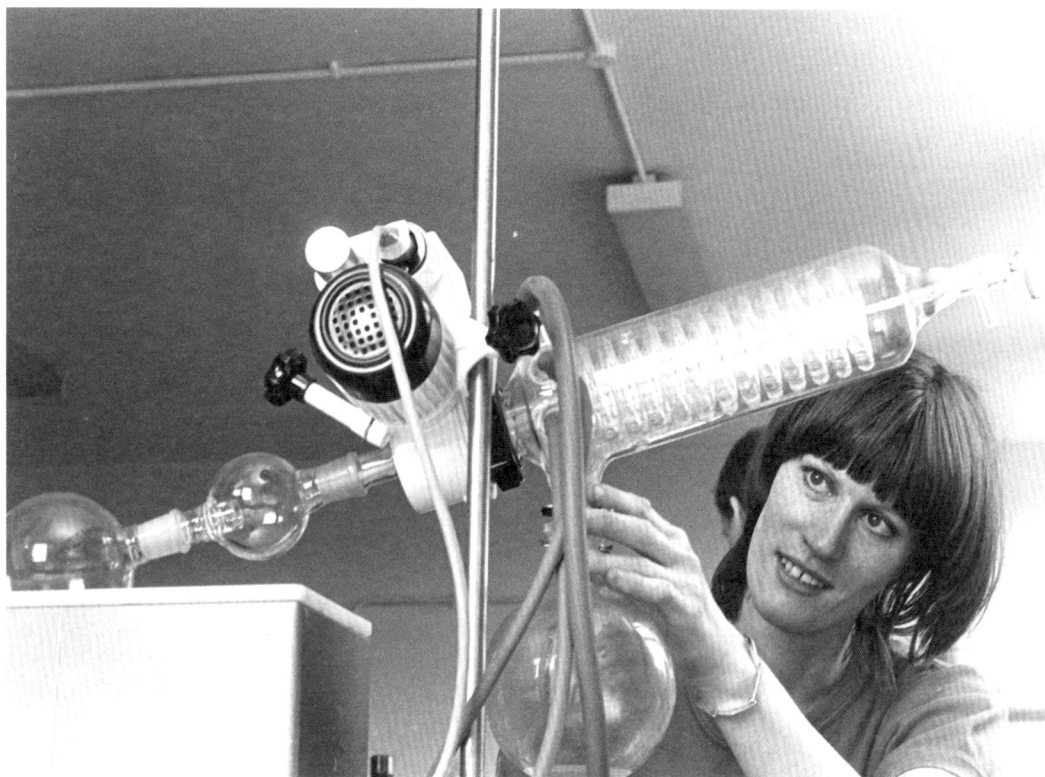

A Westfield student in the science lab, *c.*1970.
© Queen Mary, University of London Archives

The merger of Westfield College and Queen Mary College took place in two stages; though the first, the merger of the two science faculties, was certainly not planned as a prelude to the second, nor to the demise of Westfield as a separate institution. This chapter reflects on the internal and external pressures that led to the creation of a new college, officially named Queen Mary and Westfield.

Timeline

The Science transfer

For Westfield, uncertainty about the future began years before the merger with QM. In 1972 the Murray Committee, established by the University of London to consider its structure and governance, published its report. The Committee had serious concerns about the viability of the smaller colleges: could they attract and retain high-quality staff, offer sufficient choice to students, organise research and thus attract funding? Large, multi-faculty institutions were seen as the answer.

The former women's colleges were particularly vulnerable to this approach, and were named in the report. They were historically smaller than the others, and poorer. (Virginia Woolf in her polemical novel *A Room of One's Own* points out a similar difference at Cambridge between the wealthy and elegant men's colleges and the air of struggle in the women's). The Committee proposed both greater collaboration between colleges, and reorganisation.

From the late 1970s, therefore, Westfield began to strengthen its links with other colleges. Classics teaching was shared for the first time with Bedford College, not far away in Regent's Park. A full merger between the two – appropriate given their shared origins as institutions for the education of women – was discussed; but in fact both colleges were on constrained sites and in financial difficulties, and a merger would not have solved the problem. In the end, Bedford merged in 1985 with a third former women's college, Royal Holloway, situated outside London in Egham, Surrey.

This process of rationalisation began with the sciences. Physicists and chemists across the University of London agreed with the view that there should be no more than four or five sites for experimental science; Westfield was not one of those proposed. Dr Molly Scopes had just been elected Dean of the Faculty of Science, and the letter setting out these proposals arrived on the day of her first Senior College Committee meeting in this role, in July 1982. It was, inevitably, the main item on the agenda.

Westfield had taught botany since 1906, but its full Science faculty, adding physics, chemistry and zoology, had been in existence for only 11 years. Equipment was expensive, and securing adequate student numbers was difficult. Transferring to join another, larger faculty made sense.

It made sense, but it was hard for the College to accept. Molly Scopes, who oversaw the transfer, points out that the College "was fighting for its life". She adds that she was "quite unprepared for the ferocity of the storm that raged as the full impact of the situation sank in".[8] The Science faculty debated and agreed the need to move; but the College hoped at first to hold on at least to Botany and Biochemistry, plus Zoology. Eventually the scientists persuaded the College that this was unsustainable. Mathematics staff across the University of London drew up a plan to ensure that each remaining maths department had the full range of specialisms, and Westfield mathematicians went to various colleges around London. Computer Science transferred to King's. For the remaining scientific disciplines, QM was the obvious candidate, with its traditions in science and engineering, and (equally important) a new building with the space to house the new, merged faculty. Around 20 academic staff, a similar number of technical staff, and about 200 students moved over to Mile End, in a programme phased to minimise disruption to students. The first group of staff and first-year students transferred in September 1983, and the last third-year students from Westfield commuted from the Halls of Residence to QM in 1984–85. Professor Richard Clymo, who had negotiated with Professor Bevan at QM to enable the Science merger, recalled that "Westfield staff were welcomed by those at QMC… the overwhelming effect was astonishingly constructive."[9]

The Westfield College Council formally disbanded its Science Faculty on 3 July 1984. On her last day as Dean, Molly Scopes:

… went systematically around the Science block into every room, picking up rubbish, righting overturned chairs, closing windows, turning off

the dripping taps and locking the doors behind me; silence fell slowly on the whole building… The Westfield Science Faculty had ceased to be.[10]

Westfield in 1985

The previous chapter looked at the make-up of QM in 1984–85. Westfield College in the same year was a very different place. The last Science students were living in hall at Westfield but commuting to Mile End for study. The Science faculty staff had all transferred to Queen Mary College.

Departmental structure

Faculty	Department
Arts	Classics Drama English French German History & History of Art Spanish

Subjects studied

Faculty	Undergraduates	Postgraduates	Total
Arts	580	41	621
Science	225	9	234
Total	**805**	**50**	**855**

By the following year, total student numbers at Westfield were down to 644, with just 28 science undergraduates and two science postgraduates left. In the annual report, the Principal said he was "still hoping that Westfield can continue to exist in its own right, though conversations with the University make it clear that there is little chance for a small arts-only College." In 1986–87 the total number of students was 561.

8. Scopes, PM. Written contribution to this history. 2008.
9. Clymo, R. Written contribution to this history. 2008.
10. Scopes, PM. op cit.

Students by gender

Students	Men	Women
Undergraduates	315	490
Postgraduates	21	29
Total	**336**	**519**

Twenty years after its conversion to co-education, Westfield again had a majority of women: 60 per cent, compared to 33 per cent at QM. Staffing figures were strikingly low; compare the figures below to the total of 1,053 staff at Mile End.

Staffing

Staff	Posts
Academic	68
Library	7
Computer unit	7
Wardens	18
Administration	16
Total	**116**

Westfield's annual reports give a vivid sense of the intimacy of the College, every new graduate listed by name, with the subject and class of their degree.

Graduations

Class of first degree	Westfield		QM		QM 2010–11	
	1984 –85	% of total	1984 –85	% of total	2010 –11	% of total
First class honours	16	5	87	10	420	16
Upper second hons	106	35	246	28	1,192	46
Lower second hons	148	48	354	41	713	28
Third class hons/Pass	38	12	187	21	247	10
Total	**308**		**874**		**2,572**	

The total of first class and upper second degrees in 1985 was around 40 per cent for both Westfield and QM, going up to 55 per cent in 2011. Given that degrees were awarded by the University, not the constituent colleges, we can assume that academic standards in the two Colleges, within their own specialisms, were broadly the same. The 1985 UGC comparative research assessment rated Westfield's Spanish and History of Art departments as outstanding. Only six institutions in the country (including QM) had two such ratings: 23 had more than two and 20 had fewer. Although in numerical terms this placed QM half-way down the table of achievement, the then Principal proudly, and rightly, pointed out that most of the other institutions were much larger than single-faculty Westfield.

The full merger

The loss of the Science faculty, and so of student numbers, contributed considerably to Westfield's financial problems. The College set about trying to recruit more arts students, making links with the nearby Central School of Speech and Drama; but the proposed collaboration was rejected by the University. An approach was also made to King's, with a view to co-operating in arts and computing. The response from King's was to propose a complete merger.

By 1985–86, student numbers at Westfield had not risen, and the concept of a merger had to be taken seriously. The institution's finances were in a serious state:

> Whilst our carefully-husbanded resources have enabled the College to avoid deficit financing up to the end of the 1987–88 session, it is evident that our reserves will be totally expended during the course of the coming session.[11]

Talks began with Imperial College, University College, King's, QM, and (perhaps bizarrely) the Royal Veterinary College. Distances across London, and the match or mismatch of disciplines, all played their part in this exhausting series of negotiations. Professor John Chalker, at the time Vice-Principal of Westfield, recalls that each venture "developed its own trajectory of hope, optimism, obstacles, frustration and failure."

11. Annual Report 1987–88 (London: Westfield College, 1988).

Meanwhile, QM had its own financial difficulties, and was itself responding to the Jarratt report on efficiency in British universities (see chapter 2). The Classics (later Mediterranean Studies) department was lost; the Civil Engineering department from King's transferred over to QM. Other radical changes were planned. A merger with Goldsmiths College, in south-east London, was explored, but not carried through. Given the colleges' existing links, joining with Westfield had many attractions, the potential of which was clearly identified by Professor Trevor Smith (now Lord Smith of Clifton), Senior Vice Principal of Queen Mary at the time.

The choice
For Westfield the choice eventually came down to King's or QM. There were benefits to both: King's proposed to retain part of the Hampstead site as a student village; QM would use the proceeds from selling the whole site to build a new Arts building and student accommodation at Mile End. King's was seen by some as academically more advanced and financially more secure.

The crucial factor in the end was that QM expected to retain the Westfield name, and to set up a trust to fund projects reflecting Westfield's core values. The College Councils of Westfield and QM met simultaneously on 17 March, 1987. Patricia Bettis, the Principal of QM's Secretary, took the phone call from Westfield some time after the end of the working day, and went down to the Council Room to report that Westfield had agreed to the merger. Science staff already relocated to QM, including Molly Scopes, had been waiting anxiously for the result, and were delighted. Some long-standing Westfield staff felt a great sense of loss, and took early retirement, or moved on to join other institutions. The majority, however, accepted the move. The History of Art department was the only one not to move to Mile End; it had had a long collaboration with its peers at University College London, and eventually joined them.

The merger was phased over three years, from 1989 to 1992, again to minimise disruption. The valuable Westfield site was sold: half to King's College, which did not plan to use it at once. It was therefore possible to use both campuses over this period, while the funds raised by the sale helped to pay for the new Arts building, the library extension and new student accommodation, all at Mile End.

The Westfield Trust
The Trust was established on 1 November 1988, before the College's merger with QM. Its aim was to support the development of the new Queen Mary and Westfield College, especially in areas related to Westfield's history and values. These were identified as:
• teaching and research in arts and sciences
• the education of women
• the religious principles of its founders
• enhancing the College's physical environment.

Projects the Trust has supported to date include:
• providing a nursery for the children of students and staff
• helping with the costs of the Chaplaincy
• landscaping work in the Student Village
• providing accommodation within the Student Village for academic visitors
• upgrading library computers for the visually impaired
• funding prizes for second- and third-year students in humanities, science and engineering
• funding the Rosalind Hill research studentship in medieval history
• supporting the Women@QM project (www.women.qmul.ac.uk).

The Trust was wound up in 2010, considering that its aims were now completely integrated into the work of the College.

Arts building sign (now known as ArtsOne), Mile End campus.

Celebration

The Queen Mary and Westfield College Act was granted Royal Assent on 27 July 1989, and the Charter for Queen Mary and Westfield College sealed on 1 September. There was a thanksgiving service in the chapel at Westfield on 17 September. The principles stated by Constance Maynard, one of the College's founders, were restated: education for women, fellowship in a residential community, and Christian service; these were to guide the Westfield Trust. John Chalker, writing in the last Westfield Annual Report, compared the denizens of the College to Milton's Adam and Eve leaving Paradise: there were perhaps tears, but "the world was all before them".

The merger was celebrated by both parties at St Michael's Cornhill, the Drapers' Company church in the City of London. Archbishop Trevor Huddleston, always a champion of the underprivileged, applauded the coming together of two institutions with roots in educating women and the poor, male and female, of east London.

A similar view of the QM campus from the Mile End Road 'before 'and 'after' building the new ArtsTwo building. (top: after, bottom: before) See Chapter 17 to find out more about QM's buildings.

1986–1989

Outside the Informatics Teaching Lab 2012.

W hile the merger with Westfield was being planned, life in much of Queen Mary College carried on as usual: research teaching, outreach, administration. Departments were renamed, merged, relocated; new ventures were planned and came to fruition, or had to wait for a more propitious moment. This chapter outlines the major developments within QM in the late 1980s, with a snapshot of the College's less dramatic day-to-day life; and sets out the political context in which universities in England and Wales operated at the time.

The Education Reform Act, 1988

The political environment for higher education was changing. The Jarratt Committee on management and efficiency in British universities, set up by university vice-chancellors in 1984 (see chapter 2) recommended a new, more commercially-based management structure and style. The Committee's recommendations were endorsed in the Education Reform Act of 1988. Among provisions that have since become familiar – the creation of the national curriculum in schools, the provision for schools to opt out of local authority control – were two that made clear the Government's intentions for universities.

The first was the abolition of tenure for academics appointed after November 1987. Tenure was seen as a bar to the restructuring – and potential redundancies – that the Government considered necessary.

This aroused alarm about academic freedom, since tenure protected staff from dismissal for unpopular or inconvenient views, and it

was Max Beloff in the House of Lords who succeeded in introducing a clause giving constitutional protection to academic freedom, an innovation in Britain, though it was common in European countries... Significantly, this was designed to protect individuals not against the state, but against the university that employed them.[12]

Lord Beloff's amendment succeeded, but the abolition of tenure remained, leaving academic staff with far less job security than they had anticipated, or enjoyed so far (in fact QM staff had never had tenure, though Westfield's did).

The other relevant provision of the Act was the abolition of the University Grants Committee, to be replaced by the Universities Funding Council (UFC). The impact of this would take time to become clear, but Robert Anderson comments:

The change of terminology indicated that the UFC would distribute funds, but control of policy would remain firmly in government hands.[13]

Within the College

The College as a whole had important issues to address. The Jarratt report led at the start of 1986 to a new committee structure, with a Policy, Planning and Resources Sub-Committee reporting to the College Council, the College's governing body. The Nuclear Engineering department merged with Mechanical Engineering. The Science

12. Anderson, R, op cit.
13. ibid.

23

faculty was split into two: Biological and Physical Sciences; and Mathematical and Information Sciences.

And the deficit was growing: from £578,900 at the start of the 1985–86 academic year, to £672,400 at its end. Per capita research income declined in 1985–86 and 1986–87. In April 1987, there was a serious backlog of essential maintenance work needed, at an estimated cost of £9 million. In December 1987, the College Council had a meeting with the University Grants Committee to discuss the funds required for compulsory redundancies. By May 1988, the Senior Vice-Principal, Vice-Principal and Personnel Officer had interviewed all academic and academic-related staff over the age of 53 to discuss early retirement. In October 1988, the projected accumulated deficit was nearly £2 million. In the late summer of 1989, the cash flow situation was so bad that the College had to borrow from the bank just to pay salaries.

There were several explanations for all this. The College had grown; the mode of financing from the University of London had changed, putting more responsibility onto the colleges; and the College's financial management systems had not kept up. Working within a fixed budget, planning according to the budget and deleting unaffordable activities, were all new concepts to universities that had historically, as Jarratt saw, been able to do most of what they wanted. A strategy of spending to recoup, hiring more staff in key areas in the hope of attracting more funding, had unfortunately failed. In addition, there were staffing problems: in March 1989, the College Council was told that the Finance Office was having difficulty in recruiting high-level, professionally qualified staff, and so was unable to provide the management accounts which would show whether the College was meeting its financial targets. Effective governance was going to be difficult.

Not surprisingly, the impact was felt across the College. Professor Ian Butterworth, an eminent physicist who had been appointed Principal in 1986, had taken steps to re-organise the structure of the College's senior management. In line with the Jarratt report's recommendations, he had appointed three vice-principals to serve for fixed terms.

In December 1989, its newly appointed Chair, Martin Harris, reported to the College Council that he was disturbed by reports of low morale, and wished to set up a small group of lay Council members to investigate. This group, the Lindop Committee, reported back at a confidential meeting in March 1990. The same afternoon, Ian Butterworth was summoned to see Martin Harris and Sir Norman Lindop. He was given a copy of the report, which recommended that he should be asked to resign, and was invited to stand down forthwith. He reserved his position.

The next day, Ian Butterworth was away from College on prior business. Professor John Charap, as one of the vice-principals, called a meeting of senior academics to discuss the situation. The meeting passed four resolutions, including crucially: "This group believes that the best interests of the College would not be served by the resignation of the Principal"[14]. Subsequent meetings of academic and non-academic staff expressed their strong support for the Principal.

On Friday 30 March 1990 a Special Meeting of the College's Council received numbered (ie traceable) copies of the still-confidential Lindop report. The Council decided to refer it to a new College working group, the Wright Commission.

The situation had become extremely stressful for Ian Butterworth. Driving from the College to his home in Wapping, he suffered a minor stroke, and began an extended period of sick leave; early the following year he took early retirement.

John Charap recommended to the Wright Commission that the three vice-principals, Professor Trevor Smith, Professor John Chalker and himself should all resign; this had been agreed by the Vice-Chancellor as the best way forward, and was accepted. Professor Graham Zellick, of the Law Department, was appointed Senior Vice-Principal and Acting Principal. The challenge was a major one: to help the College recover both from the loss of four senior posts and from its financial crisis.

14. cited in Charap, J (2012), written contribution to this history.

Keith Aldred had been appointed Finance Officer by Ian Butterworth and arrived in March 1990, with little idea of the situation he would face. His predecessor had left in the autumn of 1989, and the role had been filled by the Deputy Finance Officer 'acting up'. By April 1990, Keith Aldred was very concerned at the state of College finances. As a result of its own enquiries, the Council set up a group including Graham Zellick to look into the matter, and then in July established a Million Pound Savings Group to advise on dealing with the

deficit. The accountancy firm Coopers & Lybrand were commissioned to carry out a detailed analysis of College finances. In early 1991 Graham Zellick and Keith Aldred set about the difficult task of establishing financial order. Patricia Bettis, Secretary to first Ian Butterworth and then Graham Zellick, comments with approval that "when Keith Aldred came in, he would simply tell people that the College could not afford to do things."[15]

Research achievements 1986–89

Physics
In 1984 (just before the period covered by this book) Professor Michael Green, together with John H. Schwarz of Caltech, started 'the first superstring revolution' with a paper on superstring theory. In 1987, their findings are published in a book, *Superstring Theory*, by Green, Schwarz and Witten. In 1989 Michael Green is elected Fellow of the Royal Society and awarded the Dirac Medal of the International Centre for Theoretical Physics. A QM team led by Professor Peter Kalmus collaborates in work at the CERN laboratories in Switzerland, which results in a Rutherford Medal for Peter Kalmus, and a Nobel Prize for the scientists leading the work. (See also chapter 22, which discusses the work of the Particle Physics Research Group.)

Chemistry
In 1987 Professor Donald Bradley receives the Ludwig Mond Medal, and the Lectureship of the Royal Society of Chemistry, for "outstanding research in any aspect of inorganic chemistry". The process he devised for purifying two compounds which ignite on exposure to air is patented by the Ministry of Defence and exploited worldwide by a commercial company. In 1998 Donald Bradley receives the Royal Medal of the Royal Society.

Mathematics
Professor Ian Percival is elected Fellow of the Royal Society for his contribution to quantum measurement.

Buildings 1986–89

Computer Science
In 1989, the purpose-built Informatics Teaching Laboratory is opened. Designed by architects MacCormac Jamieson Prichard, the award-winning building consists of open-plan programming laboratories and a robotics research lab, as well as seminar and study rooms. Richard Bornat, writing in the same year, describes the process of achieving the building the Department craved:

We wanted a striking building but we couldn't afford more than a simple box. They [the architects] came up with the floor voids which are a major feature of the building, making the first and second floors feel much larger and more open than they really are… Modern computer science teaching and research is based on large numbers of powerful workstations. They need provision for cabling and cooling. Half the City of London is being rebuilt because financial offices need the same sort of services… We wanted full disabled access and we had it – there was to be a glass-walled lift serving all floors, and a ramp to the front door.[16]

QM's programme of new building is discussed in greater detail in chapter 17.

15. Bettis, P. Interview for this history. 2008.
16. Bornat R. *The Informatics Teaching Laboratory*.

Queen Mary in print 1986–89

Some highlights:

Title	Author(s)	Department
Dorset place-names, their origins & meanings	A D Mills	English
The making of civilisation	R Whitehouse & J Wilkins	Classics
Measurement of acceleration noise & its use as an indicator of road traffic accident risk	D G Powell & K Shoarian-Sattari	Civil Engineering
Layman's guide to the aerodynamics of wind turbines	D J Sharpe	Aeronautical Engineering
Political broadcasting, fairness & administrative law	A E Boyle	Laws
A plague of voles: The search for a cure	J HW Gipps, SK Alibhai, J Gurnell & C Krebs	Biological Sciences
Selective search without tears	D F Beal	Computer Science
Optics of fractal clusters such as smoke	M V Berry & I C Percival	Mathematical Sciences
Quarks & leptons: The new elementary particles?	PIP Kalmus & R H Dalitz	Physics
The condition of East End Jewry in 1888: Reflections in retrospect	W J Fishman	Political Science [17]

As well as demonstrating the range of specialisms at QM, the list above shows how central some departments and staff were within their discipline. Bill Fishman had already published *East End Jewish Radicals 1875–1914* in 1975, and his next book, *East End 1888: Life in a London Borough Among the Labouring Poor*, would appear in 1989. Quarks and leptons, making a tentative approach in a Royal Society discussion organised by Kalmus and Dalitz, have indeed proved to be fundamental particles.

The College and the East End 1986–89

1986–87
• Four students, who entered the College via a scheme undertaken with local schools, graduate with a first in maths, and upper seconds in geography, law and chemistry.
• 1,500 students and sixth-formers attend an exhibition at QM on CERN, opened by the Principal, Ian Butterworth, formerly CERN's Research Director.

1987–88
• The Women into Science project has eight 14-year-old girls from each of three local schools, as well as their teachers, attending five fortnightly sessions with staff from the Aeronautical Engineering, Astrophysics, Earth Sciences and Mathematics departments.

For a contemporary take on the same issues, see chapter 20.

17. Annual Report 1986–87. (London: Queen Mary College, 1987).

The QM delegation to China, 1988. © Queen Mary, University of London Archives

The College and the World 1986–89

1986–87
- A College delegation to China visits 25 institutions to explore possible collaboration, including research and staff and student exchanges. (This prefigures the partnership with Beijing University of Posts and Telecommunications, featured in chapter 24, but doesn't directly contribute to it.)
- The Students' Union proposes the funding of a scholarship for a black South African student, and the College Council approves. The Students' Union and the College's Anti-Apartheid Group raise the funds for a student's airfare and living costs.

1987–88
- Under the Erasmus scheme, exchanges are agreed between the Engineering faculty and ESSTIN (The Ecole Supérieure des Sciences et Technologies de l'Ingénieur de Nancy) in France; and between the History Department and the University of Siena.
- Dr V Bulmer-Thomas of the Economics Department, and the Director of International Education, John Belcher, tour eight countries in Latin America, over four weeks, promoting the College's new MSc in the Economics of Latin America and, more generally, the opportunities for study and exchange.
- John Charap and John Belcher visit some 18 American universities to confirm their agreements to send students to QM for their Junior Year.

1988–89
- The Principal is invited to lead a British Council delegation to Iraq, to explore the possibility of enhancing higher education links, as part of the Government's wish to normalise relations with the region following the end of the Iran-Iraq war.'
- On behalf of the Royal Society, a delegation from QM's Centre for Research in Aquatic Biology, together with other senior QM staff, visits research institutions in the USSR and signs an agreement for QM to be the UK participant in the Baikal International Center for Ecological Research (BICER).

1990–1995

Senate House, University of London.
Queen Mary is one of the largest self-governing colleges of the federal University.

The Westfield merger completed

By 1990 the phased transfer of staff and students from Westfield to QM was underway; by 1992 it was complete, with the graduation of the last cohort enrolled at Hampstead. Funds from the sale of the Hampstead site paid for a new, purpose-built Arts Building at Mile End. John Chalker, Professor of English, and Vice-Principal first at Westfield, then at the merged Queen Mary and Westfield College, felt that this contributed to the success of the merger.

> One of the problems with mergers is that there are often territorial problems; where there is an established department those members of faculty coming in feel a bit like interlopers. The new Arts Building made the merger between Arts departments more harmonious.[18]

The Arts Building (now known as ArtsOne) was officially opened by the Queen in October 1992, along with the Library extension. It was designed with excellent computing facilities, and Dr Peter Denley, an eminent medieval historian, was able to bring new courses to the merged faculty: first Historical Computing (which took the use of databases as its main focus), and then the wider Humanities Computing, which looked at the range of computing techniques available for research. (There was also an MA in Computer Applications for History, taught jointly by QM and Royal Holloway, at the Institute of Historical Research. During the merger discussions at Westfield, Peter Denley says, he complained:

about the oddity of spending mornings contemplating the struggles for survival of the University of Siena in the 14th and 15th centuries, as recorded in their financial and administrative records, before coming in for afternoon committee meetings on exactly the same themes, with similar documentation.[19]

The advantages of the merger, however, soon reassured him that it had been the right decision. Other Arts staff of the period have similar, positive recollections, both of the merger itself and of the new accommodation: perhaps none more than staff from QM's Department of German, which over 40 years had inhabited in succession the vicarage of the bombed church of St Benet's (below the Aeronautics Department); its replacement on the same site, the Physics Building (the Department was situated above a wind-tunnel); the West Wing of the Queens' Building; the former Spratt's Dog Food HQ (the once-familiar 'Scottie' emblem is still in mosaic on the front of the building) and the Queens' Building for a second time.

Finances

Meanwhile, in spite of the Westfield dowry, the College's financial problems had not gone away. Graham Zellick, confirmed in the role of Principal, and Keith Aldred, Finance Officer, faced (according to Professor Richard Clymo) "a financial Augean Stables." He remembers the Chair of the Universities Funding Council (UFC) making an early morning visit to the College, followed up with notice to Graham Zellick that he had a fortnight to produce a credible recovery

18. Chalker, J. Interview for this history. 2008.

19. Denley, P. Written contribution to this history. 2008.

plan, failing which the UFC would declare the College unfit to receive public funds. The UFC, it seemed, was itself under pressure from the House of Commons' Public Accounts Committee.

Richard Clymo was Dean of Science at the time:
   Keith Aldred had just produced the first rational and understandable analysis from which departments could tell where their income came from, and what their expenditure was. This revealed that the School of Biological Sciences, in spite of the earlier round of savings, still had an annual deficit of [over] £700,000 – by some way the largest departmental deficit in the College. For several days Graham Zellick could not see how Biological Sciences could survive. But with the new Keith Aldred analyses, I was able to express all the items of income and expenditure in terms of student numbers or staff numbers (or a combination). From this it emerged (at 3.25am one morning) that financial viability needed a staff: student ratio of about 1:17. At the time this seemed very unwelcome (these ratios were still around 1:10 to 1:14 in most departments). But it did show that the problem was not the size of the deficit but the staff: student ratio. Once the number of students had been decided, the supportable number of staff would be known.
   Biological Sciences was not the only department with a substantial deficit. Graham Zellick produced a range of five plans, labelled 'A' to 'E', from 'do nothing' to 'close several departments'. A vigorous College-wide debate followed … In the end 'Option C' was settled on. This required closure of the Department of Mediterranean Studies, savings in Engineering and Chemistry, and that Biological Sciences should eliminate its deficit.[20]

Even before the adoption of Option C, Graham Zellick had ordered a freeze on new appointments, including those already in the recruitment process. It was followed with a programme of job losses, achieved through voluntary redundancies and early retirement. Biological Sciences, which had expanded considerably with the earlier Science merger, lost 50 per cent of its staff. Mediterranean

Studies (formerly Classics and established at Westfield since 1902) was lost completely.

The process was hard, but results came quickly. The Principal's introduction to the 1991–92 Annual Report foresaw the elimination of the remainder of the deficit by the end of the academic year and pointed out the need to build up the College's reserves.

The Government and universities
The 1988 Education Reform Act (ERA) was followed by its logical successor, the 1992 Further and Higher Education Act. The ERA had set up parallel funding councils for universities and for polytechnics, the latter free for the first time from local authority control. The 1992 Act abolished the distinction between the institutions, enabling all polytechnics and some other colleges to become universities and award their own degrees. From 47 UK universities, there were soon 88.

The move was highly controversial. It seemed out of character for a Conservative party that, as Robert Anderson says, "was still suspicious of comprehensive education and nostalgic for the grammar schools."[21] Critics feared that standards of education and research would inevitably slip, on the assumption that any existing university was better at both than any former polytechnic. In fact, as Anderson points out, the answer to satisfying those who wanted to differentiate:

   was to allow an informal hierarchy to re-emerge through discretionary payments allocated according to formally objective criteria, of which the RAE was the most significant. Beyond this, universities could be encouraged to seek extra revenue independent of the state.[22]

As we shall see, QM proved adept at the latter.

The new system was in any case expensive. The assumption from the mid-1980s onwards had been that student numbers would stagnate. In fact, even before the 1992 Act, they rose by 54 per cent, to 470,500. The 88 universities resulting from the Act

20. Clymo, R, op cit.

21. Anderson, R. op cit.
22. ibid.

had over a million students between them. Financing their studies became a key issue (and one which has hardly been out of the news since). The maintenance grant, the standard system of financial support, was frozen in 1990; students who couldn't finance themselves had to rely on 'top-up' loans.

The College in the early 1990s

In the third year of its new, united existence, Queen Mary and Westfield College consisted of seven faculties: Social Studies, Arts, Engineering, Basic Medical Sciences (pre-clinical), Information and Mathematical Sciences, Physics and Biological Sciences, and Laws. There were just over 6,000 students, 23 per cent of them in the arts and 10 per cent medical and dental; the rest more or less evenly distributed. Of the 1,400 staff, 427 were academics and 167 academic-related. In 1992, for the first time, 700 graduates received their degrees on the campus, rather than at the Royal Albert Hall with the other University of London graduates: 500lbs of strawberries and 480 bottles of sparkling wine marked the occasion.

This was the start of a new relationship between the constituent colleges of the University of London, and its centre. QM and seven other larger colleges had direct access to the Universities Funding Council; in due course they would be funded directly, rather than through the University. Graham Zellick commented in his Principal's report:

> The next step is for the College to acquire university status in its own right, while remaining within the University, and I am confident that a proposal along these lines will eventually bear fruit.[23]

The vision did indeed bear fruit. Today, the University of London is a federation of 18 self-governing Colleges. In 2009 QM was granted the power to award its own degrees, although this has not yet been exercised.

In late 1991 an Academic Standards Committee was set up at QM to review the College's quality assurance processes. This pre-dated the national Teaching Quality Assessment (TQA), introduced in 1991 to match the RAE, but without the latter's accompanying financial rewards. The Committee's methodology was certainly more sophisticated than the TQA's. It set about:
- considering the criteria for course and programme approval
- monitoring and reviewing of the College's teaching
- analysing the reports of visiting examiners
- upgrading staff training, and
- monitoring teaching quality via student questionnaires.

Queen Mary and Westfield College had been through very difficult times; but it was now determined to move on and flourish.

23. Annual Report 1991–2 (London: Queen Mary and Westfield College, 1992

Research achievements 1990–95

- The **Astronomy Unit** led the UK's participation in preparing the Cluster II space mission. Cluster II was a constellation of four satellites, successfully launched by the European Space Agency in 2000, which still relays information about the effect of solar wind on our planet from the outer reaches of Earth's atmosphere.

- The **Faculty of Laws** in 1991–92 had the highest level of research funding per staff member of any law faculty in the country. One example stands for the Faculty's research: a study for the Law Commission that examined the ways that accident victims use the damages paid to them, including the victims' situation some years after settlement of the claim.

- The **Environmental Science Unit** in the Geography Department directed a group of Nepalese and British scientists studying the effects of rising population, deforestation and land-use change in the southern Himalayas, north of Kathmandu, over three monsoon seasons.

- **Civil Engineering** worked on alternative technology for strengthening bridges, in response to an EU directive that resulted in heavier lorries on British roads.

- In **Physics,** the theory group played a leading role in **research** on superstring theory (see page 162) which led to the development of M-theory in 1995, an advancement that identifies 11 dimensions and has been called the 'second superstring revolution.'

- The **English Department** saw two of its staff win important literary awards: Professor Jacqueline Rose was awarded the 1991 Fawcett Prize for *The Haunting of Sylvia Plath* and Professor Lisa Jardine the 1993 Bainton Book Prize for *Erasmus, Man of Letters*.

Teaching and Learning, 1990–95

Department / School	New programme
Politics	MA Public Policy
Engineering	MSc (for BT engineers)
Russian	Language A-level in one year for those with no previous experience
History	MA Contemporary British History since 1939
Business	Joint Bachelors degrees: Business and a language, Business and Science, Business and Maths
Hispanic Studies	BA Cuban Studies

Teaching Quality Assessment, 1993–95

English	Excellent
Geography	Excellent
Chemistry	Satisfactory
Computer Science	Satisfactory
History	Satisfactory
Law	Satisfactory
Mechanical Engineering	Satisfactory

The merger with the Medical Colleges

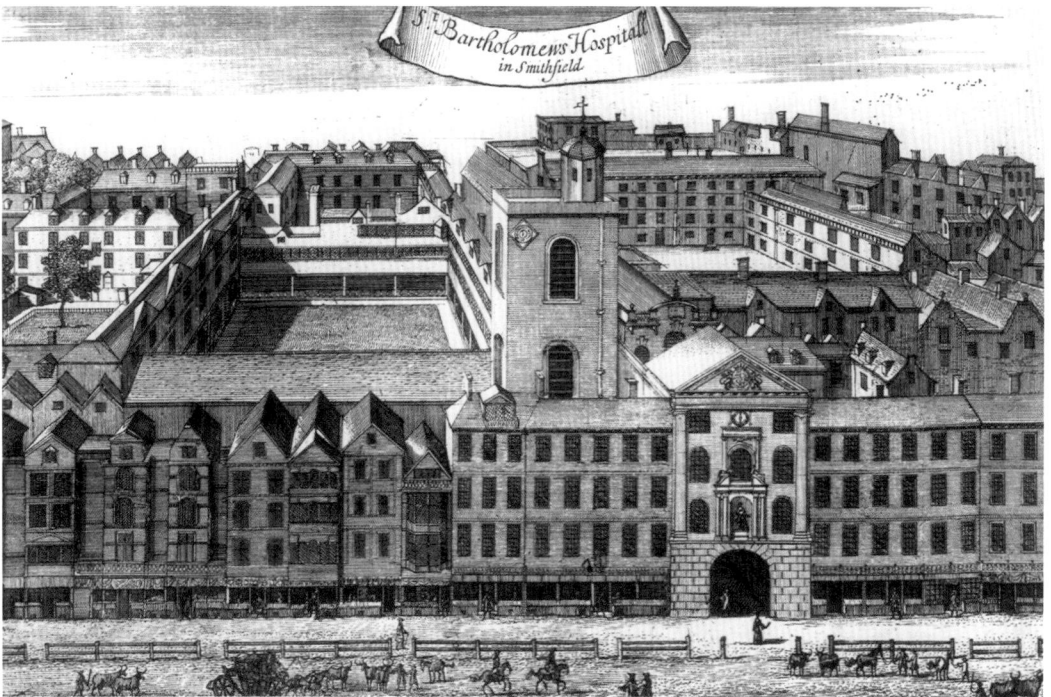

St Bartholomew's Hospital in Smithfield (engraving). Depicts Henry VIII Gate and Smithfield frontage, with tower of St Bartholomew the Less and other Hospital buildings behind. Shows the Hospital before the 18th century reconstruction. Published in J. Stow, "Survey of the Cities of London and Westminster" (1720 edition), p.184.
© St Bartholomew's Hospital Archives

The relationships between Queen Mary College, St Bartholomew's Hospital Medical College and The London Hospital Medical College went through a number of stages before Barts and The London finally came together in 1992, and then merged with Queen Mary and Westfield College in 1995.

Timeline

Pre-history

There were links between QM and The London Hospital Medical College and Dental School as early as 1917. In the early twentieth century, medical and dental students who had not taken basic sciences at secondary school spent their first year at QM, before moving to The London. This continued until the 1950s, though student numbers gradually declined.

In the first half of the twentieth century, there was a shift from vocational training for doctors to a more formal medical education. After World War II, the newly founded National Health Service needed more medical professionals. The Goodenough Report,[24] published in 1944, was a wide-reaching review of medical education in the UK. It recommended that medical students should have a broad university education, including a compulsory pre-registration year for all graduates, and postgraduate training for would-be specialists. It also suggested links between medical schools and multi-faculty universities. London's medical schools were advised to keep up with medical education elsewhere in the country, and offer equal opportunities to women. The London and Barts, along with the other London medical colleges, began to admit women from 1948.

24. *Report of the interdepartmental committee on medical schools* (Chairman: Sir William Goodenough) (London: HMSO, 1944).

35

Women in medicine

In 1944, the University of London's Senate convened a special Committee on the Medical Education of Women. It recommended that women should be admitted to every one of the University of London's medical schools.

The Dental School at The London was positive about the idea, not least because they were struggling to recruit enough students. The Medical College, however, was against the idea. A limited number of women had been allowed in for just four years from 1918, because of increased demand during and after World War I. It wasn't until 1947 that The London finally agreed to accept women as medical students.

Barts was persistent in opposing the measure. It had not admitted women at the end of World War I, and in 1945–46 made many representations expressing its opposition. Eventually, Barts acceded, but reluctantly, and in part at least because its status as a college of the University of London would otherwise have been threatened.

After extensive debate, all the London medical colleges became co-educational, including The London School of Medicine for Women, established in 1874 by Elizabeth Garrett Anderson, Elizabeth Blackwell and Sophia Jex-Blake. The University expected that "in the initial stages the proportion of women to men shall not be less that fifteen percent of the total entry."[25]

Since 1960, the number of female medical and dental students has increased, keeping pace with their male colleagues. Women at Barts and The London have made invaluable contributions in all areas of teaching and research. Today female students and teachers have a strong presence at Barts and The London. In 2009–10, 55 per cent of all QM's medical and dental students were women. QM as a whole has a Bronze (whole-institution) Athena SWAN Charter for promoting gender equality in science and technology; the School of Medicine and Dentistry hopes to gain a Silver (departmental) award in the near future.

Elizabeth Garrett Anderson, *c*.1865.
© Royal London Hospital Archives

Elizabeth Blackwell, *c*.1880.
Image from Wikimedia Commons.

25. Minutes of College Committee, 12 September 1945.

Government pressure

As medical education became more formalised, it was increasingly affected by policy and budgetary decisions made by the NHS and central government. In 1968, the Royal Commission on Medical Education, chaired by Lord Todd, reviewed the provision of undergraduate and postgraduate medical education. The Commission's report contained a chapter on medical education in London, and proposed a series of mergers to reduce the number of London medical schools from 12 to six. It expressed support for the twinning of medical schools with multi-faculty universities, as the Goodenough Committee had suggested over two decades earlier.

The response of The London to the Todd Report was generally positive, including a commitment to a 'policy of maximal collaboration' with Barts and QM. Barts on the other hand wanted to retain its autonomy. In both higher education and the NHS, however, demands for efficiency savings made mergers unavoidable.

The pre-clinical medical merger

There had been discussion of a merger of the medical schools with QM – the BLQ (Barts, The London and Queen Mary) plan – for a number of years. In the end, the merger of pre-clinical teaching was driven by both principle and necessity. It had become received wisdom that both medical schools would benefit from being part of a multi-faculty university; and BLQ would avert a take-over by one of the large London colleges, which was an even greater fear. There was considerable overlap between the medical and mainstream science curricula, and QM could offer a purpose-built building for pre-clinical studies, with large teaching labs and dedicated anatomy and dissection rooms. There was also at the time the possibility of clinical experience for these students at the nearby Mile End Hospital. These were all strong incentives; but the process was nevertheless long and often painful for all sides.

The geographical closeness of Barts and The London to each other and to QM meant that formal links were quite feasible. Professor Brian Colvin points out that "in the minds of The London, QM was not very far away, both

physically and emotionally, because The London was founded in 1740 to look after the poor of the East End, and Queen Mary College was founded in 1887 for very much for the same reason; instead of looking after their health, the College was looking after their minds."[26]

At Barts, however, there was less enthusiasm. Professor Trevor Smith, at the time Vice-Principal of QM, believes that:

> Dr Kelsey Fry, Dean of Barts, had a difficult role to play, given the entrenched feelings of his colleagues. Very adroitly, as it turned out, he had to steer between a sensible course of progressing the merger, without alienating his die-hard clinicians. To this end, he put out feelers to see if a merger of the two pre-clinical schools with QMC was a possible runner, leaving the clinical schools independent.[27]

In 1989, the medical colleges at Barts and The London finally agreed to merge and move their pre-clinical teaching to Mile End, at the newly-created Queen Mary and Westfield College. The new Basic Medical Sciences Building (now the Francis Bancroft Building) welcomed the first cohort of students in October 1990. Teaching was shared between academic staff from the two institutions. For the staff involved, there was a long period of intense negotiation over both teaching methods and the curriculum. The medical schools had each had their own approach and style, and it took intensive work to reach agreement: though that, says Dr Mark Carroll, at the time Senior Lecturer in Biochemistry at The London, was what helped bind the teaching staff together. The new syllabus was systems- rather than discipline-based, and brought together specialists in anatomy, biochemistry, physiology and pharmacology.

This was closer to the contemporary style of teaching of the rest of the College. Nevertheless, the view that 'they do things differently' in the medical school remained, and for good reason: unlike purely academic study, the course is vocational, and regulated by a professional body, the General Medical Council (GMC). In practical terms, there were still disadvantages. Staff had to move between the three sites, both for

26. Colvin, B. Interview for this history. 2009.
27. Smith, T. Written contribution to this history. 2008.

teaching and for meetings. Mile End Hospital lost the in-patient wards that had been meant to offer students clinical experience close at hand. The College got to grips with its complex finances, and a staffing of 50 across the two medical colleges was reduced to 30. As a result the medical school was forced to surrender part of its new building to other departments, and to restructure. There was also considerable hostility to the merger from some staff and many students.

Brian Colvin recalls:
> The interim period between the preclinical teaching commencing at QMW until the fuller merger of Barts and The London with QMC (*sic*) was the worst of all possible worlds. The students still had their loyalties to Barts or The London, and found themselves at QMW for preclinical teaching ... It was a way of easing everyone into the relationship, but it was essential for it to be completed as quickly as possible so that we didn't have this horrible separation between the preclinical and clinical School, especially at a time when the GMC were saying that we should be bringing clinical experience into the first two years of the course.[28]

The Tomlinson Report
In 1990, the NHS created Trusts, with the intention of allowing hospitals to regain some autonomy. The Royal London Hospital (granted the title on its 250th anniversary in 1990) became one of the first NHS Trusts, encompassing The London, Mile End and the London Chest Hospitals. At the same time, the future of Barts Hospital was called into question by Sir Bernard Tomlinson's Report of the Inquiry into the London Health Service (1992). This report argued that Barts was not viable as a hospital, and recommended its closure. The threat was to the Hospital, not the College; but closure of the Hospital would have displaced students in clinical training. The Government's response to the Tomlinson Report included three options for Barts Hospital: closure, retention as a small specialist hospital, or merger with The Royal London Hospital and The London Chest Hospital. The threat to Barts sparked an intense public

debate and a 'Save Barts' campaign, involving over a million patients, local residents, staff, MPs and councillors. In 1992, Barts, The Royal London and the London Chest Hospitals joined together to form Barts and The London NHS Trust; but the uncertainty over Barts Hospital's future remained, and contributed to the anxiety at the medical college about the merger with The London and QM.

The Tomlinson Report's recommendations reiterated those of the Goodenough Report of 1944, and the Todd Report of 1968. This time action was taken. When a Labour government came to power in 1997, the new Secretary of State for Health, Frank Dobson, commissioned a strategic review of the health service in inner London, led by Sir Leslie Turnberg. Turnberg recommended that Barts should remain open on its Smithfield site, as a specialist cancer and cardiac hospital: a recognition of its continuing innovation in these fields.[29] The Government agreed, and in February 1998, announced that Barts was to remain open. General hospital services would be concentrated in Whitechapel at The Royal London.

The full merger
The process of merging the medical schools was, of course, challenging. As well as the anticipated practicalities, there were clashes of culture. The two colleges and hospitals had their own long and distinguished histories. They were also situated in distinct parts of London – the City and the East End – and had served very different local communities.

Some of the key people involved recall the events of the time. Firstly, Professor Sandy McNeish, Warden of Barts and The London School of Medicine and Dentistry from 1997–2001:
> Each medical college had a different ethos. Many staff at both colleges didn't welcome the merger, and certainly didn't welcome being merged with Queen Mary and Westfield, because they saw it as fourth in size amongst the multi-faculty colleges of the University of London – behind UCL, Imperial and King's. Barts and The

---

28. Colvin, B, op cit.

29. Health Services in London – A Strategic Review (London: Department of Health, 1998).

The front of The London Hospital Medical College (now known as The Garrod Building) in 2012.

London both *correctly* had highly developed notions of themselves, and had a long history of taking students in clinical years who had trained at Oxford or Cambridge.[30]

Brian Colvin:

For centuries the medical schools had been independent and fiercely proud. To some extent, they punched above their weight in terms of producing leaders, but punched below their weight academically…

Each were in different kinds of ivory towers, or in the case of The London, an "ivory cesspit." Staff from The London gloried in the mess … When people came to The London from Barts, they asked why anyone would work in such an environment, it was completely unacceptable. I sympathised with the Barts people who were suddenly "slumming it." But everyone needed to just get on with their work.[31]

And Professor Peter Kopelman:

I was seen as relatively neutral, so I was seconded (from The London) to Barts to try and help with the merger of the two medical curricula. From the point of view of education and the curricula, the merger process was not that difficult. From the point of view of the histories and traditions of the two medical colleges, it was not an easy task … It took ten years, and a generation of consultants and senior academic staff to retire, before there was a true merger. From the point of view of the students, they were great and handled it well …

What I loved about the merger with QM was the interface with the other disciplines. In medicine, one is quite isolated. I enjoyed very much the Principal's 'Away Days' with all the heads, and it was excellent to be able to get to know and work with colleagues from so many disciplines …

30. McNeish, A. Interview for this history. 2008.

31. Colvin, B, op cit.

A mural of *Christ at the Pool of Bethesda* by William
Hogarth in Saint Bartholomew's Hospital.

It's important in the history to reflect on the
foundations of the two medical schools and how
the marriage between them was very much a
shot-gun marriage, and yet from that has been
born a strong and sustainable medical and
dental school.[32]

Both staff and students held strong allegiances.
Teams at the two medical colleges had competed
with each other in rugby, cricket and other sports.
These rivalries were usually jovial; but, from 1990,
when students attended joint pre-clinical lectures
at QM, lecturing staff from one college were
occasionally met with jeers from students from the
other. Staff on both sides had equally strong views,
and these clearly influenced student behaviour.
Dr Patricia Molly Scopes, who chaired a
committee dealing with student affairs, recalled
the unhappiness amongst medical students
about sharing student accommodation with
undergraduates at QM, and their insistence on
retaining separate sports clubs, to continue
competing in national medical student leagues.
For some, the vast building for Basic Medical
Sciences at Mile End did not feel sufficiently
connected with the medical world.

Barts and The London School of Medicine and Dentistry

Once the Queen Mary and Westfield College Act
1995 was passed, the work of establishing the
new School of Medicine and Dentistry began.
The first Warden was Professor Sir Colin Berry,
who had been Dean at The London. The task of
amalgamating the two schools was challenging for
anyone who had been involved in either, and after
a year Colin Berry stepped down. In January 1997,
Professor Sandy McNeish, previously Dean of the
Medical School at the University of Birmingham,
and the first Director of the Medical Research
Council's Clinical Sciences Centre at the
Hammersmith Hospital, was appointed. Sandy
McNeish described the job as attempting to join
together "two regiments that have hated each other
for the last 250 years".[33] Steps were taken to
attempt to resolve the old allegiances and divisions,
and address the much larger issues of the new
School.

The most urgent were finances and staffing. There
was uncertainty about the true situation of each of
the old medical colleges. Sandy McNeish recalled
not being able to ascertain the actual number of
staff employed by the newly merged School.
Significant deficits came to light. Keith Aldred,
appointed as Finance Director at QM in 1990,
was instrumental in getting the books straight
and reducing the deficits. Addressing the overall
structure of the School helped with both staffing
and finance; staffing levels were reduced primarily
through early retirement. The Warden and his
newly appointed management team found that
they were dealing with over 70 departments across
the merged School. As Sandy McNeish pointed
out, "the purpose of the School of Medicine and
Dentistry is to educate and to research, and if you
had a very fragmented structure, that meant the
teaching was probably fragmented and the research
was certainly fragmented".[34] Eight divisions were
created, with a clear hierarchy and structure.

The School's finances were also affected by student
numbers. Sandy McNeish was faced with this issue
on his first day as Warden, on 6 January 1997.

---

32. Kopelman, P. Interview for this history. 2008.

33. McNeish, A, op cit.
34. ibid.

Griffin House (1st and 2nd floors) and
Lansbury Lodge (day centre).

During the previous autumn, the Higher
Education Funding Council of England (HEFCE),
had begun exploring which medical schools should
take more students, to fulfil the Government's drive
for more doctors. The report on Barts and
The London was so unfavourable that HEFCE
proposed to reduce their allocation, unless
satisfactory evidence was presented by summer
1997. Lower student numbers meant less money.
A small group worked on plans for improving the
curriculum and student support. To the great relief
of all involved, the School managed to get an
increase in numbers for the next academic year.
According to Sandy McNeish, "the School had
been within six months of meltdown, but was
saved". In 1998 Brian Colvin was appointed
Assistant Warden (later Dean) for Student Affairs,
and realised that further action was needed before
the Teaching Quality Assurance visit, due in early
2000. The urgency united previously rivalrous
groups, and was, he recalls, "a crucial focal point
for the new school because … it served to fulfil
Dr Johnson's remark that 'Nothing more
wonderfully concentrates a man's mind than
the sure knowledge he is to be hanged in the
morning.'"[35] The execution was avoided.

Barts and The London Students' Association

Barts and the London Students' Association
(BLSA) was formed in 1995, from the merger of
the student unions of St. Bartholomew's Hospital
Medical College and The London Hospital Clubs'
Union with that at QM. It is now one of the
liveliest medical and dental students' associations
in the country, not least for its sense of community
and its history. BLSA's relationship with Queen
Mary Students' Union (QMSU) involves both
co-operation and constructive competition. BLSA,
like QMSU, focuses on sport, culture, providing
students with a rich social life, and charitable
activity.

The BLSA's sporting and cultural societies reflect
the radical changes in the gender and ethnic
make-up of the School of Medicine and Dentistry.
There is now a large and very successful Asian
Society, which puts on a spectacular cultural show
every year to raise money for charity; the Drama
Society and Music Society remain very active;
and RAG week regularly raises over £150,000 per
annum for the BLSA's chosen charities. The
students have strongly supported the local
community, especially in running the teddy bear
hospital (see page 80) and SAMDA, which works
with local schools to improve access to medical
and dental education (page 140).

In 1988, a group of medical students – including
Dr Veronica White, now a consultant physician at
the Trust – had the idea of raising money to build
combined accommodation for local elderly people
and medical and dental students. This became the
Griffin Community Trust; it celebrates its 25th
Anniversary in 2013. Griffin House in Poplar,
east London, was built in 1997; it provides
accommodation for 23 students from the School
of Medicine and Dentistry. Each of them befriends
an elderly resident of Shaftesbury Lodge, a
sheltered housing scheme next door, and the
students organise events and excursions
throughout the academic year.

35. Colvin, B, op cit.

In focus:
medicine and dentistry

The Dental School, 1911

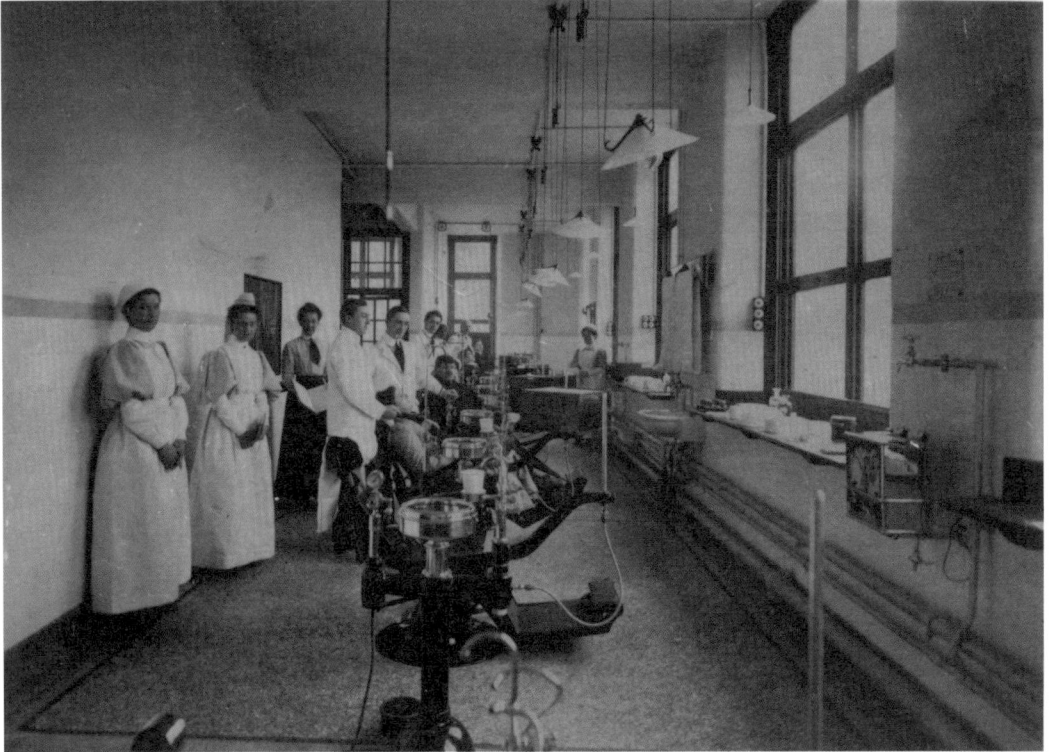

Dental Department, The London Hospital, 1911.
© Royal London Hospital Archives

Time to go to the dentist. Everything in today's surgery is familiar: the dentist with her mirror, the dental nurse; maybe an X-ray or two; maybe a filling needed. Injections, a high-speed drill, the material for filling mixed by the nurse. They make you another appointment, to see the hygienist. If you are unlucky, there is more difficult work: root-canal treatment, a crown, a bridge, implants, perhaps a referral to a specialist. Some of it is uncomfortable, rarely painful or dangerous. Time-consuming, certainly, but most of us reckon it is time well spent. Some of it is expensive, and not available on the NHS; but that's another story.

Reel back to 1855, and The London Hospital House Committee: 'It was very desirable that the tooth-drawing done at the Hospital should be superintended by a senior pupil duly appointed for the purpose'.[36] So up until then you could have had your teeth pulled out without even a medical student available to make sure it was done properly. He (women were not yet admitted) would never have studied dentistry because there was no such course; he would have been selected for his "manual capability of extraction", which sounds like brute strength as much as skill.

That committee discussion leads, slowly, over 56 years, to the opening of The London Hospital Dental School, on 3 October 1911. The story of the Dental School is the story of advances in dental treatment that would have amazed our 1855 medical student and his patients; but also of the social conditions that lead to dental ill-health, and

the political conditions that make both prevention and treatment available.

The state of the nation's teeth, 1911

In the years before the First World War, the impact of social conditions on health was taken seriously by medical authorities. The London, in the heart of the East End, where women and men had to take whatever low-paid and dangerous work was going, was bound to see the extremes of ill-health. Fumes from yellow phosphorus, used in match factories such as Bryant & May in Bow, led to 'phossy jaw,' ie decay of the jawbone; after a crucial turn-of-the century report, the factory set up an in-house dental clinic. Other industries used mercury and arsenic in manufacturing. TB was common in adults and children. Malnutrition and poor living conditions gave rise to serious dental and gum infections. Reports highlighted the appalling state of children's teeth across the country. One of the first initiatives of the new Dental School was to agree to treat local school children.

Becoming a dentist

It took a considerable struggle before dentistry was recognised as a real profession, one that required research, specialist knowledge and skill. In 1915, there were said to be 5,426 dentists in the country, of whom only 71 per cent were qualified. There was no regulation; anyone could set up as a dentist. Some of the unqualified 1,574 might have learnt their craft well and conscientiously; there was good reason, after all, not to go to dental school if you didn't have to, since the course was unsubsidised and expensive. Others were, no doubt (as a later

36. Minutes of The London Hospital House Committee, July 1855. Cited in Fish, op cit.

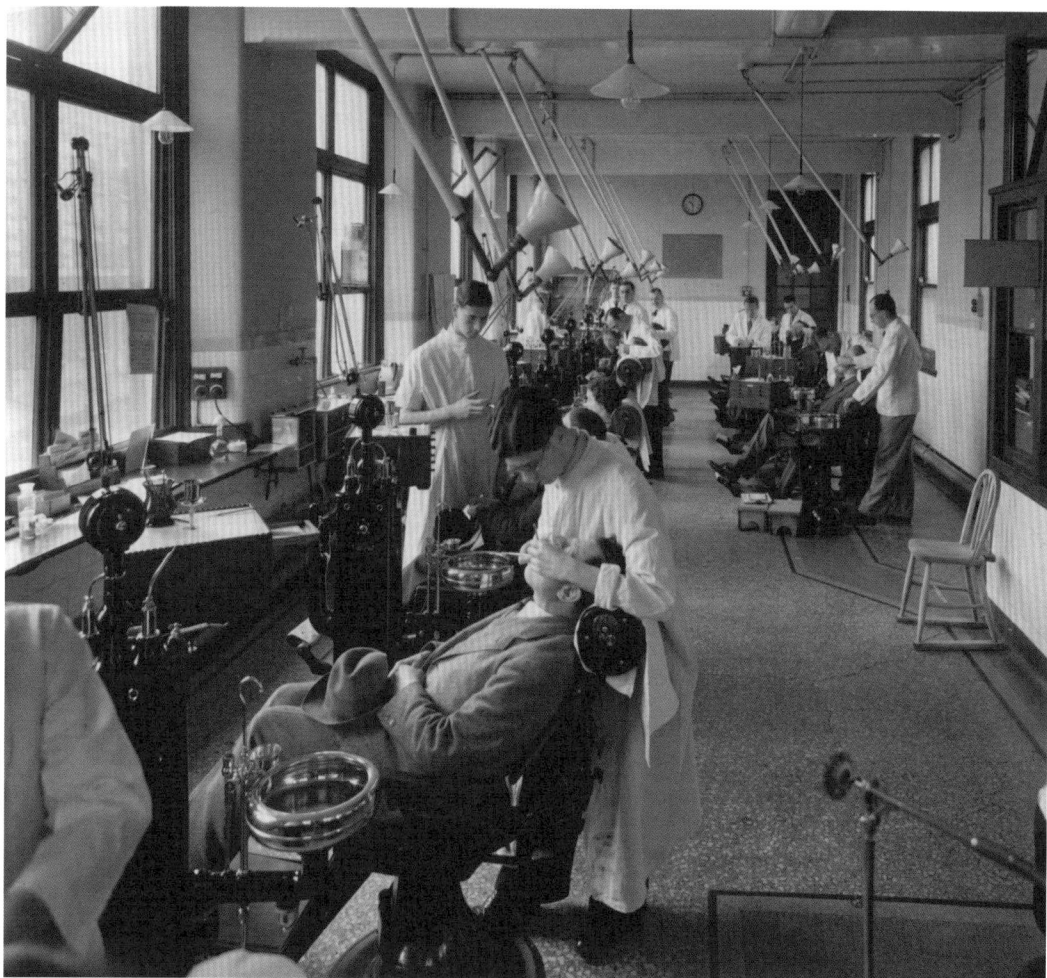

report said), "the butcher and the blacksmith", or simply men on the make.[37] Registration only came in with the 1921 Dentists Act. A few skilled but unqualified dentists were allowed to continue working; one of them was William Montague, who ran the Mechanical Laboratory at the School, and taught from 1912 right through to the early 1950s.

Not surprisingly, then, recruitment to the new School started off low, with four students in the first year, rising to only 15 after 18 months, "plus six who have gone off round the world."[38]

37. *Report of the Committee on the extent and gravity of the evils of dental practice by persons not qualified under the Dentists Act.* (1919). Cited in Fish, op.cit.
38. ibid.

Recruitment of dental students

Year	Intake
1911	4
1913	15
1919	37
1926	9
1930s	c.40
1948	44
1965	50
2011	74

During World War I, the Dental School closed for two years, with the remaining students transferring to the much larger school at Guy's Hospital. It re-opened in 1919, in the hospital's out-patients department. In 1920 there were 37 students, but

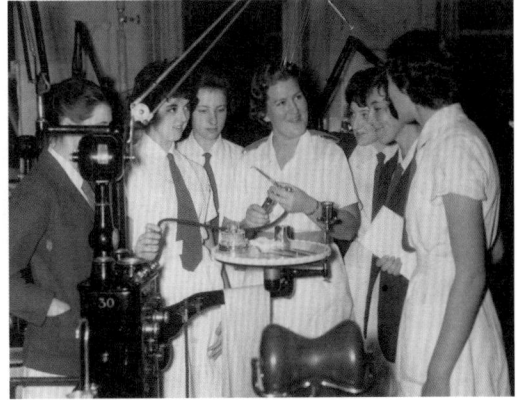

Dental Department, The London Hospital, c. 1930s (left) and c. 1970s (above). © Royal London Hospital Archives

not enough space for them to work in. Dentistry, as the hospital was realising, had particular needs, and most of the learning was practical rather than theoretical. Thirteen dental chairs were bought from War Department surplus.

None of the teaching staff worked full-time. Evelyn Sprawson was a part-time Director of Dental Studies. Other lecturers, including another founder, Harold Chapman, were paid an honorarium.

The curriculum

In the 1930s, a new undergraduate started in the lab, making dentures out of porcelain and vulcanite (of which more later). He (still only *he*) attended a range of lectures: anatomy and physiology, dental anatomy, histology and pathology, and dental metallurgy ("incomprehensible cupellations and refinements in very dangerous looking furnaces"[39]). After two years he would reach a milestone: the day he would buy his own set of instruments. His training expanded to include fillings, crowns and so on, as well as extractions on the 'phantom head' (a dummy to practise on). There were more lectures: surgery and general medicine. He might choose to study for a degree (ie Bachelor of Dental Surgery, or BDS, established in 1922), but more likely for the older qualification, a Licence in Dental Surgery (LDS). It was 1945 before all students were required to read for a degree.

Materia medica

What could be done for the people of east London and their hundred-year tooth-ache? Over the course of the nineteenth century, there were great advances in understanding dental ill-health, and in the technology available to treat it. There was also a growing appreciation of the need to prevent dental disease. Nevertheless, a great deal of dentistry was about extracting teeth and creating substitutes. Even gum disease was thought to be best treated by removing teeth (though the *British Dental Journal* in 1899 quotes someone as saying "so does the guillotine for ever cure migraine."[40]). The 1911 students did learn to do fillings, but it was considered a lesser priority.

Between the wars, treatment was not much more sophisticated. There were extractions, of course. Each student might have a hundred patients needing a full or partial denture. The base of the denture was made from vulcanite, heat-treated rubber and so the lab was filled with sulphurous fumes. Dentures may have been a boon, but with porcelain teeth fitted to a black rubber base, they were hardly flattering.

Impressions of the teeth to be cast were taken in plaster of Paris. This was a delicate process, as the cast had to be removed in the moments between the initial and final set, the plaster fractured and then reassembled outside the mouth. In the late 1920s a new, malleable impression material,

39. ibid.

40. cited in Fish, op.cit.

based on agar-agar, became available. Gold was considered the best material for fillings. Cocaine was the best available anaesthetic; local anaesthetic was rarely used. X-rays were possible; the School was concerned with the poor quality of the machine in The London's out-patients department, and acquired a new one in 1926. For abscesses, the only treatment before antibiotics was incision and drainage; given the unhygienic conditions in which people lived, and the high level of malnutrition, this was often a problem.

Dentists including those at The London spoke passionately about the need for preventive work; but it was hard to achieve. The need for oral hygiene was known, but East End patients in poor housing found it hard to practise.

Postwar

The NHS transformed the dental profession. The Teviot Interdepartmental Committee on Dentistry reported in late 1946. It recommended a comprehensive dental service, available to all, paid for out of public funds. The committee was critical of dental teaching, with its emphasis on mechanics (those vulcanite dentures) and its lack of connection to universities. Dental schools, it proposed, should be larger, with facilities for an intake of at least 50 students. That may have caused some anxiety, but in the end it suited the School's plans for development.

The inception of NHS dentistry brought, inevitably, a great surge in demand. There were not enough dentists in the country, and those there were could often offer only extractions and dentures. Dental students of the postwar years were training for a situation quite different to their predecessors'.

The students were, of course, still all male. (See chapter 6 for The London's record on admitting women). In 1942 The London Hospital's Dental Council voted to admit women, but the first female dental student, a Miss E Coates, was accepted only in 1947.

The new building

The decision to create a new building for the Dental School was made in 1947, the year before the Hospital became part of the new NHS. Space, as we have seen, had been a problem for some years. In 1948 there were 44 students working in the Conservation Room, and only 28 dental chairs for their patients. The School needed to expand in order to teach to degree level and undertake research.

The first step, in 1953, was a move into extended accommodation; but this was never going to be enough. Planning for a new building began in 1955, and got through the hospital's and the Ministry of Health's decision-making processes in 1958. A site was identified on Stepney Way, behind the main hospital building, and the School – now the Dental Institute – opened in 1965.

The new building was not only bigger, but better arranged, based on the new concept of the dental polyclinic: the conservation, prosthetics and periodontal departments would share space. There were a 133 dental chairs, with an annual undergraduate intake of 50 students. More staff arrived: 28 full-time and 18 part-time lecturers, five research assistants, four part-time honorary advisers and 15 technicians. The staff:student ratio was now 1:6.25.

The curriculum, too, was changed in 1966, to reflect the increase in student numbers, and to tackle what seemed to be the perennial problem of recruitment. Our notional student now found herself in a tutorial group, and learning a more holistic model of patient care. When she graduated, she was most likely to work in the community, and her training reflected the day-to-day demands of general practice.

The core training continued to evolve. The School urged the University Grants Committee to extend the undergraduate course to five years, and this was finally agreed in 1988. In the 1990s, new postgraduate programmes were introduced, a one or two-year masters and a three-year course for specialists in one of dentistry's 13 disciplines.

New Dental School Building, The London Hospital, 1965.
© Royal London Hospital Archives

The Experimental Dental Care Project

By the early 1970s there was a general interest in the future of dental education. At The London, one result was the Experimental Dental Care Project, set up to examine the concept of a dental care team, with the dentist as its leader. This kind of practice is now well established, but was remarkably innovative at the time. The project tested out ways of training the members of the care team – dentist, dental nurse, hygienist, dental therapist – to work together. The project reported in 1977. It compared students working alone on a given treatment with those supported by a dental surgery assistant, and found that the solitary student took three times as long. Another surprising discovery was that patients preferred to be treated by a team in an open-plan area, rather than a dentist alone in a closed room.

Over the next few years the School developed a two-year course for dental therapists (who undertake simple procedures, usually under the direction of a dentist), and celebrated the 25th anniversary of welcoming dental surgery assistants into the School.

The state of the nation's teeth, 1968

Yellow phosphorus and mercury may have been on the decline in factories, but by 1968, when a national survey was undertaken, the nation's teeth were not in great condition. 36.8 per cent of people over the age of 16 had none of their own teeth. (In some parts of the country, a set of dentures made a welcome twenty-first birthday present). 82.5 per cent had some type of gum disease. The only good news was that people who had grown up with NHS treatment had lost fewer teeth than the older generation. General opinion in the profession was that there was a serious lack of periodontal work and preventive dentistry. The fee system seemed to leave no space for either. Perhaps more work could be undertaken by ancillary dental staff.

The Dental School in 2012

What would the 1911 School's founders see if they could visit today? Space, of course: the 1965 building now houses 140 dental chairs, with another 30 in outreach centres. People: 400 undergraduates (including a hundred on the Graduate Entry Programme, a four-year programme for people who hold a first degree in a related subject) and 70 postgraduates. And such a range of people: around half of the students are women, and many (both male and female) are British, of South Asian origin. There are overseas students too, from Malaysia, Arab countries and Greece in particular. The faculty numbers over 90 full- and part-time lecturers, as well as researchers, technicians and administrative staff.

Our founders would find the same core skills taught – extractions, fillings, dentures, crowns – though the students no longer go through all the stages of making dentures themselves: the fumes of black vulcanite have completely gone. The planning and delivery of treatment have become much more sophisticated, including the use of cone

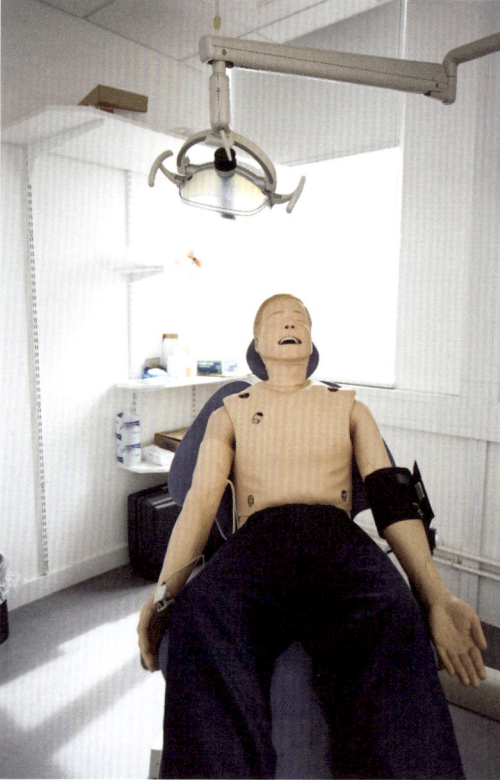

Dental students practise their skills using mannequins.

beam computerised tomography (which produces a high-resolution 3D image) and implants. The curriculum, introduced in 2001, aims to integrate clinical skills and academic knowledge, and create links between disciplines. Students now start seeing patients in their first year; Professor Paul Wright, Dean of the School from 1999–2007, says how important it is for young people to grasp the responsibility involved from early on. The curriculum also addresses the old complaint from graduates, that there was too much of a gap between taught skills and the reality of general practice. As well as seeing patients for one-off emergency care or routine and specialist care at the Institute, students work at outreach centres in the Isle of Dogs and Southend, in more ordinary primary care settings.

The findings of the Experimental Dental Care Project are embodied in the Centre for Dental Care Professionals, where dental nurses, hygienists and therapists are trained, often alongside dental students, to ensure that the team-working approach is shared from the start.

Now, as throughout the School of Medicine and Dentistry, there is a strong emphasis on research. There are three research groups: Immune and Inflammatory Disease; Caries, Hard Tissue and Materials; and Oral Cancer (with links to the Barts Cancer Institute). Research achievements include the development of a new toothpaste which uses glass to carry fluoride, the development of a protein that protects the teeth against decay, and the use of three dimensional modelling in planning veneers and crowns. Reluctant patients may also be interested by the work on managing dental phobia. In 2000, the Dental School was given the maximum score (4) in all six aspects of its work, by the Quality Assurance Agency. In 2005 it topped the *Guardian*'s university subject league table. In the 2008 Research Assessment Exercise, it was ranked second out of 14 UK dental schools.

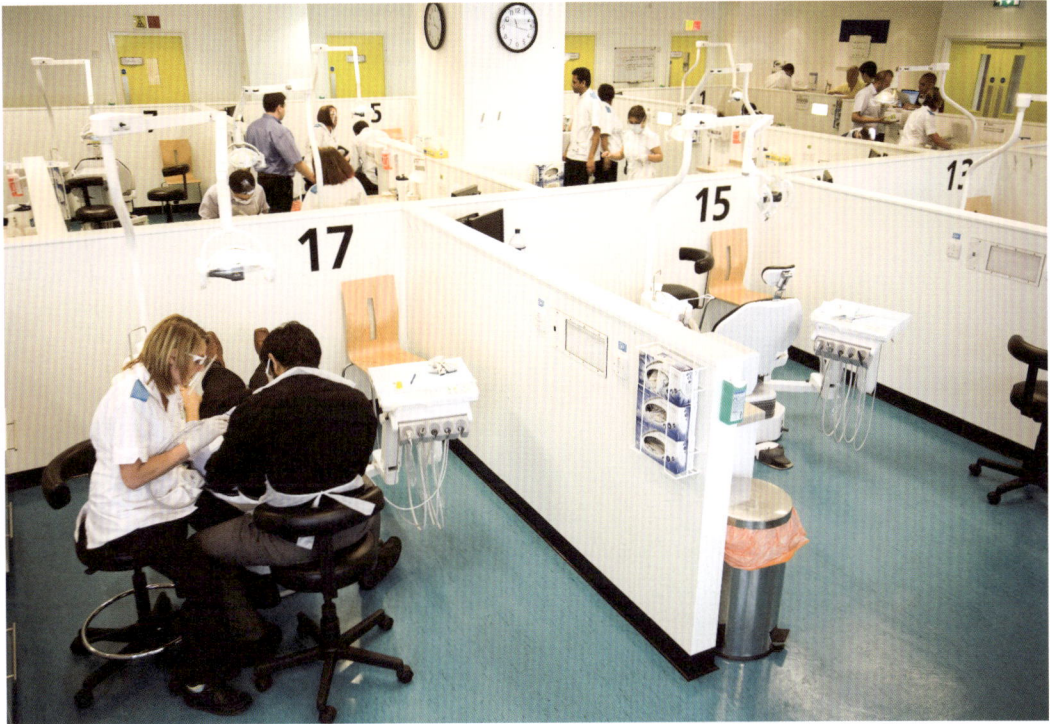

The dental clinic at Barkantine, Isle of Dogs. Students work with patients under close supervision.

Patients at the Institute of Dentistry

Come along New Road, Stepney, past the rag-trade shops in Georgian terraced houses, the office advertising Hajj and Umrah services, and you see the whole East End – Cockney, Bengali, Somali, East European – coming into the Dental Institute for treatment. If the ethnicities have changed, the basic principle has not. The East End lends itself for the training of new dentists, and in return receives much-needed treatment. One patient's experience can stand for many:

A sincere 'thank you' for all the help you have given. This has resulted in a functioning mouth again, able to enjoy a wider variety of food, and beautiful teeth – hard to tell which are mine! As a former head teacher I have been most impressed with the superb training the students receive, and how fortunate they are to have such excellent tutors.[41]

41. www.dentistry.qmul.ac.uk (Accessed in 2011)

Cardiovascular research, 1986

Stained glass window showing William Harvey in the Great Hall, St Bartholomew's Hospital.

In 1609 William Harvey, aged thirty-one, a Fellow of the Royal College of Physicians and graduate of the school of medicine in Padua, was appointed physician to St Bartholomew's Hospital in London. In 1628 he published *Exercitatio Anatomica de Motu Cordis et Sanguinis in Animalibus* (*The Motion of the Heart and Blood in Animals*), which set out his extraordinary discovery of the circulation of the blood.

Staff at Barts and The London School of Medicine and Dentistry (and allied hospitals) have continued to build on Harvey's legacy by contributing to the evolution of the modern stethoscope, a considerable advance on the device originally created by René Laennec in 1816. In addition, Barts performed one of the first open heart valve operations to narrow the mitral valve.

In 1986 the pharmacologist Sir John Vane joined St Bartholomew's Hospital Medical College from the Wellcome Foundation. Four years earlier he had shared the Nobel prize for Physiology or Medicine for his work in demonstrating how aspirin produces pain-relief, acts as an anti-inflammatory and prevents blood clots, and for his discovery of prostacyclin, which dilates blood vessels and also inhibits blood-clotting. Prostacyclin remains one of the few therapies for pulmonary hypertension (high pressure in the lungs' blood circulation) even some 30 years later.

Vane also contributed significantly to the development of drugs which block powerful blood vessel constrictors (the renin angiotensin system) and was instrumental in persuading Squibb Pharmaceuticals to develop angiotensin-converting enzyme inhibitors, one of the most widely used treatments for heart disease today.

When Vane arrived at St Bartholomew's Hospital Medical College he established a major centre for pharmacological research, specialising in inflammation and cardiovascular disease. He attracted an internationally renowned team including Professor Born (who invented the method for platelet stickiness), Professor MacIntyre (who discovered calcitonin), and Professors Angaard and Willoughby and Professor Flower (who discovered annexin). In honour of his great predecessor, Vane named this centre the William Harvey Research Institute (WHRI). The WHRI has grown over the last 26 years, and now numbers 330 clinicians and scientists, drawn from 44 nations, working on heart disease, inflammation and endocrine disorders.

Beetroot juice
William Harvey might have been less surprised at the uses of beetroot juice than we are; available treatments in his day were closer to their natural origins. Professor Amrita Ahluwalia at the WHRI has discovered that beetroot juice can lower blood pressure in healthy volunteers as effectively as the usual drugs. Beetroot is rich in nitrate, which converts in the body to nitric oxide, a gas that opens up blood vessels. A vital part of this process is the conversion of nitrate by bacteria living on the back of the tongue. (Professor Ahluwalia's team has also shown that people who use antiseptic mouthwash have higher blood pressure). The next stage, in progress at the time of writing in 2012, is to test the effect of beetroot juice in patients with

high blood pressure. The condition can affect the functioning of the heart; with high quality Magnetic Resonance Imaging (MRI) equipment it is possible to monitor the effectiveness of the beetroot juice treatment on the heart's functions.

This innovative work is possible because the WHRI has one of four Cardiovascular Biomedical Research Units (BRUs), awarded £5.45 million funding from the National Institute for Health Research in 2008, with a further £6.55 million granted in 2012. The Unit's aim is to advance the translation of scientific knowledge – such as the potential uses of dietary nitrate in beetroot – into available treatments, ie an innovative beetroot-based medicine. The BRU has a new Advanced Cardiovascular Imaging Team, a state-of-the-art Computer Tomography Scanner, and high fidelity MRI technology, to enable a far more sophisticated understanding of the way in which treatments in trial are affecting patients.

The development of the William Harvey Research Institute

1986 Foundation of the Institute, with sponsorship from Glaxo Group Research.

1990 The Institute becomes a company limited by guarantee, with charitable status. A subsidiary company, William Harvey Research Ltd, is set up to deal with the Institute's intellectual property.

1991 WHRI joins the Association of Medical Research Charities.

1996 The Institute expands with the incorporation of Clinical Pharmacology.

1997 The Board of Trustees recommends a merger with Barts and The London School of Medicine and Dentistry

1999 Transfer of the Bone and Joint Unit from The London Hospital to WHRI.

2000 Merger with Barts and The London School of Medicine and Dentistry and QM; the Division of Pharmacology is created. The William Harvey Research Foundation takes over the Institute's charitable functions.

2001 Transfer of Endocrinology from Barts Hospital to WHRI.

2003 WHRI becomes one of six institutes in the newly re-organised Barts and The London School of Medicine and Dentistry.

2004 WHRI is rated in top 20 pharmacological institutes in the World (http://highlycited.com)

2006 The Institute celebrates its 20th anniversary

2007 Two new centres are created: the Centre for Experimental Medicine and Rheumatology; and the Centre for Microvascular Research. Total of 240 staff and students

2008 65 per cent of the Institute's research is rated as 'world leading or internationally excellent' by the UK Research Assessment Exercise (RAE).

The creation of the National Institute for Health Research Cardiovascular Biomedical Research Unit.

2011 The opening of William Harvey Heart Centre (see below).

The William Harvey Heart Centre
The William Harvey Heart Centre, a new, 3,172 square metre building in Charterhouse Square, was formally opened in July 2011. The Centre represents an investment of £25 million in cardiovascular research. It has benefited from the support of partners, principally the Medical College of St Bartholomew's Hospital Trust. The Centre is unique in being able to link laboratory work with patient engagement. The Centre's Clinical Trials Unit can call on a range of clinical experts from both QM and the Barts and The London NHS Trust, to test out the findings of lab research, and the WHRI's links with GP practices in east London provide a diverse group of patients to participate in its clinical trials. This combination of factors has attracted internationally renowned scientific teams working on new therapies for disorders of heart rhythm (led by Professor Tinker), new therapies for vascular disease (Dr Hobbs), and the role of the immune system in heart disease (Professor Marelli-Berg).

The WHRI and east London

East London has some of the worst rates of ill-health in western Europe. If this disturbing fact means that the people of east London have a particular interest in the success of cardiovascular research, it also offers William Harvey researchers ample opportunity to test out their findings.

The Institute and the Heart Centre may be situated in elegant Charterhouse Square, but the catchment area of the hospitals and the School of Medicine and Dentistry includes Tower Hamlets, Newham and Hackney. The WHRI has established a network of 120 local GP practices, with a total of 500,000 patients who can be invited to take part in relevant clinical trials. Part of the Institute's commitment is also to share the results of these trials with the patients who have taken part, as well as the wider public. In 2005, 700 patients who had helped with the ASCOT study (see below) joined staff for a giant tea party in Charterhouse Square, set up to tell them the results, as well as to thank them for their participation. Many former patients continue to support and engage in WHRI research to this day.

Preventing heart attacks and strokes

Professor Mark Caulfield, Director of the Institute, and Dr David Collier, Clinical Research Scientist, were involved in a large scale study – the Anglo-Scandinavian Cardiac Outcomes Trial (ASCOT) – which tested the impact of new versus old combinations of blood pressure and lipid-lowering drugs on 19,000 high-risk patients. ASCOT reported its findings in 2005. Caulfield and Collier recruited 1,157 of the 9,000 UK patients involved in the trial through the GP practice network, and followed them for five and a half years. A third of these patients were of minority ethnic origin.

The ASCOT study showed that in people with average or lower cholesterol levels, taking a statin reduced heart disease by 36 per cent and stroke by 27 per cent. British and European prescribing recommendations are now based on these findings. In 2005 further publications from ASCOT showed the enhanced effectiveness of a combination of the newer blood pressure-reducing drugs over the older ones. The combination reduced mortality by 11 per cent, new onset diabetes by 30 per cent, and stroke and other cardiovascular events significantly.

The National Institute for Health and Clinical Excellence (NICE) guidelines (issued in 2006 and 2011) have been heavily influenced by ASCOT's work.

Genetics and blood pressure

The British Genetics of Hypertension (BRIGHT) study, established with Medical Research Council Programme funding, is co-ordinated at the WHRI on behalf of five other universities. BRIGHT is a family-based study of the genes that cause severe hypertension (high blood pressure); it offered a platform to join the Wellcome Trust Case Control Consortium.

In 2007, WHRI researchers published scans of the genetic code seen in seven common diseases in *Nature* (this was voted top paper in worldwide science in 2007). This work identified the genes responsible for many disorders, but did not find those responsible for high blood pressure. This prompted Caulfield and Munroe to establish much larger consortia, such as the International Consortium for Blood Pressure Genome-Wide Studies. This involved over 275,000 participants, and 351 scientists from 234 institutions in 24 countries (*Nature* voted this study among the top five cardiovascular advances in 2011, and *Nature Genetics* gave it the same accolade in 2009–11). To date these studies (alongside others) have identified 43 genes influencing blood pressure. This work may well open up new means of treatment.

Stem cell therapies for heart disease

A further, exciting area of research, led by Professors Mathur and Suzuki, is the use of stem cells to treat patients with heart attacks and heart failure. The stems cells are taken from the patient's own bone marrow, which means they are less likely to be rejected. (The ethical issues around some stem cell research are also avoided). They are then applied to the patient's damaged heart muscle. The example below of a fictitious patient, Patricia, demonstrates the process used in the trials and the hoped-for outcome.

Entrance to the new William Harvey Heart Centre, opened in 2011.

In addition, Professor Ken Suzuki at the WHRI has developed sheets of stem cells, which can be applied to damaged areas of the heart like a plaster, and will hopefully encourage existing heart tissue to pump more effectively. At the time of writing, this revolutionary new procedure is almost ready to be tested in clinical trials.

Patricia: a case study

• Patricia suffers a heart attack at her home in east London

• The ambulance takes her to the Barts and The London Heart Attack Centre, at the London Chest Hospital

• She has emergency surgery: an angioplasty, which opens up the blocked artery, stops the attack and reduces further damage to her heart

• A sample of stem cells is taken from Patricia's bone marrow

• The sample is prepared for use

• The stem cells are injected into the previously blocked artery

• These stem cells help the heart to repair itself and function better. They also prevent future heart failure (a common complication of heart attacks)

• Patricia returns to a far better quality of life.

The role of white cells

The work of Professor Sussan Nourshargh describes the processes and triggers that lead to white cells leaving the blood vessel in response to inflammation and infection. To do this she has developed novel approaches to imaging, so that we can now capture the movement of the cells into the tissues in real time. This paves the way for new lines of research investigating treatments that could be beneficial in treating heart disease.

Teaching

Dr Steffen Petersen and Dr Francesca Pugliese host the Barts and The London Annual Science Festival for school children, with the hope of inspiring them to consider a career in science.

The WHRI also leads 'safe prescribing training' for all Barts and The London medical students and oversees year one of the four-year Graduate Entry Programme (a four-year MBBS degree programme for students who already have a degree). The Institute also offers a one-year BMedSci (Bachelor of Medical Sciences) programme, as well as a number of masters programmes, including an MRes in the Mechanisms of Vascular Disease. There are a large number of PhD and post-doctoral students training at the Institute.

WHRI alumni include leading academics at Yale, St Louis, in Italy, and in the UK. Csaba Szabó, a post-doctoral fellow at the Institute in the mid-1990s, reflects on what he learned at William Harvey:

(1) World-class science and [the] practical implications of the research are not antagonistic, but rather, they go hand in hand.

(2) It is not the methodology you use, but the scientific questions you have in your head that should drive your research.

(3) Good things can come out of marrying and combining seemingly distant fields of research.

(4) It is not healthy trying always to be the smartest guy in the room.

(5) Sometimes when your paper is rejected from a journal, it makes sense to send it to an even better journal; and

(6) Many times the 'experts' are dead wrong.[42]

42. quoted in *William Harvey Research Institute: At twenty and beyond*. London, Barts and The London School of Medicine and Dentistry, 2006.

Barts Cancer Institute, 2003

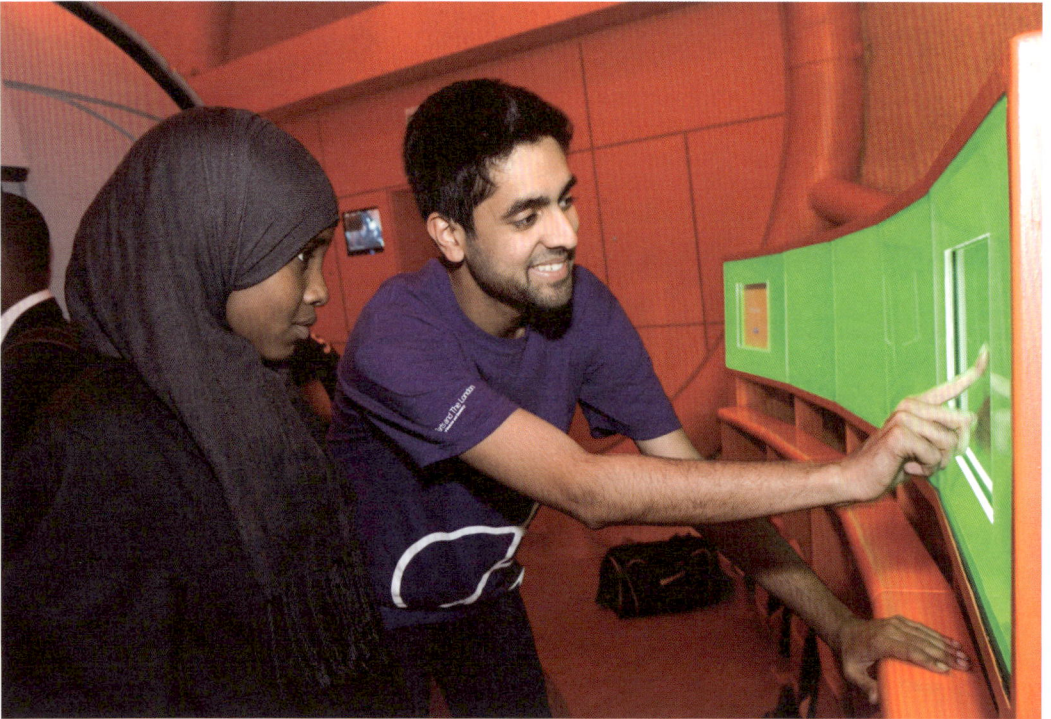

A visitor inside Centre of the Cell, the interactive educational centre
based in the Blizard Building, Whitechapel campus.

In 2010 Emma Rae, aged 24, was invited to attend the opening of the £200 million-pound Barts Cancer Research UK Centre. She was interviewed by the press, and taken into the labs behind the scenes. "It was brilliant," she says now. "People were saying they'd seen my name and they were really pleased to meet me. Normally you never get to meet the people who are checking your blood and so on."[43]

Emma was onto her third recurrence of acute myeloid leukaemia when she became one of Barts Cancer Institute's star patients. She was 15 when she had her first diagnosis: a series of apparently minor conditions had led to a blood test and then six months in hospital at Barts for intensive chemotherapy. Three years later the leukaemia returned and she had a bone marrow transplant. At her regular check-up six months later, she was told that she still had the cancer. "I was feeling really well," she says. "I kept asking, 'Are you sure?'" That was when her doctor, Professor John Gribben, suggested she might take part in a clinical trial.

"They said it was a new treatment but it had been done in Germany; and they gave me time to decide," Emma says. "I did think: 'I'm a guinea-pig – if this goes wrong …' But I've always thought positively. If there'd been another option, I'd have taken it first; but there wasn't. In the end I was more than happy to take part."

The new treatment involves chemotherapy, followed at once by a transplant of donor stem cells. It means a much shorter stay in hospital –

one month rather than six – and it has proved suitable for a wide range of patients, including those like Emma who are more vulnerable as a result of previous treatment. Emma's presence at the opening of the Centre, four years on, demonstrates the success of the experimental treatment, as well as the very well-established links between lab-based research and the treatment of patients.

From bench to bedside and back

The Barts Cancer Centre is a joint initiative between the charity Cancer Research UK, Barts Cancer Institute (BCI), and Barts and The London NHS Trust. Professor Nick Lemoine, Director of both the Barts Cancer Centre and the BCI, is clear that the strength of their work is the translation from laboratory research to treatment, and the feedback from treatment into further research. All the scientists working in the BCI's research centres are exposed to clinical reality: ie how cancer affects the lives of people like Emma. "People come to work here because they're inspired by the idea of translating their work into drugs: that can then be trialled on people with cancer; by having a real impact on patients," Nick Lemoine explains.[44]

Sarah Martin, Lecturer in Molecular Oncology, supports Nick Lemoine's view. "I decided to take up a position at the BCI, as I wanted to carry out research based on biological principles which could be translated into therapeutic strategies for cancer treatment. The BCI is one of the few research institutes where one can do this."[45]

43. Rae, E. Interview for this history. 2011.

44. Lemoine, N. Interview for this history. 2011.
45. Martin, S. Written contribution for this history. 2011.

History

When the BCI was formed in 2003, Barts and The London School of Medicine and Dentistry was facing a major challenge. The results of the 2001 Research Assessment Exercise (RAE) had been a disappointment, which inevitably meant a threat to funding. The Warden at the time, Professor Nick Wright (appointed in 2001), was faced with the challenge of improving research rankings in time for the next RAE in 2008. A massive restructuring followed, which in turn led to the formation of the Institute of Cancer, later known as the BCI.

Nick Lemoine came from Imperial College to set up and lead the new Institute. Funding from what was then the Imperial Cancer Research Fund (now Cancer Research UK) enabled whole teams to transfer to the Institute, bringing their funding with them.

Given that there are over 200 different types of cancer, Nick Lemoine's first task was to decide which areas of research to tackle, as well as who should do it. His guiding objective was to improve substantially the quality of the Institute's research and link it to effective clinical trials – and to do this in time for the next RAE.

Talented staff would be key to the success of the new Institute. Nick Lemoine went on a recruitment drive for young clinicians whose work was already funded. "We wanted lots of young, talented, energetic, ambitious people, who believed they could make an impact on the problem of cancer, both in individuals and in populations." Eight years on, the emphasis remains the same: what is rewarded is not the publication of a paper in the professional journals, but the impact on patients' lives.

The strategy paid off. In the 2008 RAE, the Institute was rated first in London and third in the UK for research into cancer. 95 per cent of its faculty was entered; 15 per cent of the work was considered world-class (4*) and 70 per cent internationally excellent (3*). It was a dazzling turn-around. At the same time, with the increased prestige of the BCI, funding has grown and staffing tripled, from a hundred in 2004, to around 300 six years later.

Working at the Institute

Below, some of our researchers describe their work at the BCI.

Dr Carla Milagre
Postdoctoral Research Assistant,
Centre for Cancer and Inflammation
My research focuses on ovarian cancer patients and the reasons why they can relapse. I hope to determine the main factors that contribute to the spread of this cancer, which kills so many women every day all over the world.

Dr Essam Kerwash Ghazaly
Postdoctoral Research Assistant,
Centre for Haemato-Oncology
My research is currently focused on the clinical pharmacology of cancer therapeutic agents … The work can be challenging and mentally stimulating, as we try to find the causes behind anomalies in our results, or try to understand the mechanisms behind observed interaction.

Sonya Mash
Research Nurse,
Centre for Experimental Cancer Medicine
I work as an Oncology Research Nurse. I provide care for patients with a variety of different tumour types, including ovarian, cervical, pancreatic, prostate and colorectal cancer … Working within the Centre for Experimental Cancer Medicine enables a nurse to feel part of an extended team, with the support of not only doctors and nurses, but also data managers and experienced trials personnel.

Dr Samira Alliouchene,
Postdoctoral Research Assistant,
Centre for Cell Signalling
Mammals have eight isoforms of PI3K [Phosphatidylinositol 3-kinases: a type of enzyme involved in cell functions], subdivided into three classes. The focus of my laboratory has thus far been almost exclusively on the class I PI3Ks, which have been implicated in cancer, inflammation and diabetes… My research work is focused on the characterisation of the role of the class II PI3Ks in metabolism and cancer… It is hoped that this work will identify new drug targets and improve the specificity of current drugs in treating cancer or diabetic patients.

Dr Michael Allen
Postdoctoral Research Assistant,
Centre for Tumour Biology

In my current research, I aim to understand how early breast cancer... progresses to invasive disease. If left untreated only around 50 per cent of DCIS (ductal carcinoma in situ) patients will progress to the potentially fatal invasive diseases, suggesting many women are over-treated. Part of my work concerns how we can stratify treatment better. Moreover, there must be a trigger causing the development of invasive disease, and thus I aim to determine what this is.

Dr Lara Boyd
Postdoctoral Research Assistant,
Molecular Oncology

I work in Dr Yong-Jie Lu's research group, which focuses primarily on prostate cancer genetics... It's great to be able to work in an institute that mixes both basic and translational science, as it means that you are always aware of the bigger picture – something that can get lost when you work at the molecular level. The Institute itself is equipped with state-of-the-art technology, meaning that you are never constrained in the research that you can carry out.[46]

Teaching

"I want medical students to be exposed to what we know about cancer," says Nick Lemoine. "I want to inspire the next generation." Undergraduates at the School of Medicine and Dentistry learn about cancer from the Institute's postgraduate students; given the prevalence of the disease, Nick Lemoine would like the subject to have a higher profile within the undergraduate curriculum.

Among postgraduate programmes, there is an MSc in Cancer Therapeutics, with electives including Paediatric and Adolescent Oncology, and Cancer Prevention and Screening; an MSc in Molecular Pathology and Genomics; an MD(Res) for clinically qualified students; and three PhD studentships and two clinical fellowships each year, funded by Cancer Research UK.

Perhaps as important as the Institute's current clinical education is the outreach work that encourages school students to consider a career in medicine. Sixth-formers are offered short work-experience placements in the BCI or Barts Hospital. The BCI firmly believes that seeing people doing their day-to-day work is the best way to persuade young people that they can try it too.

46. http://www.bci.qmul.ac.uk/research/life-as-a-researcher.html
(Accessed in 2011).

The tissue bank

In March 2011, it was announced that the BCI, along with three other UK sites, would house the world's first national breast cancer tissue bank. Every breast cancer patient at the hospital will be asked if tissue that is not needed medically can be kept for scientific research. The tissue bank will be available to doctors and scientists anywhere in the world, to provide the raw material for further research.

The Barts Cancer Institute has become one of the great successes of the School of Medicine and Dentistry, and of Queen Mary as a whole. It attracts dynamic and innovative researchers – and with these researchers comes funding and support. Cancer Research UK's funding of the Barts Cancer Centre both recognises the quality of the Institute's and Hospital's work and enables it to develop further; it also validates the Institute's fundamental 'bench to bedside and back' approach. As does Emma Rae's presence at the Centre's opening. "I even met the man who went to Germany to pick up my donor cells," she says. "That was just amazing."

The Centre of the Cell

Younger school children can explore health and illness at the Centre of the Cell, the extraordinary interactive centre based in the School of Medicine and Dentistry's Blizard Building. The Director of the Centre is Professor Fran Balkwill; she is also Centre Lead for the Centre for Cancer and Inflammation at Barts Cancer Institute. The Centre of the Cell opened in September 2009. It operates both as a physical centre where children can learn about science and medicine, and as a stand-alone website, a virtual centre. It announces:

> Our research team found that young people have difficulty understanding cells, find science boring, and think that scientists are white, male, middle-aged and mad ... Science, and the ethical issues that biomedical research increasingly raises, underpins the future development of our society.[47]

The Centre hopes particularly to provide insights into medicine for young people from east London. Its aims include to:

• inspire the next generation of scientists and healthcare professionals
• raise career aspirations and improve educational attainment
• help young people fulfil their potential.

And if that seems too worthy, the message to children accessing the site is straightforward and engaging:

> Cells are the building units of your body. Cells are so tiny you can't see them with your eyes and there are so many in your body you can't count them. Cells work together to make you think, move, talk, laugh and be you ... You started life as a single cell, smaller than the dot at the end of this sentence.[48]

47. http://www.smd.qmul.ac.uk/centreofthecell/ (Accessed in 2012).
48. ibid.

Part 2:
The complete College

1996–2000

Wolfson Institute of Preventive Medicine, Charterhouse Square campus.

The new complete College

By the start of the academic year 1995–96, the merger of QM with the new School of Medicine and Dentistry was complete. The Bill establishing the new College received Royal Assent in November 1995. The QM switchboard had recovered from the 1,300 phone calls per day of the previous summer; the recent innovation of voicemail helped to reduce the pressure. Work had started on a new £4.77 million Clinical Research Building in Whitechapel, and plans were being made for the new Medical School building. In February the church of St Dunstan and All Saints, Stepney hosted a Thanksgiving Service for 210 years of medical study at The London.

The Dearing Report

Meantime, the political situation of higher education was evolving. Faced with almost double the number of universities in the UK, and the million students enrolled in them, in 1996 the Conservative government remitted the question of higher education funding to a committee of inquiry. The Dearing Committee consisted of business people, including its Chair, Sir Ron Dearing, and university leaders, but no practising academics. Members were told from the start that no additional government funding was available.

The Committee reported in July 1997, shortly after the Labour government came to power. It recommended, among other things, an increase in the participation of young people in higher education from 32 to 45 per cent, and the setting up of mechanisms to improve the quality of teaching. Neither of these, however, was going to remedy the funding situation. The recommendation that emerged was for a flat-rate tuition fee to top up the maintenance grant, of 25 per cent of the real cost of tuition, or around £3,000; the balance would be paid by the state. The assumption behind this move away from state funding was that higher education was of benefit primarily to the individual, rather than to the society in which they would function. This, Robert Anderson considers,

> …was at odds with other aspects of the report: if higher education is so vital to the economy, for example, why should business not make a contribution too?[49]

The new government, however, rejected this system of joint state and individual payments, in favour of a flat fee of £1,000 and the abolition of the maintenance grant, which was replaced by student loans. (The new Scottish Parliament in due course replaced this with a system closer to Dearing's). At the same time, the target participation rate was raised to 50 per cent.

Finance, funding and strikes

Before the Dearing Committee had started work, the Committee of Vice-Chancellors and Principals (CVCP) had made its own proposals on funding, including a £300 registration fee. This, said Graham Zellick, Principal of QM, in his regular newsletter to staff, was not enough to make the fee worth collecting.[50] In early 1996 the finances of the College were healthy, with a projected surplus of £1.3 million at the end of the academic year 1995–96, some of which could be moved to the College's reserves. The following year, however, things were

49. Anderson, R, op cit.
50. Zellick, G. Principal's Newsletter, February 1996. (London: Queen Mary & Westfield College, 1996).

going to be difficult. The College's grant was to be cut by over five per cent, and capital funding by 35 per cent. Necessary new equipment in the Computer Science department, for instance, could only be funded out from College reserves. The Government suggested that shortfalls could be met by Public Finance Initiative (PFI) schemes; but the Higher Education Funding Council for England (HEFCE) insisted that there was no way of achieving this.

In this context, Graham Zellick concluded, a pay award to staff was unaffordable. Even a one per cent award would cost an additional £400,000. The Committee of Vice-Chancellors and Principals campaigned against funding cuts, and had delayed negotiating a pay award nationally, "in the hope that some encouraging messages may be received from the Government as to the funding position to be announced this autumn.' In the meantime, staffing vacancies could be filled only "in the most compelling circumstances."[51]

Having resolved one financial crisis in the early 1990s, a few years later Graham Zellick was facing another. His bulletins to staff over the next two years recount stage by stage the negotiations, reactions and hard decisions he faced as Principal. In July 1996 six technical staff were made redundant. The unions rejected a pay offer of 1.5 per cent. The remit of the Dearing inquiry, the Principal noted, was "impossibly wide."[52] By December there had been a one-day strike; he responded: "While I sympathise with the staff, that does not allow me or the responsible College committees to set aside financial prudence."[53] By February 1997 an agreement was made that, the Principal explained, would add £1.2 million to the College's projected deficit in each of the 1996–97 and 1997–98 financial years.

In April 1997, that deficit was forecast at £3.7 million for 1997–98, rising by 1999–2000 to £7.1 million. The main cause was the successive cut in Government funding. The Research Assessment Exercise (RAE) resulted in only a small overall increase in research funding, and a larger than anticipated reduction for the Medical and Dental School. David Blunkett, Secretary of State for Education, acknowledged that there were defects in the RAE system; but that was of no help for the immediate future.

The Council of the College decided on various measures to tackle this situation. Non-academic promotions were cancelled, academic staff vacancies frozen (again), capital allocations cut. All departments were tasked with finding proportionate savings. The Medical and Dental School would make major cuts, based on its strategic plan for teaching and research. The Humanities and Science faculties had to find £400,000 of savings per annum by reducing numbers of non-academic staff. In February 1997, the focus was on the Chemistry Department, which had performed poorly in the RAE. Should it be closed? The option was considered; but the merger with the Barts and The London School of Medicine and Dentistry had been agreed partly on the basis that QM had expertise in the natural sciences. The only other option was to invest, in order to improve research standards. Staff numbers would be increased, those taking retirement replaced, and one proposed staff transfer from another university would be accepted. The aim was to bring Chemistry up to grade 4 in the next RAE.

51. Ibid.
52. Zellick, G. Principal's Newsletter, July 1996. (London: Queen Mary & Westfield College, 1996).
53. Zellick, G. Principal's Newsletter, December 1996. (London: Queen Mary & Westfield College, 1996).

Research Assessment Exercise grading scale, 1996

5* International excellence in more than half the
  research submitted, and national excellence
  in the remainder

5 International excellence in up to half the
  research submitted, and national excellence
  in virtually all the remainder

4 National excellence in virtually all the research
  submitted, with some evidence of international
  excellence

3a National excellence in over two thirds of
  research submitted, possibly showing evidence
  of international excellence

3b National excellence in more than half the
  research submitted

2 National excellence in up to half the research
  submitted

1 National excellence in none, or virtually none,
  of the research submitted

Graham Zellick retired as Principal in the summer
of 1998, to take up the post of Vice Chancellor of
the University of London. Of his time at QM he
says:

> They have been eventful years, possibly with
> more significant developments compressed into
> that time than any other eight-year period in the
> history of any of the colleges that make up the
> present QMW.[54]

This is perhaps unduly modest. The situation
Graham Zellick inherited in 1990 was extremely
difficult, and the significant developments that
took place during his time included consolidating
the two successive mergers to create a single,
thriving institution. In fact, the work of the early
1990s created a substantial basis for the expansion
and the major successes of the new millennium.

Professor Adrian Smith, on his appointment from
Imperial College as the new Principal, recognised
the College's strengths and also its potential.
He recalls his impression of the College in 1998:

> I knew enough about the people [at QM] and
> the history to know that the College was
> unnecessarily punching below its weight. It had
> been involved in some major developments:
> the discovery of string theory, for instance, and

the work on parallel computing. It was sad that
the College was un-self-confident. I thought it
could be fantastic.[55]

Adrian Smith's analysis of the issues involved and
his strategy for tackling them are considered in the
next chapter.

54. Zellick, G. Principal's Newsletter, February 1998. (London: Queen Mary & Westfield College, 1998).

55. Smith, A. Interview for this history. 2012.

Research achievements, 1996–2000

- The European Space Agency's Infrared Space Observatory (ISO) is launched by the shuttle Ariane in November 1995. The ISO uses heat rather than light to scan the universe, enabling it to explore inside dust clouds. **Professor Peter Clegg** is the principal investigator for one of the ISO's four attached instruments. By the end of its operational phase, in April 1998, the ISO will have made around 30,000 observations, within and far beyond the solar system.

- **The Physiology Department** looks at the increased number of deaths in winter in different European countries. The puzzling fact is that countries with mild winters, such as the UK, have a greater increase in mortality than much colder countries. Successive QM internal bulletins chart the progress of this work across the continent. April 1997 finds the Department's researchers in eastern Siberia. February 1998 brings a shocking finding: the region in Western Europe and Russia with the greatest winter increase in deaths per million population is London. By the following winter we have the conclusions. In Britain 400,000 people die each year because of the cold. In Yakutsk, temperatures can reach −40° centigrade without any increase in the mortality rate; in the UK, it rises as soon as the temperature decreases. The difference is not due to climate or levels of medical care, but in the layers of clothing that each population adopts. 'Waiting for a bus for half an hour in a British winter could be life-threatening.'

- **The Wolfson Institute of Preventive Medicine** develops a new antenatal test for Down's Syndrome, the 'Integrated' test, using markers from ultrasound and blood screening at 12 weeks and 16 weeks, all integrated to provide a single test result. This test is widely adopted, in many countries.

- **The Electronic Engineering Department** receives a European Commission award for research into advanced communications in Europe: the project is a collaboration with two commercial companies investigating how to make low-cost broadband more widely available. (It is hard to remember now how remote that possibility seemed.)

The College and the Outside World, 1996–2000

- In 1997, student **Zoe Hudson** is one of 20 women taking part in the first all-women expedition across the Arctic Ocean to reach the North Pole. (She follows this up in 2000 with the first British women's expedition to reach the South Pole).

- **Geraldine van Bueren** (now Professor of International Human Rights Law at QM, and one of the original drafters of the UN Convention on the Rights of the Child) is invited by the Law Commission of South Africa to advise on reforms in juvenile justice.

- **People's Palace Projects (PPP)**, in the School of English and Drama, gets £85,000 from Comic Relief for a project in Ouagadougou, Burkina Faso. From 1997 to 2002, PPP's founder, Paul Heritage, works with the Atelier-Théâtre Burkinabè, offering training to enable people in rural areas to create their own plays, and use them to trigger debate on key issues for the community. (For more on PPP, see chapter 21).

- **The Russian Department** founds the Garnett Press, named after Constance Garnett, Russian translator and the first librarian of the People's Palace. Early publications include in 1996 *The Garnett Book of Russian Verse*, edited by Professor Donald Rayfield.

- **A pure water spring** is discovered during the redevelopment of Mile End Park. The *Bulletin* proposes Mile End as a fashionable spa.

Teaching and Learning, 1996–2000

- The College's **MA in Language, Society & Change in Europe** receives specialist status from the Economic and Social Research Council.
- A new cross-faculty **MA in Film & Communication** is launched.
- The **MA in Theatre & Performance** is created
- A cross-disciplinary **MA in Intellectual & Cultural History** is launched.
- Modules in **Jewish & Arab writing** and **post-colonial literature are now taught at the College**.
- The Business Economics course is re-named **Economics, Finance & Management,** with a dramatic increase in recruitment.
- Tutor groups are introduced for **students with dyslexia**

1999 Quality Assurance Agency assessment

Modern Languages	23/24
Biological Sciences	22/24
Electronic Engineering	21/24
Drama	21/24
Mathematics	21/24
Materials Science	20/24

2001–2005

The Octagon in the Queens' Building, Mile End campus. A library until 1988, the Octagon is now used for a variety of functions from formal dinners to examinations.

A new Strategic Plan for the years 2001–06 announces the College's ambitions. There are, at the time of its design, 9,000 students and 2,600 staff, and an annual income of £120 million. The introduction asserts that the College "is committed to the traditional values of a university, including freedom of inquiry, but with a strong contemporary and innovative approach to teaching and research."[56] The strategic aims for the period include:

- to promote and sustain a culture and environment for high-quality research and teaching that attracts and retains staff and students of the highest calibre

- to invest in new academic appointments and to conduct appropriate restructuring exercises which will ensure that the highest possible percentage of academic staff employed are research-active and judged by their peers to be of high national or international standing

- to promote a culture and infrastructure which maximises earned income in support of high-quality research and teaching

- to exploit activities which provide a third stream of funding and promote interaction with business and the community

- to achieve a balanced financial budget which enables investment in appropriate and affordable capital developments[57]

The tone, even given the professional optimism of strategic planning, is assertive and expansive. The emphasis on research and research funding acknowledges the realities of twenty-first century university life: in order to fulfil "the traditional values of a university", institutions would have to score highly in Research Assessment Exercises (RAE), and attract non-statutory funding to supplement Research Council income. Few academics would remain in post purely on the merits of charismatic teaching.

Professor (now Sir) Adrian Smith, then Principal of QM, explains the background to this plan:

> When I started in 1998, I saw that there were four linked problems. There was the financial situation. Linked to that was research: we weren't going to get funding unless our research was of the highest quality. Thirdly, we weren't attracting enough of the best students; we weren't seen as one of the best in London. Finally, again connected to student recruitment, the estate was not appealing, with decaying halls of residence out at South Woodford.

> So it was easy [*he laughs*]; it was clear what needed doing. I thought it was a ten-year job.[58]

56. Strategic Plan 2001–06. (London: Queen Mary, University of London, 2001).

57. ibid.

58. Smith, A. op cit.

Restructuring

Tackling the finances meant examining every post in every department, to see if it was viable, or could be made so. Civil engineering, a long-established discipline at QM, was struggling. Student recruitment was low, and the research profile not outstanding. It was also an expensive subject to offer, needing considerable space and equipment. The College took the difficult decision to close the department.

Other departments had similar issues. Chemistry, despite the earlier interventions, was still in difficulty. The argument about retaining a Chemistry department because of the Medical and Dental School, however, was still significant. A different approach was tried: the old Chemistry Building was not fit for purpose, and the College decided to invest in a new one. Physics at QM also had its problems; it had an impressive history, but was not attracting students in the present. The Department was supported in improving the profile of its research, and so managed to attract more funding.

Consolidating the medical merger

The two medical schools, Adrian Smith maintains, by the time he started simply "hadn't merged". Not only were the two cultures still poles apart; there was considerable duplication, and a proliferation of often tiny departments. As for the finances:

> In the last quarter of 1998 I was given two volumes of financial analysis, which said that the school would be back in the black by the following year. By March 1999 it was £5 million in the red.[59]

As in the rest of the College, financial viability depended on research. A rigorous assessment of each individual's strengths, their cost to the School and the funding they brought in, resulted in changes to 125 posts. Some posts with few teaching or research components were negotiated back into the NHS Trust. Others were redefined. 'Principal investigators' were given minimal teaching responsibility, to allow a concentrated focus on

research; superb teachers, by contrast, specialised in that, with correspondingly little research duty; and a third group combined the two, in a more traditional way. Recruitment of high calibre researchers followed: "If there wasn't someone fantastic, we didn't appoint."[60] It was too late to affect the results of the 2001 RAE, but the School was gearing up for the next round, in 2008.

Nick Wright recounts the following conversation with Baroness Elaine Murphy (then a member of QM's Council) and Elsie Gilding (then Acting Chair of the Trust) at a William Harvey Day dinner, in October 2000:

> "Are you going to apply for our Warden's job?"
> "Why should I? Barts is in a terrible state."
> "That is precisely why you should apply"
> "I never thought of that."[61]

He was appointed the following year. Brian Colvin believes:

> In the view of many of us, he rescued the new School, almost single-handedly, from the abyss. He has a remarkable style of leadership, based on a mixture of firm action and fearless delegation.[62]

With Peter Kopelman working on education issues, and Brian Colvin on student support and guidance, Nick Wright was able to focus on recruiting and retaining high-quality researchers. A second restructuring reinforced this research focus. Six Institutes were created: Cancer, Cell and Molecular Science, Dentistry, Health Sciences Education, William Harvey (see chapter 8), and the Wolfson Institute of Preventive Medicine. Nick Wright's strategy created an exceptional – and swift – improvement in research output, with dramatic results in the 2008 RAE (see chapter 12).

At the same time, a further boost to the School became possible. The Tomlinson report that set up the merger of the medical school had also resulted in funds for new building, and these had never been taken up by QM. A striking new medical

59. ibid.

60. ibid.
61. Wright, N. Written contribution to this history. 2012.
62. Colvin, B. Written contribution to this history. 2012.

research facility could now be built; but only if funding could be disaggregated from the Public Finance Initiative (PFI) pot for the Royal London Hospital. An approach was made to Frank Dobson, then Secretary of State for Health, who was persuaded to release the funds. His decision gave the School a three or four year start on the Hospital building programme, and a rebirth; without it, Adrian Smith believes, the Medical School would have folded, and dragged the rest of the College down with it. The new Blizard Building, commissioned from Will Alsop Architects after a rigorous tendering process, attracted both researchers and funding (For more detail on the Blizard Building, see chapter 17.)

All this restructuring, with the possibility of compulsory redundancies as a last resort, was bound to attract some opposition. The trade union, the AUT (Association of University Teachers), threatened a campaign in the media; Adrian Smith responded by offering to appoint an independent auditor to examine the books and verify if the cuts were necessary. As a precaution, he and other colleagues undertook some media training, including a mock Newsnight interview. The majority of staff understood the need for action. They accepted that the aim of the restructuring was not to destroy the College, but to enhance its reputation and create more jobs in the future.

The Mile End Group

In 2003, a group of Peter Hennessy's postgraduate students wanted a forum where they could discuss their relevant research. Peter Hennessy (now Lord Hennessy of Nympsfield) is Attlee Professor of Contemporary British History, and the forum became the Mile End Group (MEG), which examines issues of politics and government. MEG began by inviting speakers who excelled in their field; this evolved into a series of seminars by well-known speakers, including Dame Eliza Manningham-Buller (former Director General of MI5), Lord Malloch-Brown (former UN Deputy Secretary-General) and Alan Rusbridger (editor of The *Guardian* newspaper).

The Mile End Institute for the Study of Government, Intelligence and Society was formed in 2005. The following year, undergraduates set up the Undergraduate Mile End Group (UMEG), which seeks to engage students from across the university with issues of politics and government.

MEG has acquired an impressive reputation, and politicians, journalists and academics regularly attend the seminars, along with students and researchers. All the events are free and open to anyone.

In June 2012, the Mile End Group hosted the official launch of *The Burden of Power: Volume 4: Countdown to Iraq*; the fourth and final volume of Alastair Campbell's highly revealing and insightful diaries.

Attracting students

The College as a whole needed more students; it needed, in Adrian Smith's words, to "leapfrog" over the more visible parts of the University of London. A higher research profile was one way to do this; but something more immediate was also needed. What could be the College's unique selling point (or USP) to 18-year-olds living away from home for the first time?

The old graveyard by the Regent's Canal had already been acquired by the College and was lying idle, used only for car parking. Meanwhile students who wanted to live in halls were out at South Woodford, not only far from Mile End but also from the excitement of Central London. The answer to the USP question was to create the best student village in London. Most colleges were entering into partnership with private companies to have residences built; the College Council took the brave decision to borrow money and commission architects themselves. The gamble paid off: the Westfield Student Village is a major attraction for many students, both in the UK and internationally.

Recruiting more overseas students was the other part of the College's plan, as the fees for international students are set at a higher level than for home students. A new Director of External Relations was recruited to re-open the International Office and guide the College's strategy. The BUPT partnership (see chapter 24) was one impressive result, the first partnership in the UK with an overseas university to be granted permission by the Chinese government. At the same time, the number of students from China and across the world enrolling at QM increased substantially.

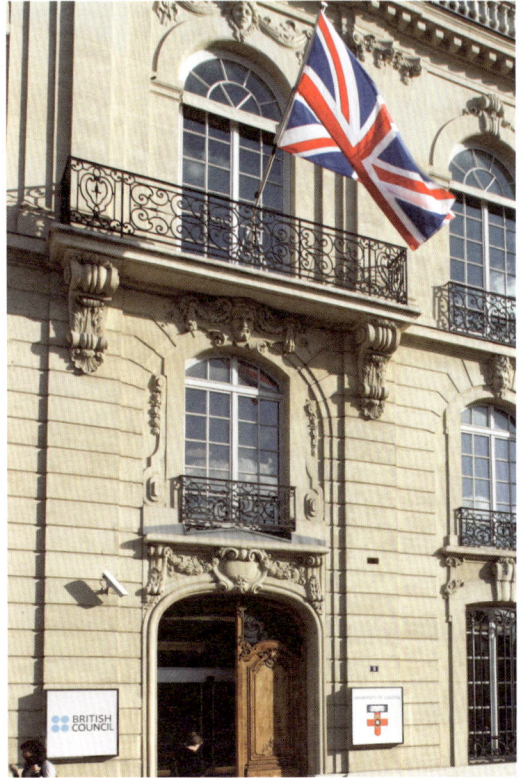

University of London Institute in Paris, *c.*2007.

The University of London Institute in Paris (ULIP)

The University of London Institute in Paris has been part of the London federation since 1969; but its close relationship with QM dates from 2004, and the formation of a Consortium that also involves Royal Holloway, University of London. Some QM students for the BA in French Studies spend a semester at ULIP; equally, undergraduates can take the entire BA programme in Paris. There is also an appealing MA in Paris Studies: History and Culture, with contributions from QM's History Department; and opportunities for postgraduate research on subjects such as French and Francophone Cinema, The Postcolonial World and North African Writing. ULIP publishes a bi-annual journal, *Francosphères*.

The future of higher education

Writing at the end of the period covered by QM's 2001–06 Strategic Plan, Robert Anderson laments that:

> Every aspect of public life is now potentially subject to central direction, and this is to be accomplished by financial incentives and proxy markets; the impression is sometimes given that without constant prodding and monitoring universities would not function at all. But social institutions can and do work independently of the state ... (U)niversities are expected to respond individually to student demand and the challenges of the market, which leaves them much more vulnerable to outside pressures.
>
> This matters because of the commitment of universities to the pursuit of truth and critical and independent thinking, which differentiates them from other social institutions, and provides a counterweight to other centres of power – politics, the media, or big business.[63]

However evident or valid these concerns may have seemed at the turn of the millennium, the challenge for QM was clearly to achieve its aims and work to its stated values within this climate. Adrian Smith recalls operating with a fair degree of independence from government policy. Some aspects were helpful: there were additional student numbers to bid for. There was also a major investment of funds in science and engineering.

In 2003, the Labour government produced a White Paper on The Future of Higher Education, which attracted much comment and debate. One issue was funding: the *Times Higher Education Supplement* (*THES*) pointed out that the percentage of GDP spent on the public funding of higher education (HE) was lower in the UK than in the US, seen as relying on private finance: 0.8 per cent here compared to 1 per cent in the United States. Nevertheless, the White Paper proposed, somewhat hopefully, the adoption of a US-style system of endowments:

> The Government will continue to be the major funder of universities but they should also have greater freedom to access new funding streams on their own account.

63. Anderson, R, op cit.

Providing incentives to build up endowments is one way. Another is allowing universities the right to secure from graduates larger contributions to the cost of their education.[64]

Commenting on the White Paper, the Royal Society noted that any increased student contribution "must take account of the varying future personal financial rewards from participation in HE"[65] (a point which seems to have been neglected since). Another controversial element was the relationship between teaching and research. The White Paper suggested that some universities might gain prestige even without a research function. The Royal Society, among others, challenged this:

> It is fundamental to the concept of HE that students, particularly those on honours first-degree courses, are both exposed to at least some frontiers within their subjects of study, and enabled to continue to keep abreast of developments in the future ... The fundamental issue is the creation of an appropriate high-quality learning environment, to which excellent teaching is a necessary but not sufficient input ... The impacts of research within a university department are many: the attraction of good staff, the attraction of highly qualified and motivated students, and the incorporation of research into the curriculum.[66]

At QM, the Strategic Plan anticipated many of these developments. It was not going to be enough, however, to attract students by means of research; their whole experience of the College needed to be positive. The first student satisfaction surveys were less than ecstatic. Swapping the tower blocks in South Woodford for the Student Village was one response; another was the creation of the post of Vice-Principal for Academic Policy. Barts and The London had a strong tradition of pastoral care and engagement with its students; the same principles were being adapted for the rest of the College.

64. *The Future of Higher Education*. (London: Department for Education and Science, 2003).
65. *Comments on the White Paper: The future of higher education.* (London, Royal Society, 2003)
66. ibid.

The state of the College

Over the first years of the millennium, student numbers at QM rose, from 9,000 students at the start of the Strategic Plan, to just over 10,000 in 2002–03 and 10,700 the following year. The breakdown by subject in 2003–04 was as follows:

Subject	Undergraduate	Postgraduate (taught)	Postgraduate (research)
Medicine & Dentistry	1,743	201	290
Natural Sciences	928	13	87
Engineering & Mathematical Sciences	2,160	322	254
Law & Social Sciences	1,548	501	110
Arts	1,382	92	72
Associates	350	—	—

Applications were also rising steadily. University league table placings were positive: 14th in the UK and 100th in the world, according to the *THES* in 2004; 12th in the UK according to the *Guardian* in 2005; 21st in the world and equal 4th in the UK for arts and humanities research, as judged by the *THES* the same year. In 2003–04, 95 per cent of QM graduates were said to be in employment or education, and those working were earning the second highest new-graduate salaries in the UK: £21,686, against a national average of £16,393.

The Research Assessment Exercise in 2001 also produced some excellent results. In the Humanities and Social Sciences in particular, research was shown to be of outstanding quality: of the eleven subject areas submitted, all but one came into the top two categories (5 and 5*), denoting work of international standard. This placed QM among the top ten universities nationally in these disciplines. There were especially good performances in Law, Hispanic Studies and Linguistics. Professor Philip Ogden, then Vice Principal for the Humanities, comments:

> These results showed what was possible at the College, showed the benefits of the merger with Westfield, and were to presage the outstanding results for the College as a whole in the next RAE.[67]

67. Ogden, P (2012): written contribution to this history

Computer Science For Fun (cs4fn)

In response to a worldwide crash in the number of students studying computer science, Paul Curzon and Peter McOwan decided to make computing fun again. They started in 2005, with a stall at an East End schools career event, teaching some workshop activities and handing out photocopied sheets. Encouraged by the excellent feedback they received, the pair decided to do more to draw those inspired deeper into the subject.

Paul Curzon and Peter McOwan created a more polished magazine and a sister website, called Computer Science For Fun (www.cs4fn.org), and told exciting stories about computer science research, writing them up in an accessible way. That initial print run of a few thousand issues has now become a twice-yearly magazine, with more than 25,000 copies distributed around the UK and in over 80 countries. The magazine includes engaging stories for researchers worldwide and over the next few years it helped to return applications for computer science courses at QM to pre-crash levels, even while nationally numbers continued to drop. The project was praised by the *International Journal of Research and Reviews in Computer Science* in 2006, and gained the largest ever awarded Engineering and Physical Sciences Research Council (EPSRC) Partnership for Public Engagement grant. Since then the project has also gained significant support from Google.

The cs4fn programme has produced two innovative books teaching magic tricks that use hidden computer science, a special on women in computing, a booklet and workshops for primary school children (supported by the Royal Society), two sister magazines on electronic and audio engineering, over a million hits a month on the website, talks to more than 3,000 students each year and trips to science festivals around the UK and Europe. The cs4fn team has produced three more exhibits for the Royal Society Summer Science Exhibition after their initial inspiration in 2005. They even had a hand in helping video games pioneer, space entrepreneur and talented amateur magician, Richard Garriott, become the first person to do a full magic show in space.[68]

68. for more on cs4fn, visit www.cs4fn.org

Double portrait of Hitler and Stalin by Alla Tkachuk, Artist in Residence at Queen Mary, University of London from 2001–06. The work was featured as Image of the Week in *The Times Arts Review*, and the 'Naked Dictators' series was published in the German literary/art magazine *Der Freund*.

Knowledge sculpture, 2003. ©Queen Mary, University of London Archives.
The statue is located in Library Square on the Mile End campus and was commissioned to celebrate the giving
and sharing of knowledge at the College. It reflects the multi-faceted, multi-cultural nature of Queen Mary
and the East End of London. The sculptor Wendy Taylor CBE, is a fellow of the College, and is from
the East End where her family have lived for at least six generations.

Graduation day

Adrian Smith vividly recalls Graduation Day 2005;
it was July 7th, the day of the London bus and
tube bombs. One was detonated just a mile away,
at Aldgate East. The news came through gradually;
sheer horror was followed by a more mundane
concern: what to do about the planned graduation
ceremony? It was agreed to put the start back by
an hour, and see if graduates and their families
would make it. "I remember looking out," Adrian
Smith says, 'and there were all these well-dressed
people walking along Mile End Road. They'd come
on foot, to make sure they got here. In the event
the hall was almost full. If parents couldn't get
home, we put them up."[69]

69. Smith, A, op cit.

The College and the East End, 2001–05

• *Transformations*: a three-year literacy scheme
works with 400 children in local primary schools.

• In 2005, a **summer school** held jointly with the
University of East London, City and London
Metropolitan universities provides intensive study
for a hundred east London school
students.

• A medical student sets up **SAMDA** (Students
Assisted Medical and Dental Applicants), to
support local children in applying for medical
and dental school places (more detail in
chapter 19).

• Students run a **teddy bear hospital,** to help small
children overcome their fear of doctors.

Awards, 2001–05

Department	Recipient	Award
Mathematics	Professor John Papaloizou	Fellow of the Royal Society
Physics	Professor Peter Kalmus	OBE Kelvin Medal
	Professor Christopher Hull	Dirac Medal of the Institute of Physics
	Professor Sir Peter Mansfield (studied physics at QM 1956–62)	Nobel Prize for Medicine
William Harvey Research Institute	Professor Roderick Flower	Fellow of the Royal Society
Wolfson Institute of Preventive Medicine	Professor Sir Nicholas Wald	Fellow of the Royal Society
Institute of Cell and Molecular Science	Professor Sir John Lilleyman	President of Royal College of Pathologists OBE
Barts Cancer Institute	Professor Fran Balkwill	Royal Society Faraday Prize
Law	Professor Genevra Richardson	Fellow of the Royal College of Psychiatrists (for work on mental health law)
	Professor Geraldine van Bueren	UNICEF Children's Rights Lawyer of the Year (2003)
	Professor Roger Cotterrell	Fellow of the British Academy
History	Professor (now Lord) Peter Hennessy	Fellow of the British Academy
English	Professor Lisa Jardine	Trustee of the Victoria & Albert Museum Member of the Council, Royal Institution

- In 2002–03 the **School of Dentistry** and Tower Hamlets Primary Care Trust identify the low uptake of dental services in local minority ethnic communities. The result is an innovative scheme to train volunteers from community groups in oral health promotion.
- Also in 2003–03, the **Institute of Community Health Sciences** administers over 5,000 doses of meningitis vaccine to pilgrims undertaking the Hajj. The intervention leads to a significant reduction in pilgrims returning with the infection.
- In the **Geography Department** Professor Jane Wills produces research showing the crucial reliance of local elderly and disabled people on the carers who help them with daily living.

Research, 2001–05

New research centres	Year opened
CELL (Centre for Editing Lives and Letters)	2002
Dr Williams's Centre for Dissenting Studies	2004
Centre for Renaissance and Early Modern Studies (see chapter 15)	2005
Centre for Anglo-German Cultural Relations	2005
The University of London Centre for Micromorphology (the study of soils and sediments), jointly with Royal Holloway, University of London	2005

Research achievements, 2001–05

- **Computer Science:** the development of a new online secure shopping system, using a mouse-written signature

- **Computer Science:** student Lila Harrar develops software to teach sign language to deaf and hearing users. Microbooks offers her a five-year contract as a developer.

- **Astronomy:** Professor Carl Murray is the only British member of the imaging team for the Cassini space mission.

- **Biological & Chemical Sciences:** researchers discover that bumblebees prefer Van Gogh sunflowers to non-floral paintings.

- **Wolfson Institute:** a symposium on folic acid and spina bifida in 2005 leads to a Scientific Advisory Committee on Nutrition, which advises that folic acid should be added to foods.

- **William Harvey Research Institute:** Atorvastatin is proved in European trials to reduce heart attacks and strokes by a third.

- **Institute of Cell & Molecular Science:** The genetic cause of the skin disease Harlequin Ichthyosis is discovered.

- **Politics:** Professor Seán McConville publishes *Irish Political Prisoners, 1848–1922*, and receives a grant from the British and Irish governments for a companion volume, covering the period to the Good Friday Agreement.

- **Geography:** Dr Simon Lewis, with staff of the Natural History Museum, find the half-a-million-year-old remains of two giant hippos in Norfolk.

Teaching and learning, 2001–05

- A new inter-disciplinary **Philosophy** programme involves staff from Physics, Mathematics and Law as well as the Humanities faculty, 2003–04.

- A new course for medical students, **The Art of Medicine and Healthcare,** run jointly by Humanities and the School of Medicine and Dentistry, looks at the use of the arts in health-care, 2003–04.

- A new foundation degree with City and Islington College, **Scene of Crime and Forensic Investigation,** is recognised as a professional qualification for police scene of crime officers, 2003–04.

- New distance learning programmes in **Computer Science and Electronic Engineering** are launched in 2002–03.

- **School of Dentistry:** Celebrates a 100 per cent student pass rate 2003–04; the School comes first in the *Guardian*'s league 2005 table.

- The Mercers' Company and the Department of Health fund a new **training programme for refugee doctors**, to enable them to practise in the UK, 2001–02.

- Nicholas Murray, biographer, and Martina Evans, poet, are the **Royal Literary Funds' Writer Fellows,** 2002–03. They help QM students in all disciplines, mainly with writing essays, but also with creative writing.

Cassini orbiter, part of the Cassini-Huygens space mission.

Professor Carl Murray.

2006–2012

Graduation, Summer 2011.

The state of higher education

In 2009–10, according to the Higher Education Statistics Agency (HESA), there were just under two and a half million students in higher education (HE) in the UK, and over 180,000 academic staff.[70] This was the largest cohort ever, and getting close to the Labour government's target of 50 per cent of 18-year-olds entering the sector.

In the 2008 Higher Education Policy Institute lecture, Professor Lord Giddens, former Director of the London School of Economics, expressed some caution:

So far as I can tell, looking back over a period of about 30 years of research work on the social background of students at universities, we've had an extraordinary period of the expansion of universities, but with a static class system. The wider class system hasn't been static at all … but nevertheless, the proportion of students from poorer backgrounds going to university really doesn't seem to have shifted across that period … 80 per cent of the sons and daughters of professional workers enter university. But only 11 per cent of the sons, and now about 15 per cent of the daughters, of unskilled workers do.[71]

He identified a number of causes of this situation, and proposed solutions, among them outreach from universities to schools, and a national student bursary scheme, given that in his view tuition fees were bound to increase (though he underestimated the extent of their rise).

In 2012, tuition fees and what is loosely called 'access' are still contentious issues (see chapter 25). However, what is notable for anyone coming to the Mile End campus is how successfully the College has tackled Giddens' main concern: inequality in recruitment to higher education. The ethnic diversity is immediately visible; other factors less so.

Of those QM students domiciled in the UK in 2010–11:

Indicator	Per cent
Normally resident in the local area	14
From state schools (first-degree entrants only)	85
Disability	6
Asian origin	40
White origin	42
From social classes 4–7 (where 4 represents small business owners and 7 routine occupations)	34
Female	52
Male	48

This breakdown is in marked contrast to many of the older universities in the UK, and is a tribute to the sustained outreach work that the College has done over many years with local schools and communities. It also bears out the research Giddens cites:

The sample that had access to those opportunities [bringing potential students to the campus, running summer schools, having students talk to schools] had not only a much

70. Students in Higher Education Institutions 2009–10. (London: Higher Education Statistics Agency, 2011)
71. Giddens, A. 'Reflections on the future of universities'. www.hepi.ac.uk/483/Lectures.html (Accessed in 2008)

higher proportion of people applying to enter higher education, but much more success in actual entry.[72]

The Women@QM project

In 2007–08, a new project highlighted a particular aspect of QM's history: its role in the education of women. The Women@QM project was the idea of Dr Colette Bowe, the first College alumna, and indeed the first woman, to become Chairman of Council (2004–09). She explains where the inspiration for the project came from:

"When I became chairman of the Council, one of the things I wanted very much to do was to make sure that this College continues to recognise and honour the Westfield tradition.

"The first fruits of that were labelling the portraits of the Westfield principals that hang on the ground floor of the Queens' Building. I wanted all the people who mill past these portraits every day to realise that these women, the first women to run Westfield, had a mountain to climb in order to make the higher education women a reality.

"I started to think about what Westfield had done in terms of pioneering women's right to be educated and take a degree and I thought to myself, that's only 120 years ago. For these young women of the 1880s, who led very circumscribed lives, Westfield was their liberation.

"I think still to this day it's quite possible that some of our female students have arrived here at the college after perhaps a little bit of a struggle to assert their right to be here and I thought, let's not forget that the fact that we now have girls all over the campus, girls doing every subject they want, isn't just something that happened by chance. It happened because a lot of very dedicated people put a lot of effort into making it happen."[73]

The Women@QM project included an exhibition, events such as a round-table discussion with alumnae of all the constituent colleges (QM, Westfield, The Royal London and Barts), from the 1940s to the present, and a book showcasing the achievements of past and present graduates.[74]

Handover

In summer 2008, half-way through this final period of our history, the Principal, Adrian Smith, announced his resignation after ten years in the post. In the May/June issue of *Bulletin* that year, he recalled the priorities for the College he'd set when he first started:

• to achieve academic excellence in all disciplines
• to raise the College's academic profile, and ensure that the image projected reflected the excellence achieved
• to improve the physical environment of the College, with major new buildings, and
• to reach a sustainable financial position.[75]

In ten years, he recorded, the profile of the College was considerably higher, with involvement in new major international projects: the Large Hadron Collider at CERN, the VISTA telescope in Chile,[76] and partnership with the Beijing University of Posts and Telecommunications (BUPT – see chapter 24 for a more detailed discussion). There were stunning new buildings, not only on the Mile End Campus, but the Blizard Building in Whitechapel and the medical labs in Charterhouse Square. As for the College's finances: a major restructuring exercise had been required – and that had not always been easy – but the College's accounts were now in order. The College's Treasurer, Charles Perrin, had worked closely with Dean Curtis, Director of Finance (subsequently Chief Administrative Officer) to achieve this, and to make sure that there was a firm foundation for the College's expansion.

72. ibid.
73. Bowe, C. (2012): written contribution to this history.

74. *Women at Queen Mary* (nd). London, QM.
75. *Bulletin* (May/June 2008) London, QM.
76. The £38m QM-led Visible and Infrared Survey Telescope (VISTA) project, initiated in 1999 and completed in 2009.

Recognition

2008 was also the year of another Research Assessment Exercise (RAE). Analysing the results, the *Guardian* placed QM 11th out of 132 institutions. The *Times Higher Education Supplement* (*THES*) commented on its own rating:

The biggest star among the research-intensive institutions was Queen Mary, University of London, which went up from 48th in 2001 to 13th in the 2008 table, up 35 places.[77]

The School of Medicine and Dentistry did particularly well: with two equal first ratings (Dentistry and the Institute of the Cell and Molecular Science), one second (the Wolfson Institute), two third (Cancer and the William Harvey Institute), and one fourth rating (Health Services Research). The collective rating for Humanities and Social Sciences placed them alongside the best universities in the country. The Drama and Linguistics departments were each first in the country, and Geography joint first, English second. Academic excellence was certainly on the increase, vindicating Professor Smith's ambitions for the College a decade earlier.

His eventual successor, Professor Simon Gaskell, discovered much that was positive on his arrival. The College had, he found, a very strong sense of community, and was welcoming and supportive to this newcomer. The finances were (finally!) healthy, and had been well managed for several years. Even more significantly, the College was at once rooted in its local community, and functioning strongly at an international level, demonstrating that the two were not mutually exclusive.

Aspirations

The current Strategic Plan, for 2010–15, states as its twin, linked aims knowledge creation (through research) and knowledge dissemination (through teaching, wider engagement and the commercial development of products):

1. To contribute to the body of human knowledge by performing research that is judged to be uniformly of international quality and that includes contributions that are internationally leading.
2. To disseminate knowledge through the presentation of inspirational and authoritative teaching programmes to a diverse constituency of talented undergraduate and postgraduate students… by public engagement with our academic expertise; and by providing leadership in areas of public interest.

And to enable this, the College aspires:

to nurture a culture at Queen Mary amongst staff and students that is mutually supportive, committed to the development of its individual members, and mindful of its obligations to the local region, to the community of nations and the needs of mankind and the environment.[78]

77. cited in *Annual Review, 2008*. (London: Queen Mary, University of London, 2008).

78. Strategic Plan 2010–15. (London: Queen Mary, University of London, 2010)

Awards, 2006–11

Year	Award / Appointment	Recipient	School
2006	Deputy Vice-Chancellor, University of London	Professor Adrian Smith	Principal
	Times Higher Education Lifetime Achievement Award	Professor Lisa Jardine	English & Drama
	Knighthood	Professor Sir Nicholas Wright	Medicine & Dentistry
	OBE	Professor Irene Leigh	Medicine & Dentistry
	OBE	Professor Sheila Cheeroth	Medicine & Dentistry
	Fellow of the British Academy	Professor Jacqueline Rose	English & Drama
	Fellow of the British Academy	Professor Michael Moriarty	Languages, Linguistics & Film
	Fellow of the Academy of Medical Sciences	Professor Nick Lemoine	Medicine & Dentistry
	Fellow of the Academy of Medical Sciences	Professor Fran Balkwill	Medicine & Dentistry
	Fellow of the Academy of Medical Sciences	Professor Malcolm Law	Medicine & Dentistry
	President of the British Medical Association	Professor Parveen Kumar	Medicine & Dentistry
2007	Fellow of the Medieval Academy of America	Professor Miri Rubin	History
	Chevalier des Palmes Académiques	Professor Jeremy Jennings	Politics & International Relations
2008	Fellow of the British Academy	Professor Trevor Dadson	Languages, Linguistics & Film
	Fellow of the British Academy	Professor Colin Jones	History
	Officier des Palmes Académiques	Professor Colin Jones	History
	Knighthood	Professor Sir Nicholas Wald	Medicine & Dentistry
2009	Sir Francis Avery Jones Research Gold Medal	Professor David van Heel	Medicine & Dentistry
	Fellow of the Academy of Medical Sciences	Professor Mike Curtis	Medicine & Dentistry
	Member of the Council, General Dental Council	Professor Liz Davenport	Medicine & Dentistry
	President of the Royal Historical Society	Professor Colin Jones	History
	Fellow of the British Academy	Professor David Smith	Geography
	Fellow of the British Academy	Professor Wilfrid Hodges	Mathematical Sciences
2010	Peerage	Professor Peter Hennessy	History
	Commandeur des Palmes Académiques	Professor Julian Jackson	
	Chevalier des Palmes Académiques	Professor Brigitte Granville	
	Chevalier des Palmes Académiques	Professor Michael Moriarty	
2011	President of the Royal College of Surgeons	Professor Norman Williams	Medicine & Dentistry
	Fellow of British Academy	Professor Jenny Cheshire	Languages, Linguistics & Film
2012	Fellow of the British Academy	Professor Miles Ogborn	Geography

Twelve QM academics were appointed Fellows of the British Academy between 1999 and 2011 –
an exceptional achievement, especially for an institution of Queen Mary's size.

Research achievements 2006–11

- In **History,** the Department's Who Were the Nuns? project considered the thousands of women who went into exile in the seventeenth and eighteenth centuries to join Roman Catholic convents that were banned in the UK.

- In **The Centre for Editing Lives and Letters** (CELL), Professor Alan Stewart prepared a new edition of Francis Bacon's correspondence; a digital calendar based on this research was made available as part of CELL's Digitalising Correspondence project.

- Dr Adam Fagan of the School of **Politics and International Relations** examines compliance with EU environmental standards in Bosnia and Serbia.

- Professor Evelyn Welch of the **Centre for Renaissance Studies and Early Modern Studies** explores fashion trends from the Renaissance to the late eighteenth century. The project secures almost €1 million funding from HERA (Humanities in the European Research Area)

Innovations, 2006–11

2006 The Medical School and the Drama Department launch the Performing Medicine project to improve the bedside manner of health professionals. Participating professionals include Professor Lois Weaver, as her alter ego Tammy Whynot (with blonde big hair), and the performance artist Bobby Baker, whose drawings on the experience of depression are shown here, and later at the Wellcome Collection.

2006 The City Centre is established in the Geography Department, and researches wage inequality in London, providing vital background research for the Living Wage campaign.

2008 The Centre for the History of the Emotions opens, the first of its kind in the UK. It provides a meeting-point for historians of culture and society, and of science and medicine.

2008 the Mile End Group introduces a module on the Blair government for third-year history undergraduates. Speakers include Alastair Campbell, Peter Mandelson, Ed Balls and Tony Blair himself.

2010 Interdisciplinary MA in Islam and the West, with specialists from the Schools of History; Politics and International Relations; Languages, Linguistics and Film; English and Drama; and Law. Students cover events from the seventh century to the present.

2011 The Leo Baeck Institute, the leading international research institute in German-Jewish history, moves its London base to QM.

2011 QM and Goldsmiths College collaborate to form **London Social Science,** an accredited Doctoral Training Centre (DTC) funded to train ten students a year until 2016.

The College and the East End, 2006–11

- **The School of Medicine and Dentistry** gets funding to study diabetes in the Bangladeshi population of east London, where the incidence is up to six times higher than in white European groups.
- The **English Department** launches a new module on the literature of the Jewish East End.
- The **Drama Department** puts on Mozart's *The Magic Flute* as a community opera, involving staff, students and local people.
- The boxer Sir Henry Cooper unveils a plaque celebrating the eighteenth-century boxer **Daniel Mendoza,** who was originally buried in the Jewish burial ground on the Mile End site.
- Three students win **London Schools and the Black Child** awards. They are:
Shardae Smith, BSc (Hons) first class, Maths & Statistics, won the girls' Outstanding Achievement in Higher Education Award; she also mentors children in Hackney.
Iskander Ibrahim, BSc (Hons), first class, Biochemistry
Hodan Suleiman, MSc first class, Mathematics.

The College and the World, 2006–11

- Researchers at the **School of Medicine and Dentistry** and Oxford University use silk to encourage damaged nerves to regrow.
- **Dr James Cho** (Mathematics) is part of the team working on the NASA Spitzer Space telescope, making the first-ever measurements of day and night temperatures beyond the solar system.
- Professors Janet Dine and Brigitte Granville of the **Centre for Commercial Law Studies (CCLS)** and **School of Business and Management** start researching the economy and structure of the Fair Trade movement.
- **Dr Toby Dodge** (Politics) testifies to the US Senate Foreign Relations Committee's Iraq inquiry, on the collapse of the state after the 2003 invasion.
- **Politics and CCLS** consider the regulation of foreign investment in Bosnia-Herzegovina and Serbia, and the potential environmental damage involved.
- Students on the **Mechanical Engineering** programme modify a plane to fly on electrical power.

Women at QM

2007 QM receives its first Athena SWAN Bronze award for promoting gender equality in science, engineering and technology.
The Bronze award is given to institutions that support female staff and students.

2010 The Bronze award is renewed. Judges note QM's Women in Science and Engineering (WISE) social and discussion group for students and staff; the Women@QM project, celebrating the achievements of women throughout the College's history (see page 86); the appointment of three female vice-principals; and the Women in Leadership group for senior female staff. They are also 'particularly delighted' by the College's flexible working policy.

In 2008, boxing champion Sir Henry Cooper unveiled a plaque to Daniel Mendoza on a wall of the college's library organised by the Jewish East End Celebration Society.

In focus:
humanities and
social sciences

The Centre for Commerical Law Studies, 1980

Entrance to QM's Centre for Commercial Law Studies, Lincoln's Inn Fields.

It is 1985, 8.30 am one weekday morning. Imagine a young lawyer in her office in the City, looking through the post. In a moment she will go back to the complex international case she is working on. Meanwhile a brochure catches her eye: *Conference and Lecture Programme 1985–86*. In October there are two evening lectures on copyright law. One on corporate insolvency – an increasingly relevant subject. Just doing those two subjects would give her ten continuing education points. And then in July 1986, there's a four-day symposium on commercial crime …

One of the things that has distinguished the Centre for Commercial Law Studies (CCLS) from the start is its constant engagement with the people beyond the university, who put the law into practice, discovering its quirks and its limitations, year in, year out. Our notional lawyer's filing system might also have the brochure for the 1985 Commercial Law Summer School, a week each on Dispute Resolution In International Contracts, International Trade Finance, and Euromarket Developments – The Legal Contribution, at both introductory and advanced level. She might have the Centre's 1985–86 prospectus, highlighting its specialisms – intellectual property (IP) law, banking law and commercial crime – and detailing possible postgraduate study, both LLM courses and research degrees. There is also a tempting paragraph on 'occasional students', the option of taking a single course without sitting an exam.

Getting started

"I thought the City, as an international financial centre, should have a focal point in the academic world on domestic and international commercial law," says Professor Sir Roy Goode, CBE, founder of CCLS and now its Honorary President. "I thought we could create a powerhouse of learning and scholarship, a centre people would look to for advanced teaching and research in the field of commercial law."[79]

In 1979 Roy Goode was already Crowther Professor of Credit and Commercial Law, he had been teaching commercial law at undergraduate and postgraduate level but he had bigger ideas, which were, as his first Director's report states:

• to promote advanced teaching and research in commercial law
• to foster the international exchange of scholars working in this field; and
• to bring together academics, practitioners, business interests and government to discuss legal problems affecting commercial operations and ideas for their solution.[80]

Where to begin? Calculated risk-taking, which became characteristic of the Centre, started here: £200 that was not in the budget was spent on a professionally designed, modern letterhead. Soon afterwards, coincidentally or not, the British Council phoned, proposing to provide scholarships for students on CCLS courses. There were at this point neither students nor courses; but that would soon change. The Centre was to become the first

79. Goode, R. Interview for this history. 2011.
80. Goode, R. *Centre for Commercial Law Studies: Director's Report, 1980–81*. (London: CCLS, October 1981).

commercial law department in the UK, and the first to teach the subject at postgraduate and diploma level.

Across London, in Chancery Lane, the Chartered Institute of Patent Agents had been considering how to mark its 1982 centenary. One possibility was the endowment of a Chair in Intellectual Property Law. Approaches were made to the University of London. Funding would be needed; but the Institute had a donor in mind. However, its concept – a professor to teach a diploma for patent agents – failed to appeal to other colleges. Fortunately, QM had the imagination to see the potential in the Institute's vision and expanded on it, as the College recognised that the Institute would naturally want international standing for its endowed Chair, as well as advanced teaching and research. The diploma, of course, would figure but much else too. The Herchel Smith Chair of Intellectual Property Law was established in 1979, and brought into the CCLS the following year.

Herchel Smith

Dr Herchel Smith, BSc, MA, PhD, DSc (Hon), was an organic chemist, born in Devon, whose research led to the first oral contraceptive. Unable to excite interest in his work in 1950s Britain, he emigrated to the United States and worked at Wyeth Pharmaceuticals in Philadelphia. When it came to getting a worldwide patent, however, he had great support from the Chartered Institute of Patent Agents in London; and when they sought funding for the Chair in Intellectual Property, he willingly provided it.

Herchel Smith went on to fund further teaching and research posts at CCLS, as well as a number of scholarships, and the annual Herchel Smith Public Lecture. The Centre continued to keep him informed of its developments and successes throughout his life. When he died, in December 2001, he left a bequest of £6.5 million to the Intellectual Property Law unit at the Centre.

Lincoln's Inn Fields. The heart of London's legal district.

The Centre's formal opening was on 20 June 1980, and Roy Goode invited the then Lord Chancellor, Lord Hailsham, to open it. But what was he to open? The Centre at that point consisted of the offices of Roy Goode, his secretary Nicola Jones, and his colleague Professor James Lahore, the first Herchel Smith Professor, all within the Law Building. The maintenance department was persuaded to add a plaque with the Centre's name beneath that of the Department of Law. Lord Hailsham duly arrived, with his two walking sticks, his dog, and his dog's minder, and despite the malfunction of the lift pronounced that the Centre would "clearly be a considerable national asset".

Early activities

In 1982 the Centre's first public lecture series, on secured transactions, filled the main lecture theatre at QM, with 221 participants (each paying £10). The lecture papers became a book, *Legal Problems of Credit and Security*, which is now in its fourth edition and is widely used by students, scholars and practitioners. Three further lecture series followed, each giving rise to a publication.

The summer schools, cited at the start of this chapter, began as week-long events but soon expanded to three. Roy Goode remembers these as one of the high points of his time at the Centre, principally for the intense interaction with highly intelligent practising professionals. Over the years, summer school subjects included The Law of Copyright and Designs, International Franchising, UK Taxation of International Businesses, and Commercial Arbitration. Demand for these summer schools and lecture series only tailed off after law firms were able to offer their own recognised continuing education programmes.

The Centre's philosophy was clear from the start. It should be a 'centre of excellence.' It would have an international and comparative perspective. It would involve close collaboration with professionals in practice. Its approach would be interdisciplinary (though Roy Goode acknowledges that this can be hard to achieve). And finally – part of the calculated-risk strategy – it would only ever do what fitted its own priorities and plans, rather than what would simply attract money.

In 1987, Oliver Letwin, then Shadow Home Secretary, wrote that:

> Over the past seven years, a remarkably distinguished group of professors, lecturers, research fellows and others have gathered together … This is no tedious cramming-house for would-be corporate lawyers… In building up its team, the Centre has concentrated on high intellectual ability… This tactic has paid off well, attracting professors with international reputations who … advise on everything from broadcasting to medical ethics, and – in short – exude interest and enthusiasm.[81]

CCLS in 2012

Thirty years on, the Centre has grown to a scale hardly imaginable at the start. There are 24 full-time and three part-time academic staff, in addition to two posts run jointly with London School of Economics (LSE), and two new posts from January 2012. There are also 16 support staff, including one and a half posts shared with the School of Law and one with LSE; and a dedicated librarian, who manages the Intellectual Property archives, now held at the Institute of Advanced Legal Studies. Chairs have been established in Intellectual Property Law, Information Technology Law, Business Taxation, Comparative Commercial Law, and Credit and Commercial Law. To mark the 30th anniversary, Philip Rawlings, formerly of University College London, has been appointed as the first Roy Goode Professor of Commercial Law.

Researchers are now organised in six institutes:
- Arbitration and Dispute Resolution
- Banking and Finance Law
- Intellectual Property
- Information Technology, Media and Communications Law
- International Commercial Law
- Tax Law.

The School of International Arbitration, established in 1985, is acknowledged as the world's leading centre for teaching and research in the subject.

81. Letwin, O. 'Academic Enterprise', *Times Education Supplement*, 11 December 1987.

The Centre actively looks for evolving areas of law that need more attention. The Cloud Legal Project, started in 2009, looks at legal aspects of cloud computing; a year later, its work made headlines in legal and IT journals, such as 'Researchers: Study Your Cloud Computing Contracts'.

A further area of interest is energy law; as this book goes to press, there is a proposal for a new Energy Law Institute at QM, examining regulation of the energy market, governance and energy security. Laurence Shore, Visiting Lecturer in Energy and Natural Resources, illustrates the urgent issues involves, saying that two things keep him awake at night: "deep sea drilling, and indigenous communities".

In the very first Research Assessment Exercise (RAE) for university departments, in 1985, the Department of Laws (including CCLS, which had only been operational for four years) was one of five law schools in the country to be given the top rating, a success it maintained in the ensuing RAE some years later. In the 2001 RAE, it was ranked 5*, again one of only five law departments in the country to achieve this rating. In 2008 the Department was ranked seventh in the UK.

Teaching at CCLS

From the outset the CCLS has engaged in advanced teaching and research.

The Centre contributes taught modules, including International Commercial Transactions, and Commercial and Consumer Law, to the School of Law's LLB courses. The School also offers 18 LLM programmes, with more than 80 modules, among them Comparative and International Dispute Resolution and Competition Law, both taught and supervised by CCLS staff. The Centre itself offers an MSc in The Management of Intellectual Property. A joint LLM in Law and Economics is in planning, to be introduced in 2012–13. There are also several part-time, taught postgraduate diplomas, undertaken by practising lawyers who study alongside LLM students: these include a Diploma in International Dispute Resolution. The Centre has between 600 and 700 postgraduate students, the largest number anywhere in QM, and the greatest proportion of them are international students.

Roy Goode is retired but remains the Honorary President of the Centre, and a member of the Advisory Board. He is still keenly interested in its work and believes that the key to continuing success is to keep entry standards high. "If we introduced more exacting standards, most of our current students would meet them," he says, "and it would make a qualification from CCLS even more prestigious. If it's known that the courses are hard to get onto, they'll look even better on graduates' CVs."[82]

In addition, true to its early and continuing relationship with the Chartered Institute of Patent Agents, the Centre has substantially expanded its tailor-made postgraduate training, through the Certificate in IP Law, for trainee patent attorneys, and the Certificate in Trade Mark Law and Practice, for both trainees and those with a wider interest in the subject.

82. Goode, R, op cit.

Location, location

Swee Ng, now Centre Manager, writes:

When I first joined CCLS in 1989, CCLS had offices in the Law Building as well as a prefabricated building off Mile End Road. It struck me as rather odd that the Centre did not even have proper accommodation to base its operation, when it evidently had a highly successful and reputable profile in conference and summer school programmes. To an extent this bears testimony to the commitment and determination of the Director and staff to ensure the success of the Centre despite its physical limitations.

Successive directors tried to relocate the Centre. The catalyst [for] the move was the last bequest by Dr Herchel Smith which enabled the IP Law unit to relocate to the John Vane Science Building in the medical campus, followed by the rest of CCLS staff to Charterhouse Square. Professor Janet Dine took one step further and the Centre was able to relocate to its present offices at Lincoln's Inn Fields.[83]

That latest move, to London's legal quarter, came in 2007; the Centre hopes to expand into two further floors of its building, with the benefit of a bespoke lecture theatre. The Centre's website offers prospective students unfamiliar with London a virtual tour of the neighbourhood, with the neo-Gothic splendour of the Royal Courts of Justice well to the fore.

The Centre and the College

The Centre's collaboration with other schools at QM has never been greater. There are joint research studentships with Science and Engineering; modules in Intellectual Property are taught to medical students; the CCLS provides input to the Joint Programme at Beijing University of Posts and Telecommunications (BUPT, see chapter 24 for further details); and a new LLM in Law and Economics is now offered jointly with the School of Economics. There is also a new (2012) LLM programme based at ULIP, the University of London Institute in Paris. The LLM can be counted as part of the Paris Bar School training, as well as being a British qualification in its own right.

Roy Goode believes that the CCLS has made a valuable contribution to QM's academic activities but he is also keen to acknowledge the great debt which the Centre in turn owes to the College, which has consistently supported a department that does not conform to the pattern of other departments and has always, in some respects, been slightly anarchic, recognising no boundaries and confident that it can achieve anything it wishes, given its commitment. That, he believes, is one of the major factors contributing to the Centre's success.

83. Ng, S. Written contribution to this history. 2011.

Linguistics, 1989

How many languages had you learned to speak before you were four? How about your parents; was it the same for them? For other members of your family? Your friends? What is the total?

If the answer is one, you are outnumbered in the present-day East End, where QM is based. This is the beginning of an exercise Professor David Adger carries out with his first-year Linguistics students: the total for the whole class tends to be around 80 languages. Once the list is established – Kazakh, Twi, Somali, Sylheti and so on – students are each assigned a language not their own, and asked to interview a native speaker. How do you say 'a big yellow ball' in your language; what order do the words come in? When you're listening to someone else explaining something, how do you show you understand what they are saying? The students then write this up as their first research project. 'I love marking these reports," says David Adger. 'I always learn something."[84]

Linguistics and east London, it emerges, have a natural affinity. In 2011, the Department advertised a new Chair of Linguistics, and many applicants cited the area's diversity as a strong incentive. There are others: the Department, though small, was rated first in the country in the 2008 Research Assessment Exercise (RAE). *The Times Good University Guide 2012* ranked it fifth in the country, after Oxford, Cambridge, Lancaster and University College London.

So what is linguistics? The attempt to understand what language is – not any particular language, but language itself. Formal linguistics wants to know about the structures that are possible in human language, and why across all languages some structures are present and others not. Sociolinguistics looks at how language is used, and what aspects of the speakers' identity or way of life are reflected in language. Formal linguistics approaches language in terms of the mind, sociolinguistics approaches it as a social phenomenon.

Linguistics and east London
Professor Jenny Cheshire and colleagues have been engaged in a study of the changing English spoken by teenagers in London. As part of this, they compare the language of teenagers in the highly diverse inner borough of Hackney with that of the more monocultural outer borough of Havering.

With David Adger, they have recently studied the use of 'who' and 'that', in constructions such as 'The man who/that I saw'. Overall in the UK, 'who' is largely being replaced by 'that' in this context. In Hackney, however (but not in Havering), young people were found to use 'who' when the person referred to was a continuing topic in the conversation. This construction does exist in some languages; but the people who use it in English don't necessarily speak them. The research argues that people are influenced not by knowing a specific language and its structures, but by living in the multilingual community of Hackney, where all kinds of grammatical constructions are available, and can be used to build new linguistic patterns.

What makes the Linguistics Department at QM special – and contributes to its success – is the

84. Adger, D. Written contribution to this history. 2011.

close collaboration between specialists in formal linguistics and sociolinguistics. A decision was taken early on to avoid the divisions and antagonisms between the two disciplines that sometimes occur. There are for instance two reading groups, one for each discipline, but graduate students are expected to attend both. Collaboration across disciplines is frequent and encouraged.

History of the department

Linguistics originally came to QM from Westfield. In 1989 Jamal Ouhalla (now Professor of Linguistics at University College Dublin) joined Westfield's Faculty of Arts; when the Colleges merged, he became a one-person department within the new School of Modern Languages. The modular system meant that students could graduate in, say, German and Linguistics. There was also an innovative three-subject degree, combining the study of a language, Linguistics and Computer Science, which ran until 2010.

In 1996 the Department expanded by 100 per cent, with the appointment of Jenny Cheshire to the new Chair of Linguistics. A taught MA in Language, Society and Change in Europe was launched, with the aid of colleagues from the School of English and Drama, and ran successfully for 13 years. Students came from across Europe, and a significant number of them stayed on to do PhDs.

Jamal Ouhalla left QM in 2002. A year later two further posts were created, and in 2004 a new Chair of Linguistics was created. By 2005 the department had three formal linguistics specialists and two in sociolinguistics.

In 2004 two new programmes opened: a BA Honours in English and Linguistics, run in collaboration with English and Drama; and an MA in Linguistics by Research. The existing Linguistics MA catered for language students with little linguistics expertise; the new one allowed for more in-depth work. At the same time, a new BA in English Language and Linguistics was planned, and launched in 2007. New appointments in 2007 and 2008 strengthened both the research groups. Jenny Cheshire says, "We strive to open up innovative sub-fields in the discipline as well as to be at the forefront of developments in more conventional areas of linguistics."[85]

Options for study

In 2011, the most popular undergraduate programme involving linguistics was the new BA in English Language and Linguistics; the first cohort graduated in that year, and by the spring, 45 firm acceptances from prospective new students had been received. David Adger believes that one reason for the popularity of the course is that linguistics is recognised by employers as requiring hard work and intellectual ability. Undergraduates engage in experimental work from the beginning; studying reaction times, for instance, as people read sentences constructed with new and familiar material. The joint BA programmes – Hispanic Studies and Linguistics, German and Linguistics, and so on – are also still available.

In addition, since 2011 the Department has offered a new MA in Linguistics. Students can choose a socio- or formal linguistics pathway, and can combine modules from each discipline. Optional modules include Bilingualism, Pidgins and Creoles, and Understudied Languages and Linguistic Theory. Students will also have the opportunity to be integrated into departmental research projects, or to connect with employers outside the college in a research practicum.

Beren Ashton-Butler, graduating in 2011, has this to say about his chosen area of study:

> Linguistics specifically jumped out at me as a result of my travels before University. I saw how cultures were shaped, maintained and passed on through language and realised there was a lot more to the everyday occurrence of vocalisations than most care to recognise. What surprised me most when simply scratching the surface was the incredible amount of systematicity found in language alongside almost impossible amounts of variation. I knew that here lay a treasure trove of fascinating insights into culture, mind, consciousness, thought, ritual and [when] I began proper research, how much it was a part of science.[86]

85. Cheshire, J. Written contribution to this history. [Nd].
86. Ashton-Butler, B. Written contribution to this history. 2011.

Research

Recent PhD research projects undertaken in the Linguistics Department include:

- What happens to the grammar of certain Northern Italian dialects when standard Italian is imposed
- The syntax and semantics of the English verb 'get'.
- The influence of bilingualism on language attitudes in Québec
- The grammar of Cypriot Maronite Arabic, an endangered contact language that combines properties of Greek and Arabic
- Cabin/flight crew communication: factors, effects and group identity construction.

As well as working across disciplines, the Department has followed a policy of focusing its limited resources on a few specialist areas. That, David Adger affirms, is how the Department was able to impress New York University with three series of lectures, by himself and two colleagues. The new appointments in 2007 and 2008 contributed to the Department's high RAE rating: "We hired the right people," he says, "and then we tried to give them the time and space". Academics from the Department have published many papers in leading academic journals, as well as monographs with major publishers. The research-group ethos, where colleagues work in similar fields and consistently support and comment on each other's work, has played a part in enabling high-quality research.

Consistently good ratings equally bring funding into the department, in a virtuous circle. Since 2002 over £2 million has been raised in research grants: a considerable sum in Humanities research, and in proportion to the size of the Department.

Close contact with the East End remains important. One study is considering how the underlying structure of English impacts on people's original language. (A phenomenon well-known to the migrant parents of children growing up in the UK: "They speak Tigrinya but with English grammar, so people can hardly understand them," says one Eritrean).[87]
One QM student is looking at what's known as 'back-channelling' – how you indicate that you're listening – in Sylheti, the language of most Bangladeshi people in east London. In Sylheti, one repeats the last word of the other person's sentence; in English one says something like 'yes', or 'mmm', or one nods. Younger people in the study increasingly use the English style of back-channelling, even in Sylheti; and that includes a Sylheti translation of that most fashionable English reaction: 'O, my God!'

Queen Mary's OPALs

Not an item from the Buckingham Palace gallery, but a series of Occasional Papers Advancing Linguistics by staff, students and external contributors. Some examples include:

- 'Was/were' variation: A perspective from London'. – J Cheshire, S Fox

- 'Incomplete descriptions and sloppy identity'. – P Elbourne

- 'Compliments and gender in French single-sex friendship groups'. – E Petit

- 'Fracturing the adjective: Evidence from Gaelic comparatives'. – D Adger

87. Deres, T. Interview for this history. 2011.

The future

A new development for the Department has
been the employment of an experimental
neurolinguistics specialist, Linnaea Stockall, whose
work has included research into the way that the
brain processes words during reading. At present
the Department doesn't have use of an MRI
scanner to further this type of work, though the
purpose-built Linguistics Research Laboratory
and Recording Studio, opened in 2005, does have
eye-tracking equipment. This lets researchers
observe tiny movements in the eye while people
read texts or look at pictures, and work out how
the brain processes information from these
movements. David Adger's vision for the future
includes a new lab with a full range of equipment,
in the basement of the refurbished Arts annexe.
The subject, he says, is a combination of
humanities, social science and science; and that,
clearly, is its great attraction:

> I think we may be at the same stage as chemistry
> in the eighteenth century. They had lots of
> knowledge, but no deep understanding that
> could bring it all together. Like us, they were
> trying to develop that understanding. And of
> course we have the same sense of excitement
> that they had then.[88]

A key debate in the development of linguistics is
that of 'nature versus nurture': to what extent is
our use of language and its structures learned or
innate? David Adger wants to test this out with a
new method: you design a new language, including
patterns of usage that no existing language has;
you give it to people to speak, and see what
happens.

88. Adger, D, op cit.

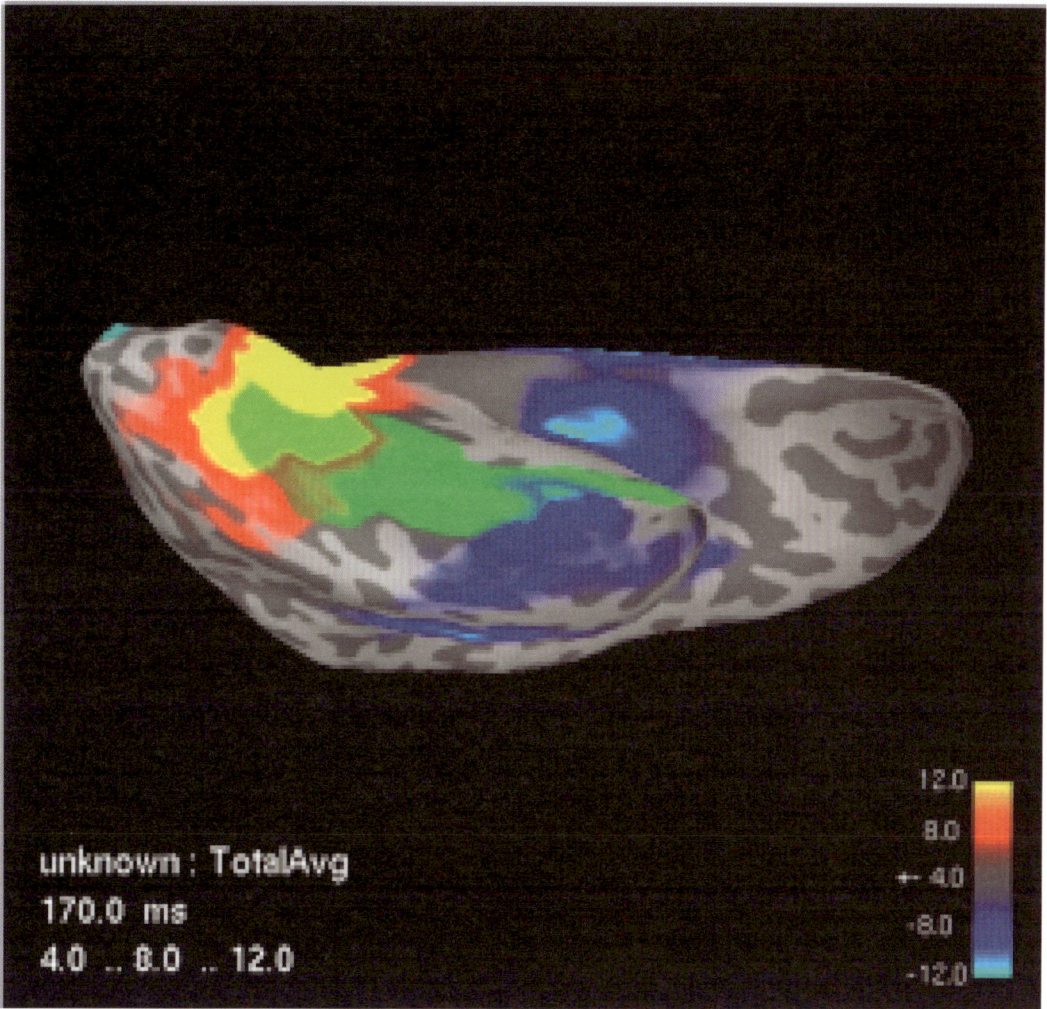

unknown : TotalAvg
170.0 ms
4.0 .. 8.0 .. 12.0

12.0
8.0
← 4.0
-8.0
-12.0

An image of the brain: the parts that are shown coloured are relevant to
how the brain 'recognises' written word forms.

The Centre for Renaissance and Early Modern Studies, 2005

William Shakespeare; copper engraving of Shakespeare by Martin Droeshout.
Image from Wikimedia Commons

Professor Kevin Sharpe came to QM in 2005, as Professor of Early Modern Culture; the highly successful Centre for Renaissance and Early Modern Studies was his creation. In 2009 he was diagnosed with a rare form of lymphoma. He appeared to have recovered after treatment, and returned to work; but the disease returned, and he died, at only 62, in November 2011. He contributed to this chapter with a piece written before his illness, and an interview while in remission. We retain the text as he agreed it, in tribute to his remarkable energy and achievement.

From the Queen Mary Annual Review, 2005:
Queen Mary has one of the largest concentrations of academic expertise in Renaissance and Early Modern Studies of any university in the UK – a rich pool which includes Professor Lisa Jardine (Director of the Centre for Editing Lives and Letters at Queen Mary), whose work stretches from Renaissance intellectual history to questions of global exchange; Professor Trevor Dadson (Hispanic Studies) a specialist on Cervantes; Professor Kate Lowe (History) a specialist on Renaissance Italy; Professor Graham Rees (English and Drama) Director of the Oxford Francis Bacon Project and King's Printer's Project, which looks at Jacobean printing and publishing practices, and Professor Evelyn Welch (English and Drama) a specialist on Italian visual and material culture.

In November 2005 these, and other academic colleagues from across the arts and social sciences sector, came together to form the core of the Centre for Renaissance and Early Modern Studies under the leadership of Professor Kevin Sharpe.[89]

Kevin Sharpe reflected on establishing the Centre:
When I was approached about a Chair in English at Queen Mary, I had just been awarded a three-year Leverhulme major research fellowship, the terms of which prohibited normal teaching duties ...

As I reviewed the situation, it seemed to me that Queen Mary had extraordinary riches in its faculty working in the period, say 1400–1750, across not only these departments but in languages, politics, geography and more. What also struck me was that that strength was not immediately visible, especially to outsiders; and that, in some measure, the excellent individuals did not add up to more than the sum of their parts. So I suggested to Adrian [Professor Adrian Smith, then Principal] and to the then Senior Vice Principal and VP for Humanities, Philip Ogden, that it might be a good plan for me to establish a Centre for Renaissance Studies, to bring scholars in different departments and faculties together and to draw attention to QM's strengths in the field. It was already becoming clear that centres improved chances for external funding and provided attractive scholarly environments for graduate work and so encouraged graduate applications. QM already had the spectacularly successful CELL [Centre for Editing Lives and Letters], established by Lisa Jardine, and plans were afoot for a Centre for Dissenting Studies under the direction of another new QM professor, Isabel Rivers.

89. Sharpe, K. Written contribution to this history. [Nd].

Having seen Renaissance centres elsewhere that had ended up as little more than sheets of note-paper, I strongly believed that a QM Centre for Renaissance and Early Modern Studies needed to be launched with a splash. I therefore proposed to bring in some of the most famous scholars in the world and to team them with QM faculty, senior and junior, to discuss key aspects of the Renaissance… After discussion with colleagues in several departments, I decided initially to run five or six seminars, with a main speaker, commentator and chair, with time in the one-and-a-half-hour slot for full discussion. Amy Neale in Events helped encourage me to see how we could make these attractive to a broad public from museums, galleries and libraries, as well as universities and colleges.[90]

The seminar series

The Centre was launched in November 2005. The first seminar, on Early Modern Empires, was led by Felipe Fernández-Armesto, then at QM, and Sir John Elliott, Emeritus Regius Professor of History at Oxford. The series continued to be graced with well-known speakers: Roger Chartier from Paris, Anthony Grafton from Princeton, and Quentin Skinner from Cambridge, who subsequently joined QM; as well as the College's own Lisa Jardine and Evelyn Welch.

What was especially gratifying was that audiences – which I had hoped might be 40 – were typically over 60 or 70, and did indeed consist of a real mix of academics, scholars in the non-university sector and, importantly, interested members of the public who joined in the lively discussion that followed. The receptions … were of no less importance than the seminars themselves. For during the drinks' hour, many a young student met famous speakers – and in some cases gleaned a future examiner; and QM colleagues engaged with, and were able to demonstrate our considerable research strengths to our international visitors.[91]

Dr Janet Dickinson, Teaching Fellow and Honorary Research Fellow in History at Durham University, has attended most of the seminars, and considers them the best seminar series outside of – and possibly including – Oxford and Cambridge. There is, she says, "a fantastic line-up of speakers, a diverse range of subjects covered and a great atmosphere afterwards, with a real effort made to involve everyone in discussion over wine and canapés… Something which really adds to QM's claim to be the centre of early modern studies in London."[92]

The seminars went from strength to strength. The second series included James Shapiro (author of the best-selling *1599: A Year in The Life of William Shakespeare* and *Contested Will: Who Wrote Shakespeare?*, and recently at QM as a Visiting Professor from Columbia), David Armitage from Harvard, and Natalie Davis, the leading cultural historian of early-modern France: over a hundred people attended her talk. There was also a colloquium on how to communicate scholarship in Renaissance studies to a wider public, led by Jonathan Bate, the Shakespeare editor and scholar, with James Shapiro; the novelist Sarah Dunant; and Penguin editor Simon Winder. The event featured in the College's Arts Week, and was extremely popular.

In addition, graduate students organised seminars of their own. Steven Cowser was part of a group setting one up in December 2008. He recalls:
Bearing in mind that the seminar panel I had organised was composed of three second-year PhD candidates (myself included), chaired by somebody awaiting their viva, and concerned with the question of the legacy of new historicism, I had anticipated that the audience would be distinctly in-house and academic. Nevertheless, in the reception afterwards, I was congratulated by a member of the public who said she had attended QM back in 1970s as an undergrad and had come to the seminar with no prior knowledge of new historicism. To my mind, this anecdote uncovers two aspects of the Renaissance Centre that should be stressed: it reaches out to the general public and also

90. ibid.
91. ibid.

92. Dickinson, J. Written contribution to this history. 2011.

maintains strong links with those once affiliated to the University.[93]

Eminent speakers have included Simon Thurley (Director of English Heritage), Peter Holland (former Director of the Shakespeare Institute, now at the University of Notre Dame), Stephen Greenblatt (from Harvard), Anthony Pagden (UCLA) and David Starkey, the well-known historian and broadcaster (with a record attendance of 200 people). QM's Evelyn Welch and Kate Lowe both gave their inaugural lectures as part of the series. Kevin Sharpe continued:

> I confess that I've begun to think that we cannot sustain for many more years a list of speakers of this international renown and calibre. But my intention always was that, having made a splash, the seminars and Centre would gain a reputation that would sustain it and develop it. It is gratifying that numbers have kept up well and that the seminars have a loyal following of many who come to each occasion, as well as those who attend for a particular speaker, or topic.[94]

Postgraduate work

As well as the seminar series, the Centre offers an MRes in Renaissance and Early Modern Studies, with core courses on interdisciplinary research in this very particular context, and options such as Understanding Religions Historically, and Urban Culture and the Book. Teaching staff include high-profile specialists in their field such as Miri Rubin, Professor of History, and Lisa Jardine, Centenary Professor of Renaissance Studies. Steven Cowser makes clear how important this is:

> As to why I chose QM and the Centre, I probably answer for most of my peers when I write that I wanted to work with the guidance of my particular supervisor. Obviously the wider London research community and facilities are an important factor but it is fair to say the key attraction for postgrads is the calibre of the staff at QM.[95]

Students also have the benefit of meeting visiting academics at the seminars. Steven Cowser recalls meeting Tim Brown, historian of Restoration

England, from Brown University, and Hannah Crawforth, at the time a doctoral student at Princeton, whose research had direct relevance to his own work.

Another considerable benefit for students is the possibility of joint supervision of their research, either within or beyond the institution. Someone exploring the links between painting and poetry, for example, while registered with the English (or Spanish, or German) Department, might have a second supervisor from Tate or another gallery. Links with Tate were firmly established in 2009, when the Centre, in co-operation with Tate Britain, hosted at QM the colloquium to launch the *Van Dyck and Britain* exhibition, for which Kevin Sharpe was the historical consultant.

The future

After five years with five or six major events each year, the Centre's visible presence was limited in 2010–11 by Kevin Sharpe's serious illness. The Centre's now established reputation, however, carries it forward. Academics who are known worldwide as specialists in this field, such as Professor Greenblatt, have been happy to participate free of charge in what is seen as an exciting and innovative venture. Within QM, too, the pattern of interdisciplinary co-operation is now well established.

International links have been forged. Thanks to Professor Miri Rubin, the Centre has developed exchanges with Freiburg (one of the German universities designated as a centre of excellence) and Princeton, and has hosted international colloquia.

In addition, the Centre can function, as Kevin Sharpe intended, as an umbrella for funding bids, its reputation as a top-class research environment established in the 2008 Research Assessment Exercise. In early 2011, for example, the Centre applied jointly with Exeter University for the funds for a PhD Fellowship in Succession Literature – the official records, eulogies and warnings, essays, drama and verse, that might face a new ruler as she or he took office.

93. Cowser, S. Written contribution to this history. 2011.
94. Sharpe, K, op cit.
95. Cowser, S, op cit.

What will the Centre look like in future?
A future Centre for Renaissance and Early Modern
Studies might have its own building, a recognisable
venue for internal and external participants in its
many activities. The Director could, for the first
time, be seconded half-time from her or his post,
in order to develop both the funding and the
substantive work of collaborations, conferences
and exhibitions as well as seminars. Over the first
five years, the plan might include one major event
per year: say, a multidisciplinary debate on staging
Shakespeare, with literature and drama specialists,
theatre directors and actors. One of many half-day
colloquia could examine how history is represented
on TV, stage and film.

An expanded Centre could provide a primary
home for PhD students, rather than having them
registered to individual departments. Graduate
students would continue to stage and lead events
themselves. The Centre would have the time to
engage more museums and galleries in its work,
with the potential for further public collaborations.

QM students inside the Lock-keeper's Cottage Graduate Centre, Mile End campus.

Part 3:
Internal and external

The Library

The Library, 2011. Refurbished in 2010, the Library offers students more space for personal and group study.

Early December 2010. The hoardings have come down, together with the signs pointing round to the back door and up the stairs. Students between lectures are queuing in the Square to come in by the revolving doors, and crowding up to the new automatic gates. Once inside, they wander into the Learning Lounge and the café, investigate the new high-tech group study rooms, sit at computer tables chatting, then spill out again, making room for the next contingent. The newly refurbished Library has opened.

The Library Building at Mile End was planned in the early 1980s, and opened officially in 1988. Even then, the committee that planned the building was aware that libraries have to be ready to adapt, given the constant changes in the way they are used. In the new millennium, reading and researching, but also academic teaching had moved on. To Emma Bull, joining as Librarian in 2007, it seemed urgent to update the Library's facilities. One group room per floor was no longer enough, when students frequently had group assignments. Encouraged to collaborate, some readers in consultation with each other inevitably disturbed others who need silence. The current extent of IT use would be unimaginable from the perspective of 1988. Students come into the library with laptops, smartphones, MP3 players, USB sticks; any library that wants to attract them now has to both accommodate and manage that reality. Students and researchers, interviewed in early 2011, commented:

> It's good they've got plugs [sockets] on all the desks on the second floor now. You used to have to get here really early to get one of the places you could plug your laptop in.

> It used to be very quiet on the first floor; then everyone had mobiles and it was chaos. But they've dealt with that.

> We had some reading to do, but having seen the condition the book's in, we've scanned what we want onto a USB stick. That way you avoid having to pay fines, too.[96]

If all that would have astonished students in 1988, how about a hundred years earlier?

The People's Palace

The first library on the Mile End site, in the People's Palace, was opened in June 1888. It was built as an octagon, with two galleries reached by iron spiral staircases, tall windows above them, and a glazed cupola. The *Palace Journal* considered "that there is nothing like it anywhere, except the Reading Room of the British Museum."[97]

From the beginning, the Palace's Library was heavily used: between 1,200 and 1,400 visitors per day, according to the second Librarian, Minnie James. (The first, briefly, was Constance Black, who as Constance Garnett became an eminent translator of Russian literature). It was of course not yet a university library, nor even the library of the technical schools, but a public library for the use of local people. By the turn of the century, the People's Palace was getting into financial difficulties, and its dual function of entertainment and education was proving problematic. The governors hoped to hand responsibility over to

96. Anonymous interviews for this history. 2011.
97. Moss, G P, & Saville M V, op cit.

The Octagon Library, *c*.1980s. © Queen Mary, University of London Archives

the local authority, and in 1902 the Library's stock and furnishings were moved to Mile End Old Town Vestry, to be run by the borough of Stepney. The magnificent Octagon building stood empty for the next seven years. It was then used by the People's Palace for a very different purpose: silent reading was replaced by the clash of billiard balls, and the clack of chess pieces. It is not clear where the College housed its library over this period; but in 1920 it claimed the space back from the People's Palace, and the Drapers' Company provided £5,000 for the Library's refurbishment.

The Octagon

This space, known first as the Rotunda and then the Octagon, continued to house the library for another 68 years. It was elegant, historic, and increasingly inadequate, as the College grew and the library stock expanded to meet new needs. An extension was built in 1964, and space below the Octagon (including a one-time rifle range) converted to book-stacks and library offices.

Neil Entwistle, who joined the library staff in 1974, recalls the advantages and the considerable drawbacks of the building:

> The Library of those days had an intimate and surprisingly functional working environment for both students and staff … It was just too small, very cold in winter, and much of the Library's stock would now be considered inaccessibly

placed on the Octagon's galleries. If you were studying English or Classics, you had to climb in order to learn. And if you happened to be, as I was, the librarian for those subjects, an important skill was being able to ascend the staircases balancing up to 30 books for re-shelving.

Working in a historic building posed other problems: heavy rain, for instance, which on one occasion:

> quickly penetrated the roof and threatened the books in the top gallery. There was no alternative but to make several perilous climbs to the un-railed cleaning gallery, somehow clutching a waste-paper bin on each trip … The bins in question were, unsurprisingly, still in position many years later even after the Library left the Octagon.[98]

A new library?

Successive librarians had made the case that the Library was inadequate for the needs of a modern college. A University Grants Committee (UCG) visitation in 1978 raised hopes of a comment to this effect, but none was made. Annual Reports and internal *Bulletins* chronicle a more-or-less resigned frustration at the overcrowding, the budget and the cold. The Library Committee (Consultative Committee) in July 1983 makes its case for a capital grant, given the obsolescence of the existing Library:

> … it is the structure and shape of the building rather than the readers' requirements that frequently decide where material is shelved or where a service point is located. Readers searching the shelves disturb those working at tables.[99]

There is only one lift, and one narrow staircase, as well as the famous iron spiral stairs to the galleries. The noise level, they say, is high.

A further paper to the same meeting shows how much thought went into the design of a replacement. These are some of the criteria:

98. Entwistle, N. Written contribution to this history. [Nd].
99. Minutes of the Queen Mary College Library Committee (Consultative Committee), July 1983. (London: Queen Mary College, 1983).

2. Unlike most public library users, many university library users remain in the building to work for long periods at a stretch. The second requirement is therefore a quiet environment with freedom from regular external noise. This implies a building well away from the Mile End Road and large, constantly used car parks …

4. The orientation of the building is important. Too much direct sunshine can cause discomfort to readers and is certainly harmful to book bindings and paper.

5. Space to extend horizontally.

A new Library will also free valuable space for the rest of the College: 2,931 square metres in all. The proposal is to convert the Octagon to a lecture theatre, mainly for pre-clinical medical and dental students. In exchange, the Committee proposes a new building of 6,155 square metres usable space. The total cost, for which the College applies to the University Grants Committee, is £3,494,960. The UGC agrees to £3,033,000.

Detailed documents on the plans for the new building still exist in the College archives. One, entitled *A Basis for a Brief to the Architect* and dated October 1983, begins with a "Statement of Aims and General Requirements". These include:

1.2 The Library should not be thought of only as a repository for books. It is a centre for information transfer and a workshop for both undergraduate students and researchers.

1.3 The building to house the Library must be modular in construction to allow the adaptability and flexibility necessary to react to changes both in technology and in teaching and research methods.

1.4 The new Library will be a prominent feature on the College campus. It must be both functional and visually satisfying. Externally, it should be memorable, internally it should feel quietly efficient but welcoming and relaxed.

Library staff and the Committee may not have known what technological advances there would be, but they were wise enough to plan for some. These requirements chime remarkably well with the Library's current (2010) strategic objectives, which include:

• to meet changing expectations

- to make our services easy to use, intuitive and coherent
- to improve our physical and online learning environments[100]

Although online learning was not yet a possibility, the architect's brief specifies 15 "consultation places" where users can check the catalogue. The IT budget, for staff and reader use, is £150,000.

In 1984 the local authority, Tower Hamlets, approves building on sites to the east of the existing campus, provided that part of the ancient Sephardic burial ground is retained as an ornamental open space (see chapter 17).

In June 1986 Lady Menter, wife of the Principal, Sir James Menter, ceremonially cuts the first turf for the new site. Work begins; with the kind of correspondence between client (in this case the Deputy Librarian, Delia Taylor), architect (Colin St John Wilson, simultaneously working on the rather larger British Library) and suppliers that will be familiar to anyone who has employed builders. It will all take three years.

Inadequate resources

Meantime, as the Librarian states wearily in his annual report:

> The Library has struggled throughout the session to provide, from inadequate resources, an adequate service to staff and students.[101]

The inadequate resources are not only spatial. A Library Finance Working Party concludes that it is under-funded for acquisitions, and that future funding should be decided by reference to a national norm. This major policy shift is agreed by the Committee of Deans, but becomes a casualty of the College's wider financial difficulties. In 1986–87 the Library is asked instead to make a £12,000 cut in expenditure. The Librarian responds crisply in that year's report that it has been impossible to cut to that extent, and that the Library has overspent by precisely £12,000. One-nil to the Library, which will get a higher percentage

of the College's finance in the following year. At the same time the UGC announces emergency funding for university libraries over the next three years. QM's is not the only library struggling.

The 1986–87 report gives us a snapshot of the Library's situation. The total stock is 294,170 items – books and periodicals – of which 277,582 are on site (the rest archived for lack of space). 120,326 loans have been made in the year. 1,600 people per day visit in term-time, 483 in the vacations. There are 5,267 registered users. Short loans are down 16 per cent on the previous year, and visits down 7 per cent. The speculation is that changes in the teaching day – now 9.00 am – 6.00 pm, from the previous 9.30 am – 5.30 pm – are making it harder for students to find time to come in. Perhaps unsurprisingly, given the financial constraints, there is no suggestion of extending Library opening hours.

The merger with Westfield

While QM was struggling with spiral staircases and overcrowding, at Westfield the Caroline Skeel Library (named for the historian who managed the College's first Library) was purpose-built, spacious and well-stocked.

Brian Murphy, Director of Information Services at Westfield and subsequently Deputy and then Librarian at QM, remembers:

> It was quite a large building … on six floors … There was plenty of spare space, so after a while we put in a bookshop, which paid a bit in rental and supplied the Library with materials … It was open for, if I remember rightly, 9.00 am until 9.00 pm Monday to Friday and on Saturdays.[102]

Westfield's was also one of the first university libraries to install computer terminals. Brian Murphy feels that in the smaller environment of Westfield it was easier to make such radical decisions:

> … if you wanted to do something, you could get round everybody in a few minutes' time, decide something, and do it … whereas here, as it is much larger it takes longer to get decisions made.[103]

100. www.library.qmul.ac.uk/strategic_objectives Accessed June 2012.
101. *Librarian's Report 1985–86*, Library Committee paper 86–7/3. (London: Queen Mary College, 1986).
102. Murphy, B. Interview for this history. 2008.
103. ibid.

By 1985 Westfield's science stock had been transferred to QM, along with the Science faculty; and discussion on a possible merger with some other college was underway. The agreement with QM came in 1988, the year that the new Library at Mile End opened. Over three years, 1989–1992, the merger brought another 600 students to use a facility designed for 3,500.

The new library opens

Finally the building discussions – there are memos about the washbasin in the disabled toilet, and the shape of the enquiry, issue and returns counter – were over. In practical terms, the new Library opened on 28 September 1988. No doubt students at the start of the term crowded in to see it, just as they did after the 2010 refurbishment.
In ceremonial terms, the Library was opened by the Queen on 14 December, the first-ever visit to the College by a reigning monarch. Neil Entwistle recalls a splendid event:

> There was much advance preparation at a College and Library level, and of course we had the inevitable security visitation, including advice on choreographing the royal toilet stop. On the day, there were crowds of local school children lining the route and waving Union Jacks! …
> I remember having great anxiety about how to interest the reigning monarch in the use of an online library catalogue.[104]

The new building brought with it new funding, and more staff; who worked, Neil Entwistle says, "in a space almost comically grand after the broom cupboard life." There was a new staffing structure, with specialist librarians qualified in the relevant discipline to serve each faculty. There was the new computerised management system, Libertas, for both users and staff. For students, there was the radical addition of a group study room on each floor, designed for 'class' or 'syndicate' study, either one under the supervision of academic staff. There were also casual reading places, a readers' lounge with ashtrays and coffee machine, an exhibition area for rare books, an archive room for the first time, and even 'dog-tethering provision' in the South porch. Using a library had never been so relaxed nor so constructive.

HM Queen Elizabeth II opening the new library in 1988.

This was Phase 1. As soon as it was complete, it became clear that Phase 2, an extension to house the Westfield stock, would be needed. The original brief had specified space to expand, and this was duly used. The extension opened in 1992.

The new building was for many years the star attraction on the site, and won the 1992 Library Design Award of the Society of College and National University Libraries. (A plaque still commemorates this).

The medical merger

The issues for the respective libraries raised by the merger with the medical schools were different. There was no question of the whole medical stock being moved to Mile End; it was a question of managing the whole as one, unified library, but on five sites. A medical librarian came to work within the team at Mile End and facilitated the relationship. In addition, the new computerised management system at QM was the one already in use by the medical schools. There was, Brian Murphy says, "a rather greater degree of independence for the medical libraries than some people thought possible."[105]

104. Entwistle, N, op cit.

105. Murphy, B, op cit.

Open plan study area on the ground floor of the Library, 2011.

The archives

From Palace to College, the previous history of QM, is dedicated "to someone who does not yet exist – the College Archivist."[106] The Library at Westfield had an archive room, though not a purpose-built storage space. The specification for the new building included an archive room, properly planned for horizontal (rather than vertical) storage of documents. An archive reading room was created, and named for Caroline Skeel. In the 2010 refurbishment, this was relocated to the second floor, and the storage facilities were extended and upgraded. There is also, finally, an archivist. Lorraine Screene was appointed on a one-year contract in 2006, and confirmed in post at the end of that year; a two-year part-time trainee post was added in 2010. The task of cataloguing the College's vast holdings continues: around 85 per cent of it is still to be done. This book, among much else, would have been almost impossible to compile without a staffed archive.

Refurbishment

The decision to refurbish the existing Library Building to meet current needs was made in 2008, and the work started in 2009. The result is modern, spacious and eye-catching. A barcoded card lets you in through automated gates; to your right is a café area and beyond it the Learning Lounge, where students can confer over a coffee and sandwich. Next to them is the Teaching Collection, multiple copies of books recommended by staff for undergraduate courses. (Though you still have to

be quick to get hold of one, students told us). Straight ahead from the gates are computer tables, and students conferring in small groups or working alone. These areas are bright and full of the sound of conversation, while upstairs, signs indicate silent study areas. There are also new group study rooms upstairs, equipped with computers and projection, where students can work on shared assignments (without, now, the assumption that a member of academic staff will be leading them).

Further student comments:
  "I come in the evenings and work on till midnight."
  "It's good there's a café now, so if I'm working here all day revising, I'm eating proper food, not just chocolate."[107]

Emma Bull has registered the complaint from students that there aren't enough computers now; she has to balance that against space for people to plug in their laptops. There is also the trickier question of fluctuating demand, with large numbers using the Library in the run-up to exams.

Revision time means more demand for quiet space; the rest of the year, group rooms are much needed. The demands of a modern library are complex and evolving. Even the redesign itself has an impact:
  More people want to come here now, it's a better atmosphere. We come here between lectures and our friends are here.[108]

---

106. Moss, G P & Saville, M V, op cit.

107. Anonymous interviews for this history. 2011.
108. ibid.

Other changes in use have other causes. The
Library manages subscriptions to a wide range of
online journals and databases; the result is that
academic staff and researchers are seen less often in
the Library Building, since they can consult these
resources at their desks. Managing e-resources is
now a major call on staff time and on the budget:
£1,750,000 in 2010. Within this decisions on
priority and usage still have to be made; but
inter-library loans can substitute for rarely used
subscriptions.

Beyond Mile End

The newly refurbished Library is modern and
expansive. Library staff have become expansive
with it, being out and about to offer help in IT or
research or whatever else is needed, in the College's
various spaces. There is now a staff of 115 working
in the four libraries: at Mile End, West Smithfield,
Whitechapel and Victoria Park. The four are very
different. In Whitechapel, at The London, the
Medical Library building is a spectacular
de-consecrated late-nineteenth century church,
which also houses the hospital museum.
The atmosphere tends to be quiet, the church
architecture perhaps instilling respect. West
Smithfield, (the Barts library) is historic and
friendly, with a small staff and many regular users.
Both of these sites have self-service and group
study facilities. The library at the London Chest
Hospital in Victoria Park, Hackney is smaller and
more specialised. All four aim to offer the same
quality of service and the same ethos of support
for learning.

And change continues. A new dedicated reading
room for postgraduate researchers opened in
February 2011. It is clear that libraries, perhaps
more than most institutions, have to be prepared
to adapt their spaces, their equipment and their
mindset constantly, as demands and students and
technology all change. No more clambering up
dizzying spiral staircases to find your English
textbook sheltering from the rain; no more
freezing in what was once an indoor rifle range.
No doubt in another 20 years – or less – today's
computers and LCD projectors will seem equally
antique.

The Whitechapel Library.

The Built Environment

Detail of the yellow, white and grey Penrose tiling on the exterior of the
Mathematical Sciences Building, Mile End campus.

April 2011. The royal-blue hoardings along the Mile End Road have come down. Instead there is a dazzling, asymmetrical wall in yellow, grey and white, along two sides of the 1960s Mathematical Sciences Building. It is one of those original pieces of architecture that makes you smile with surprise.

The yellow, white and grey tiling pattern on the outside of the building is known as a Penrose tiling. This is a tiling of a two-dimensional plane by thin and fat diamonds, which shows some local fivefold symmetry. It's different from more standard tilings of the plane, such as by squares or hexagons, because it's irregular and non-periodic: you can't translate it in some direction and exactly repeat the original pattern. The Penrose tiling was investigated in the 1970s by Sir Roger Penrose, an English mathematical physicist who graduated with a first class degree from UCL, and is now a Visiting Professor at Queen Mary.

Penrose tilings aren't just abstract. The mathematics behind their construction has applications to materials called quasicrystals, whose properties have been studied by scientists for about the last 30 years. In the 4,000-year old history of mathematics, they are relatively young![109]

The new Maths Foyer is one of numerous examples of the imaginative, functional architecture that has transformed not only the Mile End Campus but Whitechapel and Charterhouse Square in the past 25 years.

109. www.maths.QM.ac.uk/news/building-work-nearly-finished (Accessed in 2011).

Mile End: acquiring land

Long before the period of this book, the College had the foresight to acquire small parcels of land and commercial buildings between the Queens' Building and the canal: the Co-operative Wholesale Society building (1964), a Pickfords removals site (1974), the British Rail goods yard (1975), and so on. The CWS building was converted to house the Faculty of Laws, but otherwise there was no definite plan to make use of this extra land until the 1980s. Still, there was the potential for a greatly expanded College site. There were, however, two obstacles. One was the gravel yard, to the north-east of the main buildings, owned by British Rail and leased by Ready Mix Concrete. The yard was not only unsightly but disruptive: heavy lorries went on thundering up and down the cobbled road that became Westfield Way until the 1990s. It was finally acquired in 1995.

The other obstacle was more interesting, more complex to deal with, and more lasting in its impact on the site. This was the Sephardic cemetery.

The Sephardim at Mile End

When you walk east from Stepney Green station, the first College property you come to is an elegant, apparently Georgian house (in fact rebuilt in 1913), with a wrought-iron balcony, a red front door, and two terracotta plaques between the ground floor windows. This was the Beth Holim, the hospital and later old people's home of the Spanish and Portuguese Jewish community in London, founded in 1748 and moved to Mile End in 1790. The Beth Holim is now Albert Stern

above: HRH the Princess Royal visiting the Novo Beth Chaim Cemetery with Professor Geoffrey Crossick, Vice-Chancellor of the University of London; Professor Simon Gaskell, Principal, and Professor Philip Ogden, Senior Vice Principal, of Queen Mary, University of London; Rabbi Abraham Levy; and Rabbi Eiran Davis.

right: the Novo Beth Chaim Cemetery on the Mile End campus.

opposite: the Westfield Student village, Mile End campus, 2012.

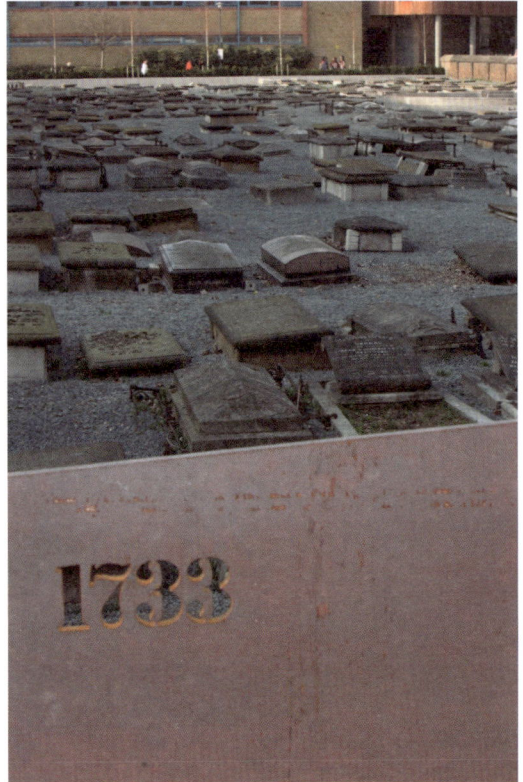

House, a student residence (named for Lt Col Sir Albert Gerald Stern, an eminent banker, developer of tanks in World War I, and sometime Chair of the College Council). The cemetery behind it is the Velho, the oldest known Jewish cemetery in the UK, opened in 1657 and closed in 1742. It was replaced by the Nuevo Beth Chaim Cemetery, opened in 1733 and closed in the 1920s.[110] The Nuevo Cemetery covered a large site next to the College buildings.

It was 1973 before long-standing negotiations over the cemetery came to fruition, with the Queen Mary College Act. This allowed the College to buy the greater part of the new burial ground. Remains over 200 years old were to be disinterred in accordance with religious requirements. The London Necropolis Company took charge of this solemn task: staff and students were forbidden

even to watch the process from the College windows. The remains were then reburied; the College made land available at Dytchleys, near Brentwood in Essex, for the purpose. Graves less than 200 years old had to stay. The College was granted a 999-year lease on this Restricted Area, with an obligation to maintain it in good order.

This explains the most extraordinary feature of the College site: the walled burial ground with its traditional flat gravestones. The wall itself is now listed as a historic structure. The Francis Bancroft Building, the catering block and the new Library were all built on the cleared site. In 2011–12, further landscaping work on the perimeter of the cemetery was overseen by Rabbi Dr Abraham Levy, the Spiritual Head of the Spanish and Portuguese Jews' Congregation. New plaques offer students and visitors information about the cemetery and its rich history.

110. see Jewish East End of London – Mile End and the Sephardim. www.jewisheastend.com/mileend.html accessed March 2012.

The Library

With the additional space available, the Westfield merger being planned (chapter 3), and the pre-clinical medical merger under discussion (chapter 6), there was the likelihood of an expansion in student numbers and the need for further building. This was the first of the high-profile buildings at Mile End, controversial at the time but now fitting perfectly into the new-look campus. (see also chapter 16).

The Westfield legacy

The governing document of the Westfield Trust, set up at the time of the merger to conserve the values of Westfield, required the Trustees to consider among other aims "the provision or enhancement of residential and academic buildings for Queen Mary and Westfield College". Dr Molly Scopes, who had become Senior Vice Principal at the combined College, remembers the early decision-making:

> The Hampstead site was to be sold and the proceeds of sale reinvested at Mile End to provide not only a new Arts Building but an extension to the new college library ... and

student residential blocks to replace those lost at Hampstead. The residences were built along the canal side. Much of the proceeds of sale were used in these major 'new-build' projects but a significant portion was also made available for small-scale works and refurbishment of older buildings ... Step by step, work was carried out on student facilities, a new Student Health Centre was created, lecture theatres were improved, a new area in the Queens' Building was re-designed for the [College's] Computer Services [administrative department] ... Improvements were made to the School of Biological Sciences and completely new departmental space provided for Computer Science in part of the same building. Conversion of the People's Palace to provide additional lecture theatres and refurbishment of the Student Union were two major projects. As the work went on, year by year I felt that I was spending the family inheritance but, I believe, to good effect![111]

111. Scopes, P.M. Written contribution to this history. 2008.

Major non-residential buildings

Year	Building	Campus	Architects
1988	Library	Mile End	Colin St John Wilson
1990	Francis Bancroft	Mile End	Feilden and Mawson
1991	Catering	Mile End	Feilden and Mawson
1992	ArtsOne	Mile End	RMJM
1996	Abernethy	Whitechapel	Llewellyn Davies
2001	Nursery	Mile End	Hassan Falahat (QM Projects Office)
2003	Joseph Priestley	Mile End	Sheppard Robson
2004	Lock-keeper's Cottage	Mile End	Surface Architects
2005	Blizard	Whitechapel	Will Alsop
2006	Octagon, restored	Mile End	Molyneux Kerr
2009	Innovation Centre	Whitechapel	NBBJ
2011	ArtsTwo	Mile End	Wilkinson Eyre
2011	Mathematics Foyer	Mile End	Wilkinson Eyre
2011	Heart Centre	Charterhouse Square	Thornsett
2012	People's Palace (restoration)	Mile End	Berman Guedes Stretton

Julian Robinson, then Head of the Projects Office at QM and later Director of Estates at the LSE, set an ambitious standard for the commissioning of new buildings. His aim was to replace the rather pedestrian style of some of the 1960s and 1970s buildings with architecture that was stylish as well as functional. The Blizard Building, the Westfield Student Village and the Lock-keeper's Graduate Centre demonstrate how successful this approach was.

Professor Philip Ogden, Senior Vice-Principal, has been engaged with the development of the College's estate for a number of years:

> [There was] a book, which must have been a history of, or guide to, the East End, which mentions the College in quite unfavourable terms... It said the College on Mile End Road, "must have the ugliest campus in the UK". This was a formative moment for me. I agreed, and I felt that something needed to be done. My passion for the built environment of the campus, getting good architects and design, was driven by the fact that people had been patronising about the College in the 1970s and 1980s.[112]

The first masterplan for the Mile End campus was devised for the College by the architects Feilden

112. Ogden, P. Interview for this history. 2008.

and Mawson in 1985; the second ten years later by MacCormack Jamieson Prichard. The latter report informed the first formal estates strategy, for 1995–2002. The medical merger had brought student numbers from 6,400 (full-time equivalent) to 8,200 in 1995, with proportionate increases in academic and support staff: the College's estate needed to be managed to accommodate these increases. As well as consolidating academic and administrative space, the College created a new Health Centre, and provided 170 more student rooms, in Ifor Evans and Lindop Houses.

Accommodating students

From the 1930s, the majority of residential accommodation for Queen Mary students was in low-rise and (later) tower blocks in South Woodford, an outer London suburb five miles from Mile End. There were also a number of small stand-alone houses, and a hostel, Luke House, in the East End. The merger with the Medical School brought a block of 32 flats, Brent House in Hackney. Marie Barter, then Director of Conference, Catering and Residential Services, recognised that these outlying properties were outdated and ill-suited to students who wanted self-catering en-suite accommodation. The properties were sold, with the aim of building new student housing at Mile End.

Mile End Campus Map

Educational / Research

ArtsOne	37
ArtsTwo	35
Arts Research Centre	39
The Bancroft Building	31
Bancroft Road Teaching Rooms	10
Computer Science	6
David Sizer Lecture Theatre	30
Engineering Building	15
Fogg Building	13
G.O. Jones Building	25
Geography	26
IRC	14
Informatics Teaching Laboratories	5
Joseph Priestley Building	41
Library	32
Law	36
Lock-keeper's Graduate Centre	42
Mathematical Sciences	4
Occupational Health and Safety Directorate	12
The People's Palace/Great Hall	16
Queens' Building	19

Residential

Albert Stern Cottages	3
Albert Stern House	1
Beaumont Court	53
Chapman House	43
Chesney House	45
Creed Court	57
France House	55
Feilden House	46
Hatton House	40
Ifor Evans Place	2
Lindop House	21
Lodge House	50
Lynden House	59
Maurice Court	58
Maynard House	44
Pooley House	60
Selincourt House	51
Varey House	49

Facilities

Advice and Counselling Service	27
Bank (£)	62
Bookshop	22
Careers Centre	19b
Clock Tower	20
CopyShop	56
The Curve	47
Drapers' Bar	8
Ground Café	33
The Hive	24
The Hub	34
Infusion	9
Mucci's	29
Occupational Health Service/ -Student Health Service	28
Octagon	19a
Police Box	38
Post Room	17
QMotion Fitness Centre	7
Residences Reception	54
Security	18
St Benet's Chapel	23
Students' Union Offices/ Blomeley Centre	48
Temporary Building	61
Westfield Nursery	11
Village Shop	52

(i) Information

Visitors who require further information or assistance please go to the Main Reception in the Queens' Building.

Please do not smoke on the campus.

These premises are alarmed and monitored by CCTV, please call security on 020 7882 5000 for more information.

Library/bookshop

Fitness centre

Bar

Coffee place

Eatery

(P) Staff Car Park

Bicycle Parking

(£) Cash Machine

Map of the Mile End campus, 2012.

The new canalside residences paid for by the Westfield Trust had begun this process. Ifor Evans House and Lindop House followed. With the sale of the outlying sites, the Westfield Student Village was created. 1,176 new study bedrooms were added: a major transformation of Mile End into a true campus, with large numbers of students living, studying (and partying) on site.

Residential buildings

Year	Building	Campus	Architects
1991	Hatton House	Mile End	MacCormack Jamieson Prichard
1992	Maynard House		
	Varey House		
1992	Stocks Court	offsite (Stepney)	Quantec
1995	Chapman House	Mile End	MacCormack Jamieson Prichard
	Chesney House		
	Lodge House		
	Selincourt House		
1996	Lindop House		
	Ifor Evans Place		
2005	Beaumont Court		Feilden Clegg Bradley
	Creed Court		
	France House		
	Lynden House		
	Maurice Court		
	Pooley House		
2007	Richard Feilden House		

The final item on the chart above was completed as part of the 2006–15 strategy, and named for Richard Feilden, the architect who had contributed so much to the College environment, and who died in 2005. Feilden House added another 250 study bedrooms, to bring the total number of bedrooms on or close to the campus to 1,923. For medical students, there are also 145 places in Floyer House, Whitechapel, and 207 in Dawson Hall, Charterhouse Square (both built long before the merger).

The impact of such accommodation on student life is significant. Young people living away from home for the first time not only feel safer not having to cross London at night, but also make friends more easily.

> The fact you were living in halls with fellow students from around the world allowed you to immerse yourself in cultures from around the world and make friends for a lifetime.
> (*Simon Barlow, Alumnus*)[113]

113. Barlow, S. Written contribution for this history. 2011.

Above all, I loved the fact that QM is the only campus university in London so everything is on campus and I can just hang out at my friend's flat if there's nothing to do.
(*Niyla Akhtar, 4th year, undergraduate*)[114]

Knowledge

Knowledge stands at the centre of Library Square, a 28-foot sculpture, a stainless steel sphere held high in sinuous steel arms. It was created by the well-known sculptor Wendy Taylor, CBE, who is a Fellow of QM and an East Ender: her family has lived in the area for at least six generations. The polished surface of the sphere makes it an image of the world, not only by its shape but by reflections of the diverse students and staff passing by. The arms, Wendy Taylor says, represent "the giving and accepting of experience, and of holding the world and therefore its future."[115]
(See *Knowledge* on p.80)

114. Akhtar, N, Written contribution for this history. 2011.
115. http://www.qmul.ac.uk/qmul/news/newsrelease.php?news_id=21 (Accessed 2012)

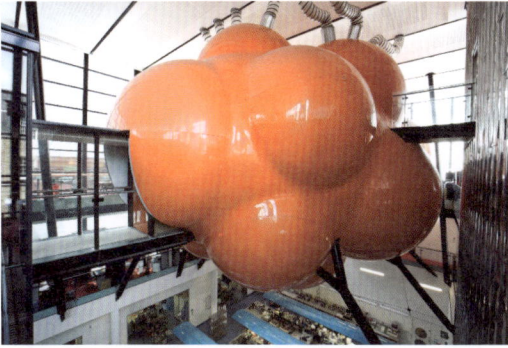

Blizard Building.

Knowledge was named Architectural Sculpture of the Year in the Building of the Year Awards 2004.

The academic buildings

The 2002–06 estates strategy also included two of the most spectacular buildings in the College: the Lock-keeper's Cottage by the canal, which became the Arts Graduate Centre; and the Blizard Building in Whitechapel. Bill Hunt, formerly Head of Projects at Queen Mary, describes the process of creating this innovative building, designed by the architect Will Alsop for the Blizard Institute of the Cell and Molecular Science:

The rationale was to provide a building that promoted interaction between a fairly disparate group of medical researchers who previously had been scattered through QM's estate. The initial designs followed a fairly conventional route… Alsops considered this did not meet some key aspects of our aspirations and we looked at how to provide a more open and interactive space. Out of this came the single lab floor concept, open plan write up and minimal cellular offices. The architects commented that the lab floor "would pancake [flatten] the site"… so the decision was made to put the labs 5.5m below ground. A very bold concept and one that took a lot of careful explaining to gain the support of the researchers… The architects made the statement that "standing on the lab floor you will be able to see the outside, sun and clouds" – they were true to their words.

The discussions with the users brought to them the understanding that rather than being separate research sections they were now forming an Institute… Sharing of space and lab function became a major aspect of the building. User satisfaction has remained high and the building is dynamic, filled with light and colour and it does work as a lab building.[116]

116. Hunt, W. Written contribution to this history. 2011.

The Lock-keeper's cottage graduate centre
seen from the Regent's canal.

Exterior view of the Lock-keeper's cottage.

The original Lock-keeper's Cottage was a simple building, like hundreds of others built along the canal network in the early nineteenth century. Until 2003 it was marooned at the edge of the Mile End site and occupied by the family of the last lock-keeper. Finally after much negotiation the College managed to buy it from British Waterways, and employed Surface Architects to develop it into a graduate centre, with workrooms, a common room and seminar room.

The third strategy

The 2006–15 estates strategy has brought in a further set of improvements and new buildings. The Queen Mary BioEnterprises Innovation Centre at Whitechapel was completed in October 2010. It offers accommodation close to The Royal London Hospital for biotechnology companies, with purpose-built laboratory space, and business support for emerging companies. Because the area with its Georgian and early Victorian terraced housing is itself of architectural interest, the College negotiated with the local authority and the Spitalfields Trust to find a modern design that would feel appropriate.

ArtsTwo replaced two rather uninspiring buildings on the Mile End Road. Designed by Wilkinson Eyre, it provides a new home for the School of History and the Leo Baeck Institute, a new studio space for teaching Film and Drama, and dedicated space for postgraduate research students. The building also houses a 300-seat lecture theatre, and five seminar rooms, which are available to

the whole College. It was formally opened on 9 March 2012 by the Princess Royal, in her role as Chancellor of the University of London. The event was part of a ten-day celebration, 'Migration, Memory and Identity', which included a concert of music of the London Sephardic community, a lecture by Simon Schama, a reading by poet Ruth Padel, and a School of Law symposium. ArtsTwo has been nominated for three architectural awards.

The Graduate Centre

The 1960s Chemistry Building was demolished in 2011, after asbestos was discovered in the structure. The space has been renamed the Anniversary Site, since the planned new building was given the go-ahead in 2012, the College's 127th birthday. This is to be a Graduate Centre, which in addition to teaching and office space will provide living accommodation for over a hundred students, reading and common rooms, a cafeteria and a glazed winter garden. (The original People's Palace also had a glazed winter garden.) Plans also include a new home for the School of Economics and Finance, with a mock trading floor and an IT lab. A combined heat and power plant will service the Centre and eight other buildings, and contribute significantly to QM's strategy for carbon reduction.

The ArtsTwo Building.

Charterhouse Square

The Charterhouse Square site, close to Barts and beside the remains of the medieval Carthusian Monastery, was vested in the Medical College of St Bartholomew's Hospital Trust and leased to the College in 1999, after the merger with the School of Medicine and Dentistry. At that time large parts of the site were still as they'd been left by World War II bomb damage. The College's lease requires the land and buildings to be used only for the School of Medicine and Dentistry. The period of uncertainty over the future of Barts Hospital stalled development for some time; but the final positive decision, that the hospital should focus on cancer and cardiac disease, enabled the College to invest in the site as the home of the Barts Cancer Institute (chapter 9), the William Harvey Research Institute and the Wolfson Institute of Preventative Medicine.

The William Harvey Heart Centre, in Charterhouse Square, opened on 7 July 2011. It houses state-of-the-art facilities for cardiovascular research (see chapter 8). What was perhaps the last remaining bombsite in Central London, on the north-eastern corner of the square, was sold by the Trust to a firm of property developers, with the condition that they built the shell of the Heart Centre as well as flats for commercial sale. Professor Mark Caulfield then succeeded in raising £25 million to fit out the building and employ staff. As well as enabling world-class research, the Heart Centre will be a focus for public engagement on issues of heart health.

Architectural awards

Year	Building	Award
1992	Library	Library Design Award, Society of College & National University Libraries
1995	Canalside residences, phase 2	RIBA Regional Award
2004	*Knowledge* sculpture	Architectural Sculpture of the Year
2004	Blizard Building	LEAF Award
2005		RIBA Regional Award
2005	Lock-keeper's Cottage	RIBA Regional Award, Civic Trust Award, shortlisted for Stephen Lawrence Award
2005	Student Village (phases 1 & 2)	RIBA Regional Award, Deputy Prime Minister's Housing Award
2006	Blizard Building	Civic Trust Award
2006	Medical School Library	DDA Award
2008	Student Village (phase 3), Richard Feilden House	RIBA Regional Award, RIBA Client of The Year Award, London Region
2011	Fogg Building re-cladding	Green Gown Award

Over the past 15 years, the College has spent around £250 million on its estate. Funds have come from the College's own capital, various charities and bequests. The result is that the three sites are all both highly functional and exciting to look at and work in. In 2006, the *Independent* newspaper acknowledged that the College "has quietly amassed some of the best new academic architecture in Britain".[117] As Philip Ogden says:

Now, there is no issue about the campus or about being in the East End. Visitors are often astounded by how the College looks, and when the next phase of development is completed it will be even better, and demonstrate just what can be achieved having a campus-based College within London.[118]

117. 'The Lock of the New'. *The Independent*, 22 February 2006.
118. Ogden, P, op cit.

Dean Rees House, Charterhouse Square.

Life as a student

Student Village, Mile End campus.

"When I came here," says Sophie Richardson, in 2011–12 President of the QM Students' Union, "it was a huge change for me. I'd never written an essay of more than 300 words. After six weeks here, I had to write 1,500. I had to learn to become an independent learner."[119]

Learning independently – learning to think, analyse, know what else one needs to learn – is perhaps the most profound change that undergraduates go through, and arguably the purpose of higher education. It is an experience that can be enormously liberating, but also alarming, if one's education to date has involved learning to replicate 'correct' answers. For the new undergraduate, though, it's one of many adjustments to be made. Some, like Sophie, are living in London for the first time, coming from towns and provincial cities, from other European countries or across continents. Some have learnt English at home, but are still faced with rapid, constant communication in a foreign language. Some students live at home and commute across London to QM; others share accommodation in the Student Village. Everyone, whatever their background, has to adapt to the particular culture of British university life.

The Westfield Student Village

Probably the greatest change in student experience since 1985 has been the development of accommodation on campus, in the Westfield Student Village. The Student Village began in 1990, with the first residences on the banks of the

Regent's Canal. It now has almost 2,000 places. Priority goes to first-year students whose family home is beyond the boundary of the orbital M25 motorway (so there is no option to commute). Like all the best villages, it has other facilities: a shop, café, restaurant and launderettes. For young people who find it hard to get up in the morning, there is the traffic-free five-minute dash to lectures; those studying late in the Library can get home quickly and safely. And more than anything, there's the social side:

> [The highlight was] undoubtedly the friends I made as a student and all of the simple things we were able to do together on campus; whether sharing a pizza in Café Amici or playing a game of pool in the SU bar, those are the memories I shall retain for the rest of my life.
> (*Humayon Pramanik, graduated 2005*)[120]

> With some help I managed to drag my entire luggage into my small but pretty room with a view on the Regent's Canal. It was a very happy moment, especially when it turned out I have really nice and easy-going flatmates, that there is never a queue to the shower, and the School of Law is just two minutes away.
> (*Dominika Jankowska, 3rd year, Law*)[121]

The multicultural and international life of the College is cited by some students as exciting, by others as reassuring:

> I felt it was very important to be in an environment where I can practise my religion

---

119. Richardson, S. Interview for this history. 2011.

120. Pramanik, H. Written contribution to this history. 2011.
121. Jankowska, D Written contribution to this history. 2011.

Assistive Technology Room on the Mile End campus.

comfortably. QM ... has two prayer rooms/
multi-faith centre, it was easy to find a restaurant
serving halal food and there was even halal food
being served on the QM campus... And because
I wear the hijaab, I felt at ease at QM because
there were many students who also wore the
hijaab and face veil.
(*Niyla Akhtar, 4th year, Law with German*)[122]

Some first-year medical and dental students live in
the Student Village, and have a chance to meet
their counterparts in other disciplines. There are
also residences on the other sites, at Whitechapel
and Charterhouse Square, and bars and other
social facilities for students living close to the
two hospitals.

Disabled and dyslexic students
The issue of access to higher education for
students with disabilities came into focus with the
Disability Discrimination Act of 1995, and the
concept of making "reasonable adjustments" to
ensure equal access. In the context of education,
this might mean providing lecture handouts in
different formats, or allowing students to submit
assignments electronically. SENDA (the Special
Educational Needs Discrimination Act of 2001)
clarified the situation further: universities are
expected not simply to react to students' requests
for reasonable adjustments, but to anticipate them.

However, what really made a difference to the
recruitment of disabled students, says Simon
Jarvis, head of QM's Disability and Dyslexia
Service, was the introduction of the Disabled
Student's Allowance (DSA) in 1991, and its
extension to all disabled undergraduates, without
means-testing, in 1998. The DSA provides vital
funding to cover some of the extra costs disabled

122. Akhtar, N, op cit.

students incur – a note-taker or reader for someone visually impaired, for instance, or taxi fares for a person with restricted mobility. From the mid-nineties onwards, the numbers of disabled students in higher education rose dramatically. (In 2010–11, 941 students at QM disclosed that they had a disability; only two years previously, the figure was 639). Also in the 1990s, many more students disclosed that they were dyslexic, encouraged perhaps by the new recognition that with appropriate support, academic achievement was perfectly possible. Over the last ten years, another taboo has been broken, with more students feeling they can acknowledge mental health needs. Institutions, too, have been more ready to work on mental health issues, recognising among other things that the key question of student retention is closely linked to mental well-being.

The Disability and Dyslexia Service at QM was created in 2007. Before that, support was divided between the Advice and Counselling Service, and the Language and Learning Unit. They did much good work; but Simon Jarvis believed referrals between the two could involve delay and so a dedicated disability service was vital. The department now has specialist staff working on dyslexia and mental health, as well as disability advice. Services include study skills for dyslexic students, with seven tutors providing individual support; note-takers and mobility helpers; and since 2010 a support group for students with Asperger's, including a tailor-made induction. At the end of their first academic year, all the members of this original group were thriving.

The service also works with academics, supporting them in making the necessary adjustments to their teaching and assessment practice; and with the rest of the College. A Disability Discrimination Act audit in 2008 raised a number of issues, to which the College has been quick to respond. For example, the newly refurbished Library has a dedicated assistive technology room for visually impaired students, with large screen computers, text-enlargers and height-adjustable desks; there's a similar room for students with other disabilities or dyslexia close to the Disability and Dyslexia Service offices. There are also 15 adapted residential rooms in the Student Village.

The service's best achievements, Simon Jarvis says, are the successes of students it has supported: just two examples speak for themselves: a visually impaired student with a PhD, and a wheelchair user who lived on campus for three years and got an upper second. Without the College responding to their needs and understanding their potential, this would never have happened.

The Students' Union

The social life at QM was fantastic. Draper's Bar was still being refurbished when I started in 2007 so the Students' Union organised regular trips to some of London's best nightclubs, which was a great way to explore London nightlife at student prices. When Drapers' Bar did open in September 2008 it was so exciting to have a brand-new bar. Being the main social area on campus, it meant students flocked there in [their] masses every night of the week so it always had a fantastic atmosphere. On top of the nightlife, Queen Mary offered clubs and societies for almost anything you could think of! (*Alice Carney, graduated 2010*)[123]

A few friends and I restarted the QM Polish Society, which not only attracted Polish people, but also many people of different nationalities who just happen to be interested in Polish culture. Being international and foreigner-friendly is one of the greatest features of Queen Mary. (*Dominika Jankowska*)[124]

The Drapers' Bar is, as Sophie Richardson, President of the Students' Union, confirms, extremely popular; it hosts comedy evenings, club nights, and a monthly Wednesday evening session, hosted by each of the sports clubs in turn after all the teams have been playing. Students who for reasons of religion or preference avoid the bar have plenty of other events they can attend, including 'QMSU Loves U' evenings and a civilised Sunday session of Scrabble and other games in the coffee shop. In honour of former College differences, there's also an annual Merger Cup, with rugby, football, tennis, netball and hockey teams from the School of Medicine and Dentistry playing their counterparts in the rest of the College.

123. Carney, A. Written contribution to this history. 2011.
124. Jankowska, D, op cit.

As well as organising events – political as well as social at times – 200 students attended the tuition fees demonstration in late 2010 – the Students' Union has an important role in representing student interests in the College's decision-making structure. When results of the National Student Survey showed that assessment and feedback were areas of concern at QM, the Students' Union did further research on student views, and presented a paper with recommendations to the College Council. Since February 2011, the Students' Union and the College have been working on making changes that, the Union hopes, will eventually set standards of transparency and specificity for assessment and feedback.

The Students' Union believes as a matter of principle in free education. However, Sophie Richardson understands that the tuition fee issue exists, and that the College had little option but to raise fees to £9,000 per year for home students. "My main concern was keeping the College accessible for students from lower income backgrounds,' says Sophie. "I think the amount committed to bursaries should be enough to continue supporting those students who need it most. I'm also very pleased that the College is continuing to fund the East London Aimhigher programme [a scheme that encourages disadvantaged school students to consider university] when the government has scrapped it nationally." (See chapter 25 for more on tuition fees).

> "It's a very positive working relationship. I know in some universities, the Vice Chancellor won't even open the door to the Students' Union. Here, it's very student-focused. The relationship's evolved over time. Students' Union officers have been very active and responsive, and I think that's helped build up trust."

A recent collaboration with the Mental Health Co-ordinator (in the Disability and Dyslexia Service) resulted in a session on general mental wellbeing, timed for National Mental Health Day, and one on stress-busting in exam time. Sophie and her colleagues work closely with the College's support services, referring students to the Advice and Counselling Service when appropriate. "I've never had anyone come asking for support and found it wasn't available." [125]

Advice and counselling

Professor Brian Colvin, formerly Assistant Warden (and later Dean) for Student Affairs in the Medical and Dental School, credits the Advice and Counselling Service with changing students' attitudes. "When I became Assistant Warden … in 1998, medical and dental students were very reluctant to seek or accept Advice and Counselling's help. By 2008, when I retired from the post, the situation had changed completely, largely because of strong leadership at the Service." [126]

The Advice and Counselling web page, listing information leaflets and application forms, gives some idea of the range of issues the Service covers, noting, as it does, the following topics:
- Access to Learning Fund
- Banking
- Managing your Budget
- Extenuating Circumstances
- Immigration
- Resitting, Interrupting or Leaving Your Course
- Childcare
- Part-time and Vacation Work

As well as offering one-to-one support, the Service provides a great deal of information on the web. One self-help page, for instance, tackles the common but sometimes hidden issue of homesickness:

> It is really important to realise that you are not the only one feeling homesick and that it doesn't in any way mean you are inadequate. Suddenly, you find that, instead of being a central person in a small unit with plenty of peripheral activities and friends, you have become an anonymous member of a 5,000-plus community, where you know no-one. Understandably, you feel shaken and lonely and you long for the secure and the familiar. Sometimes the emotions are completely overwhelming. [127]

125. Richardson, S, op cit.
126. Colvin, B. Written contribution this history. 2012.
127. http://www.welfare.qmul.ac.uk/selfhelp/changes/index.html (Accessed 2011).

What the students say

I found the teaching stimulating and enthusiastic. The lecturers couldn't fail in transmitting their particular passions for whichever field they specialised in and this passion was infectious. I felt I was able to pursue any field I encountered whilst studying, as the guides I had didn't only *know* the greatest in their field, more often than not they *were* the greatest in their field. (*Beren Ashton-Butler, BA (Hons) English Language and Linguistics, 2011*)[128]

The Film Department is fairly small so it was easy to get to know both staff and students. It meant a lot that my lecturers knew my name and meant I felt comfortable going to them with any problems I was having. What really came across in their teaching was the academics' passion for the subject, which was really inspiring. (*Alice Carney, BA (Hons) Film Studies, 2010*)[129]

My first year in the University has been a very rewarding experience. QM, just like the education system in Singapore, seemed to have adopted a 'teach less, learn more' strategy, where students are allowed to explore their academic subject in more depth, after their curriculum time. (*Leong Qi Xiang, 1st year, BSc Economics*)[130]

The social life at uni is the best. There's none of that bitchiness that you experience at school and college, because everyone is older and a bit more mature. I met a lot of people and made a lot of friends, and there is always an event going on which, guaranteed, someone else will be attending, so you will have something in common. Undoubtedly, my experience at QM has been the best, I can't fault it! (*Niyla Akhtar*)[131]

128. Ashton-Butler, B. Written contribution to this history. 2011.
129. Carney, A, op cit.
130. Xiang, LQ. Written contribution to this history. 2011.
131. Akhtar, N, op cit.

Our students
in the future

QM students on the Mile End campus, 2012.

Since its inception as the People's Palace, QM has been committed to providing education for people who might otherwise struggle to obtain it. Recent years have brought a wider public debate; who goes to university? Do the best opportunities always go to the best applicants, regardless of background? With long-standing links to its diverse local community, QM's staff and students have found a variety of ways of encouraging young people to consider higher education, at the College itself or elsewhere, and of preparing them for it.

Student to student

SAMDA, Student Assisted Medical and Dental Applicants, is an innovative and effective student-led project. Set up by a medical student in 2000, SAMDA gets current students in the School of Medicine and Dentistry to help a new cohort of school and college students with their applications each year.

One volunteer, Shabaz Ahmad, himself a beneficiary of the scheme, tells of a teacher in a sixth-form centre who "spent three hours trying to convince me not to apply to medical school. The more he tried, the more determined I was." For prospective students like him, the application process was alien and bewildering. He and his colleagues now speak to whole classes in ten local sixth-form centres; they also mentor individual applicants, helping them write their personal statements, offering mock interviews and introducing them to the examiners who will be assessing them. SAMDA invites clinicians to speak at specially planned events, and offers contact with a range of medical schools, so that

applicants are clear about what's available to them. The message to would-be doctors and dentists, Shabaz says, is "Don't lose hope. Be yourself, and be honest, and work hard. Then at least you'll have the grounding for doing what you want." [132]

Working partnerships

Outreach is not left to committed students. St Angela's and St Bonaventura's Sixth-Form Centre in Newham is one of 13 schools and colleges across east London with which QM works in partnership. The 'Destinations' board in the school's entrance has photos of the latest group to succeed, with the name and the chosen university beneath each student. "Aspiration isn't the issue," says Sakhdeep Sohi, Assistant Head at the Centre. "We don't have to persuade students to go to university; but we have to provide realism, to make it viable for them. We need to get information to parents and pupils. Parents here want this for their children, but they can't offer the contacts and experience that other families might have." [133] The school is Catholic. Most students are of minority ethnic origin: African and African-Caribbean, Asian and now Eastern European; there's also a proportion of Muslim, Sikh and Hindu students.

The range of support offered by QM is impressive. Year 12 students have a three-day programme of talks and meetings at QM: the Admissions Tutor tells them about the process, Student ambassadors take them round the campus and discuss their own experience, academic departments accept them for an insight into subject teaching. There are talks on finance – increasingly important as tuition fees rise.

132. Ahmad, S. Interview for this history. 2011.
133. Sakhdeep, S. Interview for this history. 2011.

There are taster days in a range of subjects: Sakhdeep's own French class has spent a day in the College's French Department, and she hopes to build a similar link for her students with Film Studies.

Student volunteers come into the school to mentor small groups on their A-level subjects, and to help one-to-one with personal statements. Like SAMDA – which also works at the school – the Education Liaison Service offers mock interviews: "I send them to Queen Mary," says Sakhdeep. "They need to find their way around the campus, get the timing right, work out what it's appropriate to wear."[134] Many sixth-formers have never been on a college campus before; it's important for them to see where they're applying, whether it's Queen Mary or elsewhere.

"It's very powerful, having students talking to students," says Sakhdeep. Recently 96 per cent of St Angela's and St Bonaventure's sixth formers have gone on to university, to QM or further afield. In 2010, 14 came to QM, to study subjects from dentistry to drama, biomedical science to business management. Perhaps like many of their predecessors, in due course they'll be coming back to the school, to work with younger students and demonstrate just what can be achieved.

Strategic input
Outreach programmes like this, though greatly appreciated, have their limitations. In the past three years, QM has pioneered an in-depth approach to working with local schools. Anne Setright, Head of Outreach and Widening Participation, explains:

We want to get in while the children are still young, to build up a relationship with them and get them thinking about their aspirations and the options they have. It's also about preparing children from early on, so that they're choosing subjects that won't limit their options in future.[135]

In practice this means far more than an extended outreach programme; it involves a sustained relationship between the College as a whole and the whole school. Two east London schools, St Paul's Way in Tower Hamlets, and the Drapers' Academy in Havering, are benefiting from this new approach.

St Paul's Way Trust
St Paul's Way Trust School has probably the most exciting new building in Poplar, an area of the East End now largely overlooked, though in the 1920s it was briefly famous. (The radical Mayor, George Lansbury, led the Poplar Rates Rebellion, distributing local tax revenues directly to the poor instead of forwarding them on to the London County Council). With its glass frontage on a main shopping street, and a canopy sheltering the wide, welcoming entrance, the building demonstrates that the school both values its pupils and is open to its local community.

The immediate catchment area has a sizeable community of Bangladeshi origin. Parents, says the Head teacher, Grahame Price, are not without aspiration for their children; many came to the UK precisely in the hope of giving their children a better education than they themselves had: "The issue is how much first-hand knowledge they have of what that would look like in practice." By now some of the school's students have cousins or older siblings in higher education, but predominantly in the most local institutions, QM or London Metropolitan or east London. "We want to make sure that our students can choose the best course for them, whether that's at Queen Mary or elsewhere in the country. It can be difficult for students who stay living at home to take full advantage of the whole experience of university, particularly if those homes are overcrowded."[136]

A recent report from the education charity the Sutton Trust showed Tower Hamlets eighth from the bottom in terms of access to the top 30 UK universities, and fourth from the bottom for access to Oxbridge.[137] This is the context for QM's engagement with St Paul's Way.

---

134. Ibid.
135. Setright, A. Interview for this history. 2012.

136. Price, G. Interview for this history. 2012.
137. Degrees of Success: university chances by individual schools. (2011) London, Sutton Trust.

"The local authority removed the previous governing body, because the school was struggling," Grahame Price explains. "I was appointed Head teacher by an Interim Executive Board (IEB) in 2009. The IEB created a Foundation Trust, a completely new model of governance, with a Trust Board overseeing the work of the Board of Governors. We wanted a strong alliance with higher education. We approached Queen Mary to ask if it was willing to take part, and ideally to become the lead member of the Trust. The College was enthusiastic. They wanted a greater input into education in the borough, and they saw it as an opportunity to support the school's strategy for improvement."[138]

QM became the lead member of the Foundation Trust, with Nigel Relph, Director of Corporate Affairs, and then Professor Philip Ogden, Senior Vice-Principal, as its Chair; other Trust members include King's College London, the University of East London and the University of Warwick. Peter Heathcote, Professor of Biochemistry at QM, chairs the Board of Governors, accountable to the Trust. The commitment of the entire College hierarchy is, Grahame Price believes, vital for such a radical project to succeed: "It is a huge commitment." QM has demonstrated to the whole school that the relationship matters to both sides: the QM Council has even met on the school premises; QM students come to use the school's sports facilities.

In practical terms, the partnership means that the school benefits from informed academic and professional input into its planning processes. An example: St Paul's Way is the first London Faraday specialist science school. The issue for the staff and the Trust Board is how to teach science effectively. One answer has been to give all Year 7 students a whole day of science every fortnight, so that they have time to follow through on projects and fully grasp the concepts involved. The same process happens in Year 10. "Of course, we don't want them to be thinking, '*Oh no, a whole day of science!*' So we've had to work hard to make the learning both stimulating and *deep*."[139] Students from every year group visit the College

and attend lectures, for a taste of university life. Parents have come with Year 9 students, to get a sense of the experience their children may have. The whole ethos is of encouraging higher aspiration, from parents, pupils and teachers. And already the results are dramatic: from an intake of just 100 three years ago, St Paul's Way Trust now has 240 youngsters in year 7, with a waiting list. The school's new reputation has attracted a greater mix of pupils from across the borough, with benefits for all involved. ("We now have five oboeists in year 7," says Grahame Price. "The sound of the oboe is a new experience in the corridors of the school.") The Government's measure of success is the percentage of students getting 5 GCSEs, including English and Maths, at grades A–C. St Paul's Way Trust has gone from 23 per cent three years ago up to 60 per cent, above the national average. While the school has been led by Grahame Price and his colleagues, the input of QM has been irreplaceable, he says. "They are part of the team".

The Drapers' Academy
Harold Hill, home of the second school whose relationship with QM also forms a new kind of partnership, could hardly be more different from Poplar. It is right on the eastern edge of London, bordered by woodland. The area was developed in the 1940s, soon after the war, to rehouse families from the heavily-bombed East End. The idealism of that postwar reconstruction is still visible, in the open spaces with mature trees, the good-sized semi-detached houses. In the view of Matthew Slater, the Head of Drapers' Academy, however, one planning decision has had a major impact: an underground link to Harold Hill was mooted but never developed. The result has been the dramatic isolation of the community. To reach Central London – or QM, at Mile End – you need to take a bus to the nearest mainline station, Harold Wood, and a train to Liverpool Street or Stratford. The journey can take an hour; at 2012 prices, it would cost a family of four £21.40. "People live and die on the Hill. They work here. They never leave. Many of our students have never been as far Romford, let alone the West End."[140]

138. ibid.
139. ibid.

140. Slater, M. Interview for this history. 2012.

The school had been through several incarnations before its partnership with QM, with increasingly dilapidated buildings, reducing enrolments and a general sense of struggle. Many of the parents of the present students were themselves past pupils, and the new school has had to deal with their preconceptions. One masterstroke, as the school was in the process of transformation, was to take a shop in the centre of Harold Hill as a project office, so that parents could drop in and discuss the plans: "We could have had an office in Romford Town Hall, but no-one would have come."[141] Another was holding an open day for the community before the school re-opened.

There are many differences to Harold Hill's secondary school, this time around. Its academy status means that it is no longer managed by the local authority. Instead it has two sponsors: the Drapers' Company and QM. (For more on the Drapers' Company, see chapter 1). The Company wanted a close involvement with a school, and QM has been the Company's education partner since the College's inception.

As at St Paul's Way, a new building was seen as crucial to the new vision, a symbol of the availability of innovation and excellence to a community that has felt excluded from both. It will open in September 2012, appropriately the first educational building the Drapers have sponsored since the People's Palace. Meantime, organisational change has not waited for physical redevelopment. "The main change has been in expectation," says Matthew Slater; "what we expect in terms of achievement, behaviour, attendance, everything." The vision, shared from the start by the Headteacher, the Drapers and QM, is of high academic achievement, and strong discipline, within a calm, welcoming environment.

Input from the College has helped the school to develop its approach to education and to particular issues in teaching. One innovation has been to have some students work towards the English Baccalaureate, with the aim of giving them a better chance of entering higher education. In a radical move, matching this ambition, QM has guaranteed a place to any student from the Drapers' Academy who gets the necessary grades.

From September 2012 there will be a sixth form for the first time, and teaching staff who have not taught at that level before have support from subject specialists at QM. The new approach has had an impact too on the calibre of staff applying to work at the school. "At the start we advertised four vacancies and had one applicant," says Matthew Slater. "Now if we advertise we're inundated. Teachers can see that it's a good environment to work in, and that they have the chance to connect with some of the best academics in their subject at the College."[142]

Communication with parents has been vital. A new parent-teacher association has been formed, the Friends of Drapers' Academy, and all the parents of Year 7 have signed up. Matthew Slater holds Options Evenings, aimed at helping parents support their children. "I tell them to check what their children are putting on Facebook, and to blame me if the children complain." The school keeps in close touch with parents throughout the year: a surprise to some, but attendance has improved dramatically, perhaps as a result. The borough of Havering, unusually in London, has falling demand for secondary school places; in spite of this the 2011–12 intake was 124, a 15 per cent increase on the previous year. Harold Hill is a predominantly white working-class area, but increasingly children from the Nigerian community in Havering are applying, their parents attracted by the School's academic aspiration and its ethos of discipline.

Sponsors of academies such as the Drapers' play a significant, strategic role in governance. The Board of the Drapers' Academy consists of four members of the Drapers' Company and three staff from QM, plus representatives of the local community. QM Vice-Principals Professors Morag Shiach and Susan Dilly, and Professor Mike Watkinson, have been instrumental in specifying the school's vision. The College has also had an input to the design of the new building – QM being highly experienced in this field – and runs workshops for the school on community development. The success of Drapers' Academy is seen as essential to any improvement in the lives of local people, present and future. Matthew Slater quotes the opinions of pupils

141. ibid.

142. ibid.

who have lived through the transition to the new
Academy: that they behave better now; that they're
expected to do more, and work harder because
they want to; that they like the lunch-hour and
after-school activities, such as fencing and boxing
(good for self-control). "They say they like
coming in."

Monitoring the impact

All this involves a major investment of time and
expertise from the College, and the effect has to be
monitored. A new student information system
allows the College to track those from partner
schools who apply to QM; in future the College
hopes to track outcomes for all school students it
has worked with. "We take a wide view of
community engagement," says Anne Setright.
"It's not only about our own recruitment. We're
not saying either that everyone should go to
university. We just want school students to make
an informed choice about the path that's right
for them."[143]

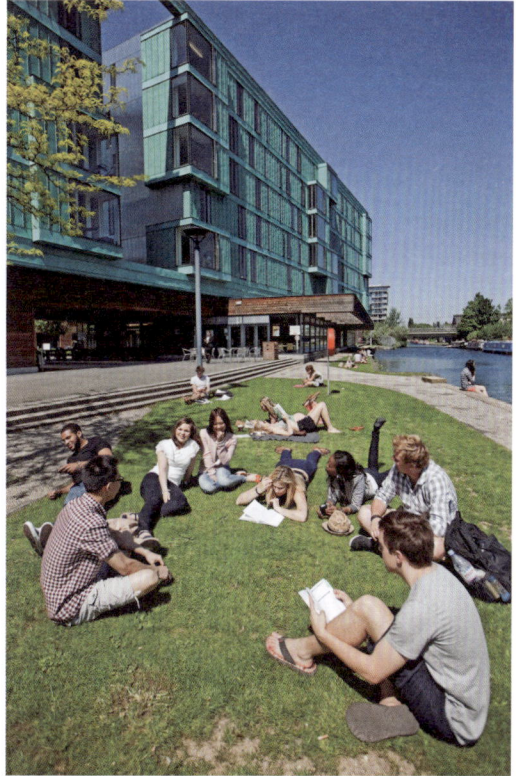

QM students on the Mile End campus, 2012.

143. Setright, A, op cit.

The College, the East End and the Olympics

The Sunday flower market at Columbia Road.

High Street 2012 is a project celebrating the route from Aldgate, at the eastern edge of the City of London, to the Olympic Park at Stratford. The route includes Whitechapel High Street and Mile End Road, sites of the medical school at the Royal London Hospital and the main QM campus respectively. The College is running two High Street 2012 projects. Walk With Me explores experiences of cinema in the East End, mixing interviews with local people with archive footage of the area. Contributors include users of the Stepney Jewish Day Centre, representatives of the old Jewish East End, along with children from the Osmani Primary School in Banglatown (around Brick Lane). The films made for Walk With Me by Mile End Films, the College's in-house video production unit, will be shown online and in public spaces along the High Street 2012 route.

Walk With Me brings together the past and present of the East End, the historic area of London where QM is based. As its oldest and youngest participants show, the East End has always been a place of arrival and settlement for people from across the globe: Flemish weavers and silk-merchants, impoverished Germans, working in the harsh conditions of the sugar refineries, Jews from Russia, Poland and the Ukraine, who staffed the numerous garment factories, Somali seamen and later their refugee grandchildren, Bangladeshis after Partition and civil war. At the same time, an indigenous East End population worked in the docks while these were still functioning, and serviced much of the city's infrastructure of markets, shops and transport. Proximity to the docks brought widespread bomb damage during the Second World War, and rebuilding and resettlement after it.

The signs of this historic diversity are still visible: the silk-merchants' elegant houses in Spitalfields and the disused synagogues next to them, the beautiful Hawksmoor churches, the Trinity Green almshouses on Mile End Road (built to house "twenty-eight decay'd Masters and Commanders of Ships, or ye Widows of such," as the plaque says), the flourishing 'Indian' (in fact Bangladeshi) restaurants of Brick Lane, the minarets and dome of the East London Mosque. Meanwhile, the once-isolated Isle of Dogs has been transformed into Docklands, with high-rise office buildings and warehouses converted to upmarket housing. The demographics keep changing: City workers commute on the Docklands Light Railway, visual artists turn Hoxton and London Fields into cultural centres. The latest signs of this evolving local culture are the buildings of the Olympic site, close to the College on Hackney Marshes, and the associated sporting and cultural activities of London 2012.

As Walk With Me indicates, QM has always had a productive, reciprocal relationship with the East End. Established to provide both entertainment and education for the people of east London (see chapter 1), it is now closely involved both with the diverse population, its opinions, needs and aspirations, and with the dynamic events of the Olympics and Paralympics. Chapter 19 looks specifically at the College's wide-ranging involvement with local schools. The present chapter considers the ways in which the College works with the East End: by studying it, by offering support, and by using the occasion of the Olympics for engagement, entertainment, research and education.

Whitechapel market outside The London Hospital.

Canary Wharf, east London.

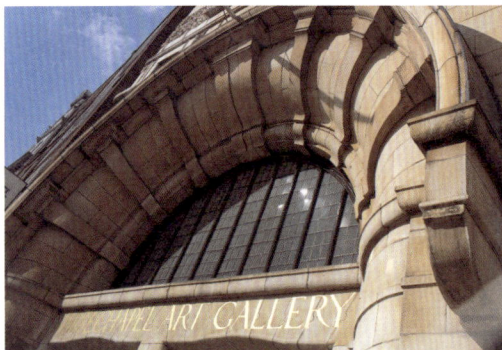

The Whitechapel Gallery, east London.

Studying the East End

The College's location has been a fertile research ground for a number of departments at QM. We have seen in chapter 14 how local cultural diversity provides material and recruitment incentives for the Linguistics Department. In the 1980s and 1990s, Politics established the Centre for the Study of Migration, and Geography, a Centre for East London Studies, whose work included a commission from the London Docklands Development Corporation on the projected travel-to-work area and skills profile of future employees at Canary Wharf, the financial and administrative hub of the Docklands.

In 2006, the School of Geography established the City Centre, another interdisciplinary and collaborative effort to focus research on urban lives and connections across the globe. The East End is very much part of this. Research at the Centre addresses a range of themes, from economic, political, health and environmental issues through to urban cultures and art practice. The recent Global Cities at Work project, for example, focused on the role and significance of foreign-born workers in low-paid jobs in London. Funded by the Economic and Social Research Council (ESRC) between 2005 and 2007, it demonstrated that London has a clear "migrant division of labour" that allows the city to function. While the city's professional jobs are filled by an international elite, so too the lowest paid jobs are filled by a workforce that comes from all corners of the globe.

The School of Geography sees its work as a collaboration with the communities and individuals involved, rather than a distanced study of them. It has hosted the London Women and Planning Forum since 2003, and has been a member of the broad-based community alliance London Citizens since 2005. As part of their studies, undergraduates take part in research for London Citizens, and are invited to attend leadership training and apply for internships with the organisation. In 2010 the School also launched a postgraduate programme to study community organising – the first of its kind in the UK – taught in partnership with Citizens UK.

A Living Wage

Professor Jane Wills and her colleagues have both supported and researched the London Citizens' Living Wage campaign, mapping the gap between the minimum amount needed to get by in London and the actual statutory minimum, and charting the adoption of the living wage across the city. The campaign, a broad coalition including community organisations, faith groups, trade unions and academics, has used direct action, demonstrations, lobbying, conferences, public meetings and the media, to publicise its demands. Over 8,000 low-paid contract workers in cleaning companies have benefited from the campaign; high-profile firms such as HSBC, Barclays Bank and Hilton Hotels have been forced to concede better conditions; the London Organising Committee of the Olympic Games (LOCOG) agreed to pay the London Living Wage to workers in construction and on the Games themselves, and the results have been monitored. In November 2002, a march in support of the living wage progressed along the Mile End Road and culminated in a large public meeting at QM, appropriately in the People's Palace. In April 2006, QM was declared to be the first living wage campus in the country; two years later most of the previously contracted-out cleaning service was brought in-house, with significant improvements to pay and conditions for cleaning staff. The School followed this success with research into the impact of the move for both cleaners and the College.[144] At the time of writing, the charity Trust for London has funded additional work on the costs and benefits of the living wage across the city at large.

Queen Mary was the first 'Living Wage campus' in the UK, bring domestic cleaning services in-house and offering employees a decent salary and better working conditions.

144. Wills, J, with Kakpo, N & Begum, R. (2009) *The business case for the living wage: the story of the cleaning service at Queen Mary, University of London*. (London: Queen Mary, University of London.)

Collaborative Doctoral Awards

In 2012, seven new Collaborative Doctoral Award studentships were announced (*detailed in the table below*). These are funded by the Arts and Humanities Research Council and offer students an experience of working outside an academic environment, with supervision by both the College and the partner organisation. QM has a strong record of winning CDAs. In 2012, existing partner organisations include the Barbican, The Museum of Childhood (also in the East End, in Bethnal Green), the British Museum and the Globe Theatre.

Title	QM School	Partner organisation
Domestic servants and domestic space in London, c.1650–1820	History	Geffrye Museum of the Home
Domestic labour, metropolitan households and the wider world, 1850–1914	Geography	
Home, work & migration in the East End of London since 1945	Migration Studies & Geography	
Men juggling work, home and family in contemporary London	Geography	
Health, environment & the institutional care of children in Late Victorian London	Geography	Ragged School Museum
Putting nature in a box: Sloan's vegetable substances	Geography	Natural History Museum
Maritime masculinities and material culture in the Royal Navy, 1758–1815	Geography	National Maritime Museum

Supporting the East End

The College's long-term involvement in the London Living Wage campaign is one instance where research and support for the local community have coincided. There are numerous others. The people hurrying down New Road and into the Institute of Dentistry's clinic are helping students practise their discipline, as well as getting relief from toothache (see chapter 7). The patients of local GP surgeries who take part in clinical trials are assisting cardiovascular research at the same time as hoping for an improvement in their condition. The people with housing or employment problems who come to the free Legal Advice Centre have a similar, mutually beneficial relationship with the College's Law students.

Volunteering

QM students undertake a number of voluntary roles in the East End. Provide Volunteering, based in the Students' Union, was started in 2002 with funding from the Higher Education Funding Council for England (HEFCE). In 2011 around 2,000 students were registered with Provide, and about 350 are currently active. They offer one-day volunteering, student-led projects and volunteer placements with local not-for-profit groups. Some students help on environmental clean-up days, clearing litter and graffiti from Regent's Canal, which runs behind the Student Village. Others turn up early in the morning at the Whitechapel Mission to cook breakfast for the many homeless people for whom this will be the one hot meal of the day. Some mentor young people, helping with both homework and after-school activities. Sarah Gifford at Provide talks about the benefit to volunteers as well as to the people they work with:

> They get involved in the local community, feeling a real part of it. They meet new people and make friends. They get to see other parts of London – for instance, we always have people stewarding for the London Marathon, so they're out in places they might not visit otherwise. And of

course it's good for their CV and their employability later on.[145]

Provide is also hosting a volunteering programme, Aspire, linked to the Olympics and particularly the Paralympics. Devised by students, Aspire involves students working with local young people to raise awareness of Parasport. Volunteers give lessons, as well as offering school children the chance to try out sports such as goalball (played by blind athletes) and sitting volleyball for themselves. Ruth Faulkner, the Aspire project leader, hopes that both QM students and the young people they work with will get the "Paralympic buzz."

The NGO Clinic
Newham Monitoring Project is a long-established anti-racist organisation, based in QM's neighbouring borough. The project was set up in 1980, following the racist murder of a young local man. It provides casework, a 24-hour emergency helpline and outreach and educational projects, as well as campaigning, and monitoring the response of statutory organisations on issues affecting the black community. In the 1980s, Newham Monitoring Project became a model for a number of NGOs (Non-governmental organisations) in raising awareness of institutional racism racially motivated crime.

The project is one of a number of local organisations supported by the School of Business and Management's NGO (Non-Governmental Organisation) clinic. The School has evolved from a much smaller department and has developed a unique approach among the many business schools in London, focusing on corporate social responsibility and a critical approach to mainstream management theory. Professor Stefano Harney and Dr Emma Dowling set up the NGO clinic. Stefano Harney explains:

I wanted to do something concrete in the business school to indicate that our knowledge of organisations can also be constructive in society. It was fine to see business schools making noises about adding more modules on ethics, but I thought it was time for them to put their money where their mouth is by donating

the free labour of their academics to civil society organisations.[146]

What this means in practice is that Stefano Harney and his colleagues make use of their understanding of organisations and their related research to help small and emerging not-for-profit organisations. At Newham Monitoring Project they work with staff and trustees on organisational change and development. The Clinic works with local groups, but equally with overseas NGOs: in Istanbul, for example, it supports a coalition of community development organisations.

Olympic QM
On 23 February 2010, the second in a series of lectures with an Olympic theme took place at QM. Entitled 'The Politics of the London Olympic Games', it considered the three occasions – 1908, 1948 and 2012 – and the impact of each of Olympic Games held in Britain on the politics of its time. The speaker was Dr David Runciman from the University of Cambridge. Other lectures in the series have considered the 1972 Munich Olympics, community participation in the planning of the current Games, and the original Olympics compared to London 2012 and Rio 2016. The lecture series, devised by Professor Miri Rubin of the School of History at QM, brings together specialists in cultural history, classics and political science, from QM and beyond.

This was an early response to the Games, dreamed up while the event's spectacular new facilities were still half-built. An even earlier response was purely practical: in 2005, the College signed up to provide accommodation for Olympic and Paralympic officials. The Games take place during the summer vacation; 1,000 student rooms have been made available for the Olympians, and 900 for the Paralympians.

145. Gifford, S. Interview for this history. 2011.

146. Harney, S. 'Universities Lead the Way to the "Big Society"' *The Guardian*. 9 November 2010.

Women and the Olympics

The London Women and Planning Forum held a seminar at QM a year before the Olympics, on 6 July 2011. Entitled 'London Olympics: What's In It for the Women?', the conference examined whether the needs and preferences of women had been taken into account in the design of facilities, and whether the profile of women's sport would be raised, as the Games organisers intended. Other topics were the provision of women-friendly venues in the Olympic boroughs, and policies designed to widen the participation of women in sport.

Pop Up

Phakama is a worldwide experimental arts organisation. During their residency at QM, in collaboration with the Drama Department, Phakama held a pop-up festival, Velela!, for local young people. 50 young people who were not in employment, education or training were trained in the skills needed by the UK's creative industries, including performance, production and front- and back-of-house skills. The two-week festival in June 2012 was followed by a year of weekly sessions, work experience and apprenticeships, which would culminate in a second festival a year later, staged by the participants themselves.

ORiEL: the Olympic Legacy

London's Olympic bid promised the Olympic Committee and Londoners a major and lasting impact on east London: employment, housing, improved transport and urban regeneration at all levels. The likely effect has been much debated by the organisers, sceptics and local communities themselves. ORiEL – the Olympic Regeneration in East London Study – has been designed to assess the legacy of the Games.

Steven Cummins, Professor of Urban Health in QM's School of Geography, is leading the five-year longitudinal study and a team comprising three postdoctoral researchers and ten investigators from QM, the London School of Hygiene and Tropical Medicine, and the University of East London. The Olympics are, he says, the largest infrastructure project of their kind in Europe, and "a dream come true for someone interested in urban regeneration. It offers a rare chance to assess

impacts using a "before and after" approach in a very controlled way."[147]

Around 1,800 school children and their parents in the east London boroughs of Tower Hamlets, Newham and Barking and Dagenham will be given questionnaires at the start of the Games to assess their health and wellbeing. The numbers of pupils coming to live in and leaving the area will also be tracked, along with socio-economic data, to measure changes in the local population. In addition, researchers will work closely with 20 families over the course of the study, to gain insight into their experience before, during and after the Olympics. "We want to know how involved they feel, as well as … the changes they see and how it affects their daily lives. We'll be looking at the whole picture: from income and employment, to health and housing quality."[148]

Government ambitions for the Olympics include inspiring people to "try new activities, learn new skills and extend their links to reach new people, not just in the UK but worldwide."[149] ORiEL offers an unrivalled opportunity for QM's researchers and their colleagues to contribute insight to future regeneration projects. They will be able to draw on their experience of one of the greatest events London has witnessed.

---

147. http://www.qmul.ac.uk/research/olympics/index.html (Accessed 2012)
148. ibid.
149. 'Before, During and After: Making the Most of the London 2012 Games'. (London: Department for Culture, Media and Sport, 2008.

The Geffrye Museum, London.
© Heather Cowper

153

Our international outlook

QM students, 2012.

In a 2010 paper, the Principal of QM, Professor Simon Gaskell, identifies four ways in which the College and others like it transcend national boundaries. They are:

- Knowledge creation through international collaboration
- Internationalisation of the academy (one in three academic staff and more than half of QM's research associates are from outside the UK)
- Internationalisation of the student body, and
- UK contributions to university education overseas[150]

All four make a crucial contribution to the fundamental aim of higher education: to advance and disseminate knowledge, wherever it comes from.

International students

QM has an inbuilt advantage in spreading its reach beyond the UK: many of its home students already have links across the world. Young people recruited from schools in the East End and the other multicultural areas of Britain may have family in Somalia, Bangladesh, Nigeria, the Caribbean and beyond; they may have been born in one of those countries, or visit regularly, or simply be aware of their parents' complex heritage. An existing cosmopolitan environment is a good starting point for a culture of international exchange.

Home students abroad

The Erasmus scheme is a programme of the European Union. Launched in 1987, it has now

150. Gaskell, S. 'The Modern UK University as an International Institution'. (London: Queen Mary, University of London, 2010.

provided over two million students with the chance to study in another European country. For many, it represents their first experience of living abroad. QM has over a hundred partnership agreements with universities in 16 European countries, within the Erasmus scheme. Some examples can be found in the table below:

School	Country	University
Engineering & Materials Science	Bulgaria	Technical University of Sofia
Politics & International Relations	France	Institut d'Etudes Politiques, Rennes
Biological & Chemical Sciences	Germany	Johann Wolfgang Goethe Universitaet, Frankfurt am Main
Economics & Finance	Italy	Universita Commerciale Luigi Bocconi, Milan
Law	Denmark	University of Copenhagen
Film Studies	Spain	Universitat Jaume 1, Castello de la Plana
Dentistry	Czech Republic	Brno University of Technology
Geography	Slovakia	Comenius University, Bratislava

Another option for UK-based students is the international exchange programme, which moves further afield. Undergraduates can spend either the first semester or the entire second year of a three-year programme at one of five universities in the United States, the University of Melbourne, or Nanyang Technical University, Singapore. Sara Hammond, reading for a BA in English and

French, spent her second year in San Diego, at the University of California:

> UCSD was a fantastic experience for so many reasons. There [was] a huge variety of courses with a lot of different approaches to my subject and a lot of excellent teachers. I also learnt a lot outside the classroom. San Diego is a fun city to be in and I had the chance to learn to scuba dive, go surfing, run a marathon, visit Mexico, ride on the equestrian team, swim with a club… I met a lot of really great people that I will be keeping in touch with.[151]

Pat Power, Deputy Director, Marketing and International, regrets that not more students take up these opportunities. "It's partly for financial reasons," he says. "Many students have enough problems financing their studies, without having to manage for a year abroad."[152] Even when money is not a problem, however, he feels that students may be cautious, and unaware of the benefits of living and studying in another country.

International students at QM

Much of the work of the International Office involves recruiting students from abroad to study at QM. In 1985, when this history begins, 3.5 per cent of students were from the countries that then constituted the European Union, and 22 per cent from beyond the EU, notably Hong Kong and the USA (see chapter 2). In 2010–11, international students from 122 countries took up 7,000 of the College's 16,900 places: almost 44 per cent of the student body. Demand in some countries is so great that the College has offices in Lagos and Lahore, with locally recruited staff who have studied in London (one at QM). "Prospective students can read about the College on the web," says Pat Power, "but they appreciate being able to talk to someone face to face."[153] The success of these in-country centres has led to plans to open others in India and China.

The International Office in its present form was established in 2000. Some of its functions had been undertaken far earlier (the 1986 deputation to

China, for example). A previous International Officer had visited Latin American countries in the early 1990s, to market the College to potential students. These initiatives, however, became a victim of the financial crisis of that time. In 1999, Nigel Relph was appointed with a brief to revive international activity. He recruited three staff, who between them travelled widely, visiting higher education exhibitions around the world. The British Council at that time still organised the circuit of visits for UK institutions; since then the organisation has withdrawn substantially from this role, and universities have taken the initiative themselves.

In 2012 the International Office had 12 London-based staff, a regional manager for India and Sri Lanka, and three business development managers, covering China; Nigeria, Kenya and Ghana; and Azerbaijan. There are also a number of international research assistants, undergraduate and postgraduate students working in the International Office.

Life as an international student

> Moving to London and the Queen Mary campus has been both an adventure and a challenge to me. I have been to London before and I knew it quite well already, so I was not worried that I was going to a foreign country. I had also seen the campus during the summer prior to my arrival. The sun was high in the sky and all the trees and flowers were blooming. I had confidence I would be just fine and this turned out to be the case! (*Dominika Jankowska, 3rd year, Law*)[154]

QM provides extensive induction and orientation for international students, from its summer and academic-year English language courses to guidance on using public transport. There are group outings within Britain and around Europe – this may be the only chance some students have to visit York or Paris – and events organised for both home and international students that are always sold out and could, staff believe, usefully be extended. Young international students have high priority for accommodation on campus, and some

151. Hammond, S. www.qmul.ac.uk/undergraduate/exchange/universities/index.html (Accessed 2012)
152. Power, P. Interview for this history. 2011.
153. ibid.
154. Jankowska, D, op cit.

International students enjoy QM's Welcome Week – a week of acclimatisation and social activities especially for international students.

residences organise international or country-specific days. With all the support available, anyone living and studying abroad still has to adjust to a change of culture, both social and academic. Some students are surprised at being expected to speak in class; others are more vocal than their UK counterparts. Some come from a culture of copying verbatim from given texts, and find the practice frowned upon here. Teaching staff have the delicate task of matching their own practice to a range of learning styles.

> The style of teaching was quite different to what I was used to. Back home we have marked tests and essays almost every week, while in Law here there are four, not obligatory, essays per semester and no tests, so I had to get used to the fact that studying is my own responsibility now, and my success will be marked at the end of the year. I have to admit it is quite a shock, and at the beginning it feels like there is so much free time; it takes a while to appreciate that this time is needed for reading and trying to understand the concepts. (*Dominika Jankowska*)[155]

The greatest adjustment for many, according to Andrew George, who has worked in the International Office since 1999, is to multiculturalism. For anyone, from any part of the world (including the UK), who has grown up in an environment with a single culture and an unchallenged set of beliefs, London's sheer diversity can be bewildering. It is also, of course,

one of the great strengths of the College and one of the gifts it offers its students: being prepared for diversity enables you to work anywhere in the world.

> I'll never forget the first time I came to London. I was immediately enchanted by its mixture of historical centres and modern architecture, its multicultural hub, its fast-paced tempo, and its seemingly endless alleyways. Walking the urban landscape is one of my favourite pastimes and is definitely the best way to experience London. As an arts student, London is the perfect place with theatres, art galleries, museums and exhibitions taking up large portions of the city. Every time I go out I discover something new. Although I've only been here for a year and a half, London has quickly become my home. (*Ashley Steed, MA Theatre & Performance, 2011*)[156]

International students and UK policy

At the time of writing, the British government has reduced the number of student visas granted. The College is trusted by the UK Borders Agency (the immigration authority) and QM applicants may suffer less than those to less prestigious institutions. The likely impact, Pat Power believes, is more indirect. As Professor Laurie Cuthbert has found in China, potential students perceive the UK as less welcoming than other countries, as the result of such political statements. Other governments make it easier for people from abroad to enter, study and work; the UK seems to be making it harder. The College sees that the benefits to the UK of hosting the most dynamic and intelligent young people from across the world are not simply short-term – their fees contribute substantially to the economy of universities – but lasting, with highly skilled graduates both staying to contribute to the UK, and creating links for the future. (Many current and past heads of state have studied in Britain). Simon Gaskell believes that the Government was naive in thinking it could make belligerent noises on overseas student numbers, to quell British fears about immigration, without having a much wider, negative impact. The College now has a harder task: countering the impression of general antagonism.

155. ibid.

156. Steed, A. Written contribution to this history. 2012.

International collaboration

Some of the partnerships entered into by academics at QM have already been logged in the chronological chapters of this book: the Cassini-Huygens mission to Saturn, led by NASA and the European Space Agency with the participation of QM's Astronomy Unit; the work on the Large Hadron Collider at CERN (see chapter 22).

The NGO Clinic of the School of Business and Management (described in chapter 20), works not only with local organisations, but in 2012 with NGOs (Non-governmental organisations) in Hong Kong, Palestine, Vietnam, Indonesia and Brazil. The School of Medicine and Dentistry has also been working across borders: in 2006, for example, the Barts Cancer Institute and Zhengzhou University, in Henan Province, China, created the Sino-British Centre for Molecular Oncology (the study of cancer by examining the functions of the cell). The Centre is jointly funded by the National Science Foundation and Henan Province. An exchange programme provides training for Chinese scientists in the latest technological advances in oncology. The Centre is engaged in exciting new work, the development of viruses that will treat cancer. Clinical trials will take place in due course both at the Institute and in China.

The partnership with the Beijing University of Posts and Telecommunications (BUPT), which is discussed in detail in chapter 24, provides one model for QM's international reach. Further collaborations with Chinese universities are planned. Nanchang University has proposed that UK students could help their counterparts improve their English. In the 2011–12 academic year, Mandarin speakers on the staff at QM tutor a small group of British students in the language. The idea is to equip them to go to Nanchang in the 2012 summer vacation, courtesy of the Chinese university, and return the compliment with students there: an extraordinary opportunity to travel, for QM students who might never afford a gap year.

QM and the wider world: Theatre in Brazil

Professor Paul Heritage was already working on HIV/AIDS awareness in the prisons of Brazil, when he was appointed to the Drama Department of QM, and set up People's Palace Projects (PPP) to allow him to continue and expand his work. The title was a conscious link to the cultural as well as educational aims of QM's founders: the mission to bring opportunities to disadvantaged and oppressed people remained, the catchment area had grown.

Staging Human Rights started off in the state of São Paulo. With UK research money and Lottery funds, we worked in 37 prisons, working with [the famous activist and theatre director] Augusto Boal's Centre for the Theatre of the Oppressed to train prison educators to implement their own mini-projects, which we guided and supported. Interactive forums looking at human rights within the prisons led over time to a declaration of human rights, devised by the participants at a final event at the Parliament of Latin America in São Paulo. And then the Brazilian Ministry of Justice asked us to extend the project across other states.[157]

Further work in Brazil focused on young people in trouble with the law, and perhaps inevitably drew Paul Heritage into conflict with civic authorities: 'At times we achieved big changes in juvenile prisons, but if you win these small battles too often, someone is going to plot your downfall.'[158] The project moved from within the juvenile justice system to the favelas – shanty-towns – where young people returned to live. With Grupo Cultural AfroReggae, based in one of the favelas, and a cast of Brazil's TV and cinema stars, PPP staged *Anthony and Cleopatra* and *Measure for Measure* in the favelas' public spaces.

We searched for locations in communities with a lack of public amenities of any kind. We decided to launch the project on one of Rio's most violent frontiers, a no-man's land known as 'the Gaza strip', located between two favelas controlled by rival drug gangs, where gun

157. quoted in Tyndall, K. *The Producers, Alchemists of the Impossible.* (London: Arts Council England & The Jerwood Charitable Foundation, 2007.
158. ibid.

Professor Paul Heritage and members of Afroreggae at the Southbank Centre in July 2010, part of the *Favela to the World* project.

murders are committed daily by the young men from the drug factions. A ceasefire was negotiated to allow the opening performance to take place on the shooting gallery that was the border between two communities, the first ceasefire in the 20 year-long war that has raged between these gangs. We rehearsed in the evenings, and during the night I negotiated with the traffickers. All of us involved agreed that if ten people came to claim this frontier as a place from which to watch Shakespeare, this would be success. We put out 200 chairs. Two thousand people turned up. The site, the audience and the actors were overwhelmed. No-one can say what were the impressions and the impact which will survive, but the ceasefire itself lasted 18 days.[159]

Paul Heritage was knighted by the Brazilian government in 2004, and awarded the Orilaxé Prize for Human Rights in 2006. His work has extended beyond Brazil, to Burkina Faso and back to the UK. *Staging Human Rights*, begun in São Paolo,

later worked with female prisoners in both the UK and Brazil, and culminated in 2002 in a play for BBC Radio 3, *Carandiru*. In addition, *From the Favela to the World*, a partnership involving AfroReggae, the Barbican, the Black Police Association and others, ran from 2006 to 2012, working in east London, Manchester, Newcastle and Liverpool and examined how the arts could help to promote social justice.

159. ibid.

In focus: science and engineering

The Particle Physics Research Group, 1960

ATLAS detector, CERN laboratory, Switzerland.

The structure of matter

Particle physics is a discipline that combines the study of the minute components of everything around us, with vast quasi-philosophical questions. The realisation that the great diversity of the world stems from a handful of elementary particles, acting under the influence of a few fundamental forces, was one of the scientific triumphs of the last century. The field now extends beyond the sub-structure of the atom, and connects with astronomy and cosmology. Since the Large Hadron Collider at CERN was first switched on in September 2008, the subject has increasingly caught the imagination of the public. The 2012 discovery of the Higgs boson made headline news around the world; a discovery in which physicists at QM played an important part.

The Particle Physics Research Group at QM has been engaged in this work over 50 years, at laboratories in the UK, Germany, USA, Canada and Japan as well as at CERN, and its staff have been involved in some of the major international discoveries. The Group is primarily engaged in research, but there is also significant outreach work to schools and the wider public, as well as opportunities for undergraduates to take part in short-term projects, and a three- to four-year PhD programme.

Because particle physics can be confusing as well as enthralling for the non-physicist, this chapter includes brief definitions and explanations.

Some definitions

- *Atoms* consist of a *nucleus*, which has positive electric charge, and *electrons*, which are negative.
- The *nucleus* consists of *protons*, which are positive, and *neutrons*, which have no charge.
- *Protons* and *neutrons* are composed of *quarks*.
- All matter is made up of *quarks* and *leptons*. These are believed to be *fundamental particles*: ie they can't be broken down into further components, as far as we can tell.
- For every kind of *matter* particle, there is a corresponding *antimatter* particle, which has some opposite properties such as electrical charge.
- The *Standard Model* explains the hundreds of particles, and the interactions between them. It says that there are just:
  - six quarks, in pairs, called *up/down*, *charm/strange* and *top/bottom*
  - six leptons: three charged (*electron*, *muon* and *tau*)
  - three uncharged *neutrinos*, which have very little mass, and are hard to find
  - and *force carrier* particles.
- There are four fundamental *interactions* between particles, which between them create the universe. They are:
  - gravity
  - electromagnetic
  - strong
  - weak
- *Force carrier particles* carry these interactions. *Gluons* are the carrier particle of the strong force. *Photons* are the carrier particle of the electromagnetic force.

Early work at QM

Particle physics work at QM was started in 1960 by Alick Ashmore (later Director of the Science Research Council's Daresbury Laboratory and recipient of a CBE in 1978). When Peter Kalmus joined in 1964, about ten academics, postgraduate students and technicians were involved in the work. Early experiments, mostly on hadron physics (the study of strongly interacting particles), were carried out at the Proton Linear Accelerator and the Nimrod synchrotron in the UK, and at the CERN proton synchrotron. (A synchrotron is a type of particle accelerator, where the magnetic field – which turns the particles so that they circulate – and the electric field, which accelerates them, are synchronised with the particle beam). In parallel, David Bugg, John Edgington and Reg Gibson studied lower energy interactions at the TRIUMF facility in Vancouver.

Experimental particle physics, Professor Kalmus emphasises, is a collaborative activity, not only within one institution but across international borders, and involves postgraduate students, postdoctoral researchers and support staff, as well as academics. The QM experiments, together with many carried out by other groups, contributed to the understanding of the quark structure of matter. The field has changed tremendously: half a century ago quarks were purely theoretical constructs, and there were only three of them; only two leptons were known; and the only verified force carrier was the photon.

W and Z

In the early 1980s, four members of QM – Peter Kalmus, Eric Eisenhandler, Reg Gibson and Graham Thompson – were engaged in a large international collaboration at the CERN proton-antiproton collider, and discovered two particles, which were named W and Z.
The experiment showed that electromagnetism (which generates electricity), and the weak interaction (which allows the sun to shine) are aspects of the same force. Carlo Rubbia and Simon van der Meer from CERN received the 1984 Nobel prize for the discovery, and Peter Kalmus received the prestigious Rutherford Medal (for distinguished research in particle physics) for his contribution, and later also an OBE.

This discovery caused a great deal of excitement. A camera crew from the BBC had been following the experiment for three years. In January 1983, within a week, the discovery was announced at CERN, a *Horizon* TV programme about the work was broadcast, and Peter Kalmus gave a seminar to a packed audience at QM. The then Prime Minister, Margaret Thatcher, who had previously visited the experiment at CERN, sent a letter of congratulations. Since then, pictures of the apparatus, and of proton-antiproton collisions, have appeared in many physics textbooks and popular science books.

Probing the proton

Starting in the late 1980s, a group from QM joined a collaboration using the world's only proton-electron (and proton-positron) collider HERA, in the DESY Laboratory in Hamburg. High energy electrons, which appear as point-like particles, are ideal for investigating the structure of complex objects. Before HERA closed in 2007, significant results included detailed measurements of the structure of the proton.

In his early career, as a PhD and postdoctoral student at University College London, Peter Kalmus helped to build a small electron accelerator to measure the sizes of nuclei. He was ending his research career with electron scattering again, but now at 10,000 times the energy. After Peter Kalmus became Head of Department at QM, this work was led by Graham Thompson and Eric Eisenhandler. Many experiments were carried out. One result showed that whereas the "static" proton consists of three quarks held together by gluons, when probed at high energies, the proton can be seen to consist of a swarm of quarks, antiquarks and gluons.

Some acronyms:
- ATLAS: A Toroidal LHC Apparatus; particle detector experiment at CERN
- CERN: Conseil Européen pour la Recherche Nucléaire, or European Council for Nuclear Research; now called European *Organisation* for Nuclear Research, but the original acronym has stayed.
- DESY: Deutsches Elektronen-Synchrotron
- HERA: Hadron Electron Ring Accelerator (at DESY)
- LHC: Large Hadron Collider
- LEP: Large Electron-Positron Collider
- LEAR: Low Energy Anti-Proton Ring
- PPRG: the Particle Physics Research Group at QM

The present-day equipment required is vast in scale – the Large Hadron Collider at CERN, for example, is a hundred metres underground, and uses a tunnel 27 km in circumference. Both theory and practice also require extraordinarily sophisticated technology. The Group at QM has contributed to both developing such equipment and analysing its findings.

CERN in the 80s and 90s
From 1989 to 2000 OPAL, another experiment at CERN, absorbed the attention of two further QM staff, Professors Steve Lloyd and Tony Carter, who built and then used LEP, then the largest particle accelerator in the world. They were able to study in great detail the W and Z particles that the previous team had identified. LEP produced millions of Z particles, and 12,000 pairs of W particles. One early result of the OPAL experiment was the discovery that there are only three families of quarks and leptons.

A further Rutherford Medal was given in 1996 to David Bugg, who worked on low energy antiproton-proton physics at another CERN facility, LEAR, and on hadron spectroscopy, the study of the mass and decay of hadrons.

Accelerators, colliders and detectors
The key to studying the subatomic world is to use accelerators to boost the energy of particles before a collision, then use detectors to find out what is produced, and hence deduce what has happened. The more energy you put into the particles, the more 'stuff' (matter) can be created in a collision. Particle physicists are interested in studying the particles created in high-energy collisions, because some rare and unusual ones may appear for a fleeting moment.[160]

The Particle Physics Research Centre (PPRC) in 2012
The PPRC currently comprises about 30 staff and 13 PhD students. Their work is focused either on the discovery and identification of new particles, or on testing features of globally unifying theories.

The Particle Physics Research Group (PPRG) is involved in six major experiments. Two – ATLAS and T2K – are just starting; H1 and BaBar have completed their data-taking and are in the analysis phase; and SNO+ and SuperB are at planning stage.

ATLAS is a general-purpose detector, the largest and most complex yet constructed, for the Large Hadron Collider at CERN. Its development and use form one of six current LHC experiments. It involves 2,900 scientists from 37 countries, and is at the forefront of world particle physics. A number of physicists from QM have been involved since ATLAS was first proposed in 1994, contributing to its design and construction; they now also lead the dedicated Software Infrastructure Team. The 'Grid,' which links computers seamlessly, so that users can make use of all available computer resources worldwide, has had significant input from the PPRG since 2001, and the College also hosts one of the largest computer clusters. The ATLAS Group at QM is studying the properties of the heaviest known quark, the top quark, as well as investigating how knowledge gained from the electron-proton H1 Experiment at DESY can be applied to the proton-proton experiment at ATLAS.

160. adapted from *CERN: The miniscule challenge*. http://public.web.cern.ch/public/en/research/MinChallen.html accessed June 2011

On 4 July 2012, the QM Communications team issued the following press release:

> Scientists at Queen Mary, University of London taking part in the ATLAS particle physics experiment at the Large Hadron Collider (LHC) in Geneva are ecstatic about new results released today which confirmed the discovery of a new particle consistent with the Higgs boson.
>
> The Higgs boson is the elementary particle needed to explain why and how particles have mass. Until today, the 'Standard Model' of particle physics was unable to fully explain why the most fundamental particles of the universe had mass and why they were different. The discovery of the Higgs boson is the first step towards filling this gap.
>
> The particle physics group at Queen Mary has been involved in the design and construction of essential components of the ATLAS apparatus, as well as analysis of the data.
>
> "The group at Queen Mary have worked very hard for many years now and we are one of the leading UK hardware groups in this area," said Steve Lloyd, Professor of Experimental Particle Physics at Queen Mary.
>
> "It is great to see even this hint of a discovery from work done here at Queen Mary. We can't say it's definitely the Higgs but it sure looks like one."[161]

T2K is an experiment in neutrino oscillation. Neutrinos were once considered to be massless, but in certain circumstances they show changes that demonstrate that they must have some small amount of mass. T2K began at the end of 2009 and will run for around five years. It uses technology 20 times more sensitively than any previously available to search for neutrino interactions.

Other experiments have considered how quarks and gluons form hadrons (H1); and the asymmetry between matter and antimatter (BaBar).

Students and PPRG

Physics undergraduates at QM have the opportunity to take part in PPRG projects, either on summer internships, or on modules in their third year. Recent topics available for undergraduate work include:
- global warming and cosmic rays
- micro black hole production at the LHC
- review of production, decays and properties of the top quark.

The PhD programme runs over three to four years. Students attend lecture courses in the first semester, and undertake a first-year project, before embarking on their specialist field. Suggested research topics include top quark mass and the study of sterile neutrinos. PhD students attend national and international workshops, conferences and summer schools, and take part in outreach work.

Taking particle physics out into the world

Peter Kalmus, officially retired since 1998, is still heavily involved in engaging young people and others in the fascination of particle physics. He has received the Kelvin Medal and the European Physical Society Outreach Prize for this work, (as well as the 2010 Institute of Physics Branches Prize and an honorary Fellowship of the Institute).

A major outreach project, currently organised by Dr Lucio Cerrito, a member of the ATLAS team, is the annual High Energy Physics Masterclass, which introduces A-level students to the subject. Participants have the chance to perform crucial measurements on real data, and experience on a small scale what it is like to be involved in cutting-edge experiments; as well as getting a glimpse of university life in general.

161. http://www.qmul.ac.uk/media/news/items/se/78681 .html Accessed July 2012.

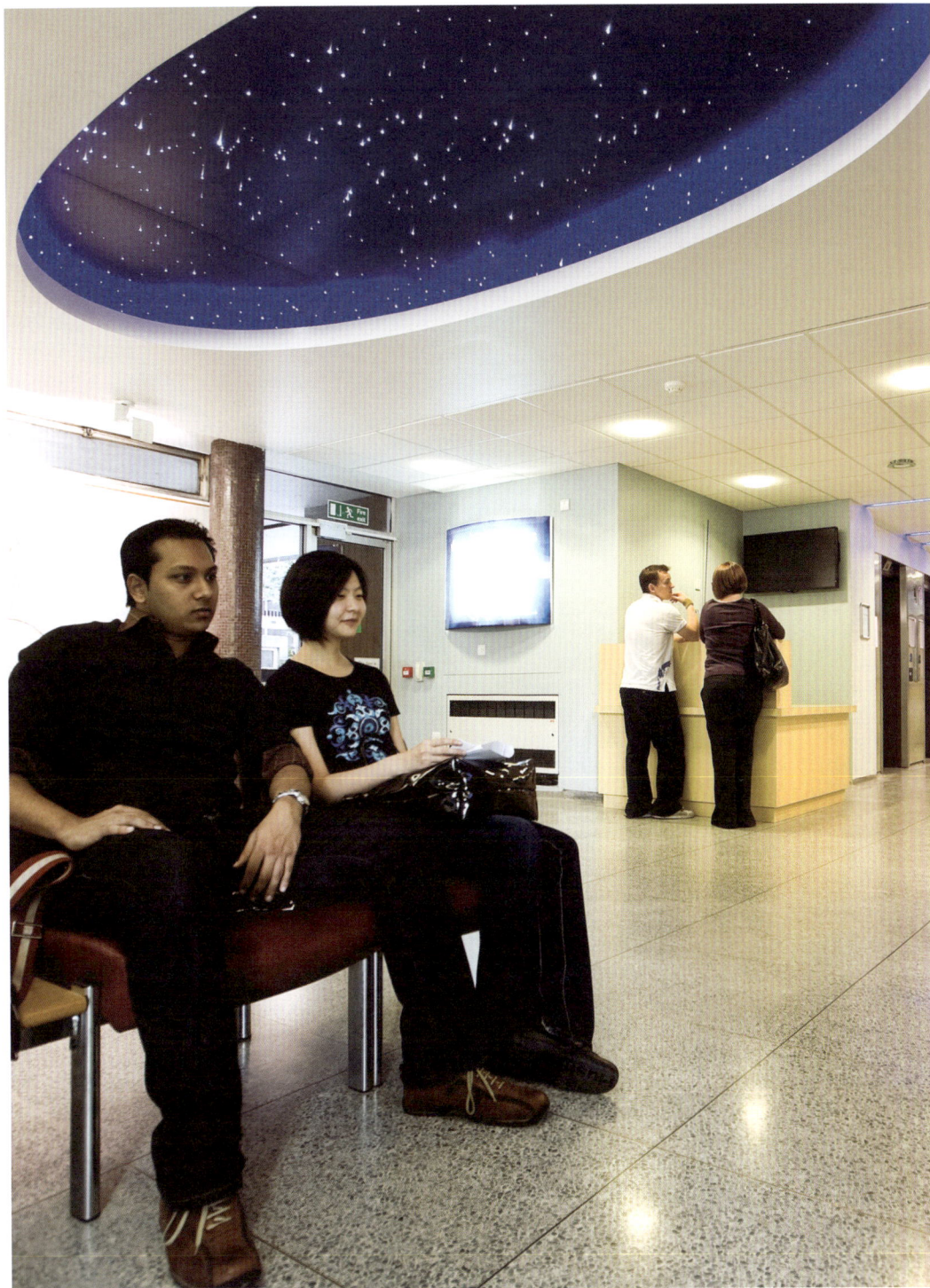

Students sitting in the foyer of the GO Jones Building, 2012.

Apa Tech

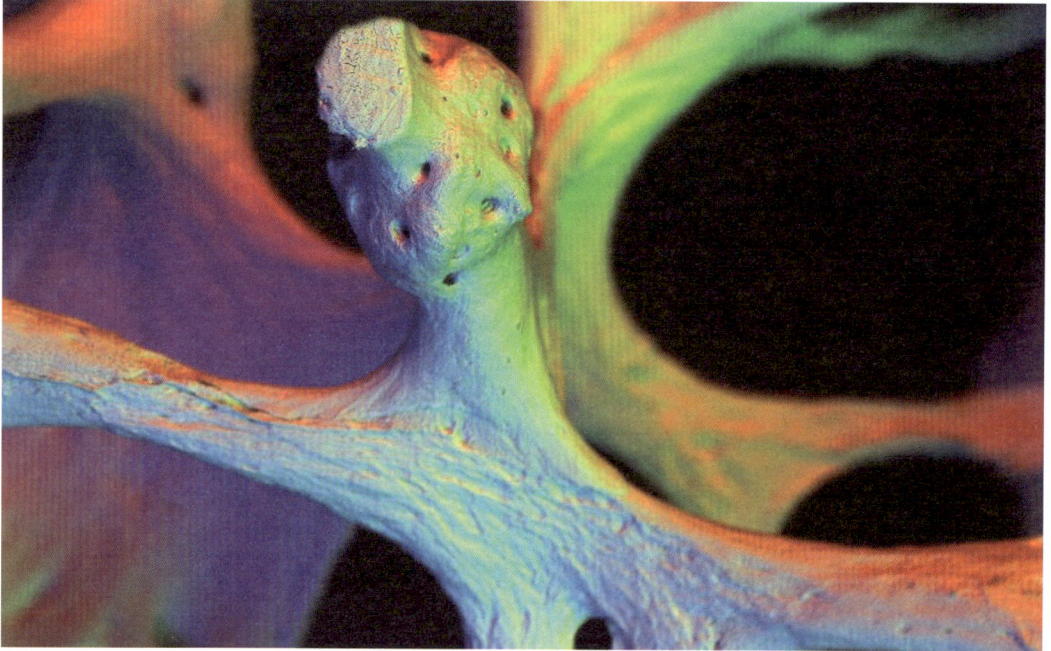

'Porotic bone' scanning electron micrograph captured by Alan Boyde.

There has been a road accident. The patient, Alan, was knocked off his bicycle. His left leg is badly broken: a complex fracture of the tibia. Too complex for the doctors to expect it to heal on its own.

Amina, aged 13, has cerebral palsy, and a severe curvature of the spine, which could get worse. Amina is due to have an operation: spinal fusion, which will weld the vertebrae together and straighten the curve.

Adele had her first hip replacement 15 years ago; the replaced joint has worn out. The second operation – the 'revision hip replacement' – will be more complicated.

These patients are fictional, but by now we are all used to stories like these: surgical work that would once have seemed impossible, but is now carried out routinely in hospitals across the world. We are so used to them in fact, that we may not consider what they involve.

Bone is an amazing material. We tend to think of it as growing until we reach adulthood, then simply stopping, or, worse, decaying. In fact bone can and does grow. It can heal itself; if Alan's accident had been less serious, he would have expected after a time in plaster to have a healed, functioning tibia. As his case suggests, though, for this regeneration to take place, the bone needs either to heal over a very small space, or to have something else – a 'scaffold' – to bridge over. Hence bone grafts. The missing pieces of bone are replaced, so that new bone can grow over the gap and complete the healing process.

Interdisciplinary Research Centre (IRC)

In the late 1980s, the Science and Engineering Research Council decided to fund a series of Interdisciplinary Research Centres (IRCs) in topics of strategic importance for the UK, including biomedical materials. Professor William Bonfield, Head of the Department of Materials at QM, and distinguished for his research on bone, put together a consortium consisting of colleagues from The London Medical College (pre-merger), the Royal Free and Royal National Orthopaedic Hospitals, and applied to become an IRC. Against tough competition from all the leading UK universities, the College's application won the IRC programme grant: a major achievement for QM. William Bonfield became the first Director of the IRC, in 1991.

One of the IRC's strategic aims was to develop a synthetic material for bone grafting. At the time, surgeons had two main options available. They could use bone from hospital bone banks, that is, donated after death. Dead bone, however, doesn't promote bone growth, and is inevitably of variable quality. Or they could transplant bone from another part of the patient's body; but this causes additional pain, and can sometimes result in infection. A synthetic material might avoid all of these problems. A team at the IRC, led by William Bonfield, began exploring.

HA

A compound called hydroxyapatite (HA) was already being produced commercially. HA is similar to bone mineral, and can stimulate bone growth: but the version available at the time was little used for bone grafts, because the growth was so slow. The IRC team set about analysing the commercially available HA.

Stoichiometric ratios

Compounds like HA are created by a chemical reaction. The precise ratio of one component to another needed to create the compound is known: for HA, for instance, it is thought to be ten parts calcium to six parts phosphorus. This is the 'stoichiometric ratio': there is no shortfall, and no residue left over.

William Bonfield and his colleagues discovered two things about the available HA. First, it was not stoichiometric: the ratio of calcium to phosphorus was not exactly 10:6. And secondly, unless it was made using distilled water, there were unwanted traces of heavy metals. Both these factors, they found, got in the way of bone growth.

The next step was to make stoichiometric HA in the laboratory, and test it out. The result could hardly have been more satisfying. New bone growth took place not within 40 days, as with existing HA, but in 28: four weeks instead of almost six. This cleaned-up HA would later become the team's first commercial product, ApaPore.

Silicon

Twenty-eight days was good, but it could be better. For the next three years, the team went through the elements and ions that are found in bone mineral, adding a trace of each at a time to the stoichiometric HA and observing how long it took for new bone to grow. Sodium, magnesium, carbonate – then finally the discovery: silicon. If added in the right proportion, silicon permitted bone growth in just seven days. Further, more sophisticated screening tests confirmed this. The new, *silicate-substituted* HA provided the best possible chemical basis for the growth of new bone.

One additional, crucial step was the development of a new process for making HA granules composed of interconnecting pores, to create the best possible scaffold for bone growth. For William Bonfield, these two achievements transformed the task: "With scientific control of

both chemistry and structure, we now had the basis for a world-leading synthetic bone graft."[162]

Going commercial

What we did next was quite unusual in academe at that time. Instead of publishing our results immediately, we patented the key findings and became canny about 'know how.' Every development or discovery, from how we manufactured silicate-substituted hydroxyapatite to processing its porous structure, was assessed for its patentability. Very soon, a raft of applications had built up so in 1996, we launched a virtual company – Abonetics – to act as a locker for these and later patents.[163]

By 2000, interest in synthetic materials for bone grafting had increased, and the IRC team decided it was time to turn Abonetics into a commercial venture. This, inevitably, meant finance; which meant venture capital, start-up funding from commercial sources. The venture capital company 3i plc, the UK's largest at the time, rightly saw orthopaedic surgery as a growing market, and offered £3 million; £1.2 million more than the team had asked for.

The new company, ApaTech, was established in June 2001, and based at QM, with Dr Peter Lawes as its first Chief Executive, and William Bonfield a non-executive Director. Its first commercial product was ApaPore, the stoichiometric HA the team had first made several years earlier. Clinical trials had already started: in Aberdeen, with 30 people undergoing spinal fusion, and in Exeter, for people needing a second hip replacement operation.

Production

By 2004, William Bonfield recalls, ApaTech had 'progressed from making our product in small beakers to big beakers,'[164] and was keen to move on to large-scale production and marketing. With a second round of venture capital (£6 million from

162. Bonfield, W. *Engineering Business Success.* (London: Royal Academy of Engineering, 2011.
163. ibid.
164. ibid.

MTI and 3i), a production plant was established in Elstree, just outside London, and expanded to create a bespoke processing plant. A new Chief Executive, Simon Cartmell, contracted out distribution in the UK and Europe, and set up a subsidiary in the United States. The second product was the silicate-substituted HA, marketed as ActiFuse, and this got an enthusiastic response from surgeons, especially in the US. In 2005, sales of both products were at £270,000; two years later, with the addition of a subsidiary in Germany, the figure was £3.1 million: over a thousand packs of ApaPore or ActiFuse per month.

Even this, it seemed, could be bettered. In 2008, with $45 million in funding from 3i plc and HealthCare, a US-based company, ApaTech recruited a hundred more staff (six years earlier there were just ten), and built a second facility at Elstree, to quadruple manufacturing capacity. Already, before the formal opening of the new facility, ApaTech had been rated by the *Sunday Times* every year from 2007 to 2009 as the UK's fastest growing medical technology company. In June 2010 it won a PraxisUnico Impact Award for 'outstanding business impact through successful knowledge transfer.'

How to use ActiFuse
In putty form:
• mould it into shape and use it to fill a hole (eg after a small bone tumour is removed)
• place directly on broken bone to mend a fracture
In granule form:
• mix with blood or bone marrow and apply to bone graft
• inject a slurry of granules into a gap

The sale
By summer 2010, however, ApaTech had been sold. There had been previous buy-out offers, turned down because the Directors felt there was still work to do; this time one was accepted, because of the potential for greater outreach for the technology. Baxter International, a global healthcare company based in the United States, acquired the company for $330 million: around £220 million.

Graeme Brown is Director of Queen Mary Innovation which supports the development of spin-out companies. ApaTech, he says, having moved up to Elstree, maintained excellent communications with the College, but had become less visible: "So the sale was a big surprise to 99 per cent of the College."[165] A pleasant surprise: QM held around eight per cent of shares at the time of the sale, and received a substantial addition to College funds.

How it all happened
William Bonfield reflects on the reasons for the project's success.

> First and foremost, we produced world-leading science. From the outset, our research was distinctive and the clinical results have been outstanding. Second, we were developing materials for a growing market … Third, patenting proved crucial. From day one, our researchers not only took a strategy of patenting first and then publishing, but also ensured that the applications stood up against the competition. Fourth, the ability to raise money was vital – no money, no company … People were the overall factor contributing to our success. While ApaTech required exceptional researchers to produce innovative science, we also needed talented individuals with commercial experience to market our products.[166]

These days, Graeme Brown adds, although there are successful spin-out companies, it would be hard to replicate ApaTech's success. "The investment environment is different. Venture capital companies wouldn't put in such large sums at such an early stage."[167] The amount that the IRC was able to spend on its numerous patents would also be hard for the College to match.

The precedent, however, is not lost. ApaTech was an early example of the College using its scientific expertise not simply to publish in the leading academic journals, but to translate its results into production, for the benefit of the public.

165. Brown, G. Interview for this history. 2011.
166. Bonfield, W, op cit.
167. Brown, G, op cit.

The BUPT partnership

The HongFu campus, Beijing University of Posts and Telecommunications, Beijing, China.

How many people using a mobile think about climate change? The impact of mobile phone use is now as great as that of air travel. A call on a mobile uses 30 times as much energy as the same call on a landline. But mobiles aren't going away; the phenomenon known as 'fixed/mobile substitution' may be irreversible. If there's no going back, there needs to be a better way forward: green technology for telecoms. That is just one area of research explored in a unique international partnership.

The Beijing University of Posts and Telecommunications (BUPT) is a prestigious institution, specialising in telecommunications including electronic engineering and computer science. It is designated a 'key university' – one of the top hundred of the 2,000 universities in China – by the Chinese Ministry of Education. The School of Electronic Engineering and Computer Science at QM has had a productive working relationship with BUPT since 1999, based on shared research interests, in addition to the number of BUPT graduates who came to Mile End for masters programmes. In 2003, however, the relationship moved to a different level, with a radical proposal from the anglophile President of BUPT, Professor Lin Jintong. He suggested that the two universities should develop a joint programme of study, operated at BUPT but using academics from both institutions, with a jointly devised curriculum. Students would graduate with degrees from both BUPT and the University of London.

Getting the Joint Programme underway was hard work but not problematic. Each side needed to understand the other's systems and procedures, to arrive at a qualification that would have recognition in both countries and beyond. The nature of the subject certainly simplified things: the content of engineering, unlike politics, say, or philosophy, is not affected by culture. Teaching styles, however, do differ, and this precisely is one of the strengths of the programme: Chinese education focuses on mathematical rigour, UK on problem-solving and the need for students to think for themselves; the combination gives them an adaptability that a single academic culture would find hard to emulate.

The visionary aim of the Joint Programme is to create graduates who can operate successfully in the global community. BUPT on its own can teach the engineering elements. What QM can add is the Western perspective, the skills and awareness that enable engineers to function in the commercial world: the legal framework, understanding of management systems and styles and focus on personal development. Professor Lin saw that the growth in the Chinese economy and the rise in manufacturing capability made it essential for Chinese engineers to understand the international context of their work, whether they aimed to work in China or abroad.

Undergraduate programmes
The Partnership offers three undergraduate programmes: BSc(Eng) E-Commerce Engineering with Law; BSc(Eng) Telecommunications Engineering with Management; and BSc(Eng) Internet of Things Engineering. All three run over four years, the standard duration for a Chinese first degree; the first year includes an intensive English language course, as all teaching is in English.

Joint Programme E-Commerce Engineering with Law:

Examples of taught modules

Module	Taught by
Advanced Mathematics	BUPT
Digital Circuit Design	QM
Internet Programming	BUPT
Probability Theory & Stochastic Statistics	BUPT
Introductory Java Programming	QM
Computer Crime	QM
Intellectual Property Foundation	QM

The programme brings together two academic cultures, and has to meet the criteria of each for degrees to be awarded. For example, all BUPT students are required to pass every module, including the Chinese compulsory ones, to graduate. Although QM has no such requirement, the more demanding standard prevails. Equally, QM requires the use of an external examiner; this is unknown in China, but is adopted for the Joint Programme degrees.

Laurie Cuthbert, Dean for China Operations, reflects on the experience of teaching at BUPT:
It's possible to do more, and in more depth, than on a UK undergraduate programme. That's partly having more time: it's a four-year degree, and there is space in the programme for approximately 25 per cent more material than in the UK. Chinese students also have a much better grounding in maths before they start.

We thought that it would be very different teaching here, but students are the same everywhere; they're just normal 18- to 22-year-olds. But they are more demanding; they complain if anyone ends a lecture early, or if you don't make it interesting. There's a greater value put on teaching and learning, just as the Scots generally value education more highly than the English.

One cultural point we see is that students don't like asking questions in class; instead they'll crowd round afterwards, to ask you one-to-one. So you could have 50 people raising questions at the end of a lecture. We have different techniques

to get round the reluctance. You can ask for volunteers to act something out, for instance, and that'll be fine.[168]

Zelun Zhang, now a PhD student at QM, reflects on the experience of learning in a different way:
Because I was from the Joint Programme between QM and BUPT ... the QM staff taught us when I was an undergraduate. The style is like kindly supervision and teaching, but lets you think and apply the knowledge by yourself. This kind of style gives us enough space to absorb and apply knowledge, but guides us when we are lost.[169]

Results from the undergraduate programme have been impressive. A hundred per cent of graduates to date have gone on to postgraduate study or employment. In 2011 84 per cent progressed to a masters or PhD; 68 per cent are going abroad to the UK and, increasingly, the United States. This is a record for QM, for BUPT and, according to a Vice-Director of the Ministry of Education, a record for China.

At the graduation ceremony in June 2011, when acknowledging the students' achievements, the current President of BUPT, Professor Binxing Fang, said how proud he was to be able to claim that the young people in front of him were students at his university. Professor Simon Gaskell, Principal of QM, noted that there were now over 1,600 graduates of the Joint Programme who were making huge inroads in employment, postgraduate study and research, as well as fostering wider knowledge about the importance of an international education. This was a theme also touched on by Mr Christopher Wood, Deputy Minister at the British Embassy in Beijing, who saw graduates making important contributions to the social and economic development of both countries.

The obvious destination for Joint Programme graduates would seem to be QM; but sadly, given the success of the Joint Programme, numbers are declining. 'The perception is that the UK government doesn't want them,' says Laurie Cuthbert. 'It's harder to get visas, the fees are

168. Cuthbert, L. Interview for this history. 2011.
169. Zhang, Z. Written contribution to this history. 2011.

Professor Simon Gaskell, Principal, shaking the hand of a student graduating from the joint QM / BUPT programme.

going up. By contrast America is very welcoming.'[170]

Xiaofei Wang graduated in e-Commerce in 2008. She went on to a Masters in Industrial Engineering at the University of Pittsburg, and from there to a post in a US manufacturing company. 'The Joint Programme,' she says, 'taught me strong communication and trouble-shooting skills, both of which are indispensable in my current job.'[171]

Xiaofei was by no means alone as a female engineering student in China; in fact almost 50 per cent of the Joint Programme students are female. Their grades are overall better than the men's: in 2010 80 per cent of the female students on the Telecommunications Engineering programme got a first. In a culture where the one-child policy still makes boys seem more important, many young women feel they have to work extra hard to prove themselves, and the results demonstrate their success.

170. Cuthbert, L, op cit.
171. Wang, X. http://www.qmul.ac.uk/alumni/profiles/ (Accessed 2012)

Research
The Green Telecoms project is just one research collaboration between QM and BUPT. Some results have already been published, and patents acquired. Staff are working closely with the Chinese telecoms industry: two of the four main telecommunications manufacturers worldwide are now Chinese, so researchers are extremely well placed to contribute to future developments. This again makes the programme highly desirable for students.

Working across disciplines
Engineers do not just work with technology: they are involved with management, financial control, ensuring systems are safe and do not harm the environment, complying with regulations, ensuring an ethical approach, and so on. While an engineering degree needs to cover the basic science and technology, it must also include these non-technical aspects to be accredited under the Washington Accord on worldwide recognition. These competences are new to the Chinese education system, and the Joint Programme is

the first degree of its kind to be accredited in mainland China – in this case by the Institution of Engineering and Technology.

Management is a common component of many engineering degrees. What is less common is the addition of law; but engineers need to work in an industrial and commercial framework where legislation has an increasing impact on their work. The modules are not intended to turn Joint Programme graduates into lawyers, but to give young engineers an understanding of legal principles. The content is based on the very successful LLM degree in Computer and Communications Law given by the Centre for Commercial Law Studies (CCLS) at QM, one of the leading institutions for the study of commercial law in the world (see Chapter 13). CCLS staff modified the course's content to suit undergraduate engineers.

A new feature, added in 2011, has experts from the CCLS giving one-week guest appearances on the law modules to ensure that students on the Joint Programme learn the very latest concepts.

Logistics

Logistics is not only a taught module on the undergraduate programmes, but a vital skill for QM staff travelling to and from Beijing. All of them also teach at QM, so to minimise disruption, the programme at BUPT is arranged in week-long teaching blocks, four per module. Each block consists of five two-hour lectures (one per day), plus tutorials; with travelling time it means that staff are away for two weeks for each block. Most staff travel to and fro roughly once a month. The best planned schedules, however, are not proof against the vagaries of international travel: ash clouds and stolen passports all mean that cover has to be found for unavoidably absent lecturers. QM may well be Air China's most loyal customer – and of course, BUPT staff also visit London for meetings and conferences. In 2010–11, staff made a total of 200 round trips: but, Laurie Cuthbert points out, if the 2,000 students all came to the UK to study, that would be 2,000 round trips, and an even greater carbon footprint.

The future

The model of collaboration with BUPT is one that Laurie Cuthbert can see being replicated by other Schools at QM. It is based on a keen and practical respect for both academic traditions: it is not a British degree being taught in China, nor a new, confected institution, but a programme tailor-made for the needs of Chinese electronic engineers who will have the skills and confidence to work wherever their discipline takes them. (See chapter 21 for other initiatives).

Originally only open to Chinese students, the Joint Programmes are now open to students from the UK and around the world. For students planning to work in the field of communications, systems and networks, these Joint Programmes represent an incredible opportunity.

The international nature of the telecommunications industry, and the size and influence of China, means that employers everywhere will value graduates' knowledge and understanding of local conditions. Not to mention their mastery of the Chinese language.

Part 4:
The future

2012 and beyond

Tickets to Researchers' Night 2011. Researchers' Night is an EU funded, Europe-wide event bringing together the public and researchers once a year to celebrate research and show how it helps improve people's lives.

The future of higher education

In February 2012 the report was published of work commissioned to supplement the Coalition Government's 2011 White Paper on Higher Education entitled *A Review of University-Business Collaboration,* written by Professor Sir Tim Wilson. The report begins by stating its philosophy:

> The economic and social prosperity of the UK depends upon a healthy knowledge-based economy. In our globally competitive economic environment, never before has there been a greater need for a talented, enterprising workforce, for constant innovation in product and service development, for a thriving culture of entrepreneurship, for dynamic, leading-edge scientific and technological development and for world-class research that attracts investment. In collaboration with business, and with the support of government, the UK has the capability ... to be the source of strength in the UK's knowledge based economy of the twenty first century. [172]

The Department for Business, Innovation and Skills, announcing publication of the report, summarises its recommendations as:

for universities to be at the heart of the economy, promote growth and improve the employability of our graduates. [173]

The concepts and the wording are hardly new: this history has seen both repeatedly, in the twenty-seven years it covers. For universities and those concerned for higher education, it raises familiar questions. The model is encouraging for – say – biomedical research, and potential spin-offs such as ApaTech. It is presumably supportive of cardio-vascular research, though the benefits to the economy are more indirect (fewer days lost to illness; lower healthcare costs). But where does the Dr Williams's Centre for Dissenting Studies fit into this model? Does studying Drama in QM's top-rated department make a graduate more employable? By whose criteria?

The ongoing public debate on the function of higher education has become more public and more articulate. In August 2011, Professor Stefan Collini of Cambridge University published an extended article in the *London Review of Books,* responding to the White Paper. Early on, he comments:

> Since perhaps the 1970s, certainly the 1980s, official discourse has been increasingly colonised by an economistic idiom ... British society has been subject to a deliberate campaign ... to elevate the status of business and commerce and to make 'contributing to economic growth' the overriding goal of a whole swathe of social, cultural and intellectual activities which had previously been understood and valued in other terms ...

> Higher education policy has been something of a barometer of the growing dominance of the worldview expressed in these phrases. [174]

172. Wilson, T. (2012) *A Review of University-Business Collaboration.* London, Department for Business, Innovation and Skills.
173. retrieved from www.bis.gov.uk/policies/higher-education
174. Collini, S. (2011) *From Robbins to McKinsey.* London, *London Review of Books,* vol 33 No.16.

The White Paper that Stefan Collini examines moves the higher education debate from tuition fees to the wider issue of university funding. It proposes a complex system for the allocation of student numbers, and therefore fee income. Its express intention is to create competition between universities and to privilege student choice. While Stefan Collini queries the latter – 'The paradox of real learning is that you don't get what you "want"'[175] – the journalist Simon Jenkins believes the emphasis on students' experience of learning is essential. After 1988, he writes:

Teacher contact time with students dwindled and staff student ratios tripled. Ask any student: in many universities the teaching is nowadays plain awful. Yet the appetite for research grew to a third of budgeted academic time, and was met … The monasteries abandoned the laity and spent their money on private prayer.[176]

While this debate continues, the Higher Education Funding Council for England has announced its new Research Excellence Framework, to replace the Research Assessment Exercise. Funding bodies, the HEFCE announces, will 'use the outcomes to inform the selective allocation of their research funding to HEIs [Higher Education Institutions] with effect from 2015–16.'[177] The precise impact of this change is not yet known, but the implication of increased competition has caused concern.

Whatever the pressures of funding, universities can of course aim both to provide excellent teaching and to conduct excellent research. Professor Susan Dilly, Vice-Principal for Teaching and Learning, states:

Teaching and Learning at QM has developed significantly over the last decade with increases in undergraduate student numbers and the quality of their entry qualifications. The period has also seen major improvement in our research standing nationally so that we should naturally move to having a greater number of postgraduate taught and postgraduate research

students who would benefit from Queen Mary's research strengths.[178]

It is an uncertain time for universities, and QM among them. As this history indicates, however, in the past quarter of a century times have not often been certain. There are significant questions for the College as it considers how to maintain its core values of excellence and accessibility while adapting to external changes that it may either welcome or deplore.

The issue of student tuition fees has already had to be addressed. The new system allows universities to charge home students up to £9,000 per year from 2012–13. QM has opted for this maximum charge, backed up by a substantial bursary fund for students from low-income families. The Principal, Professor Simon Gaskell, explains how this difficult decision was reached.

I found the early response of some institutions – essentially, 'because we're worth it' – offensive. I thought we should work out the actual cost to the College of providing these courses, using the best possible methodology. That meant taking into account not only teaching but infrastructure costs, the component of academic research that feeds into undergraduate teaching, and the cost of providing bursaries. It came to £8,900 for Humanities and Social Sciences, going up to £10,600 for Science and Engineering, and £16,000 for Medicine and Dentistry, even taking into account some continuing direct government subsidy for the latter areas. The question for us has become: how can we ourselves subsidise these courses?[179]

There will inevitably be more than one answer. Further use of the College estate – renting out student accommodation in the vacations, for example, as is happening for the 2012 Olympics. Some measure of cross-subsidy will be feasible. Financial planning was at its most difficult in this period before the new fees system began, and when the linkage between lower fees and potential student numbers was abruptly announced. Other initiatives can also be at once useful and a

175. ibid.
176. Jenkins, S. (15 March 2012) 'Universities need the guts to break this Faustian pact with research'. London, *The Guardian*.
177. retrieved from www.hefce.ac.uk/research/ref
178. Dilly, S. (2011) written contribution to this history.
179. Gaskell, S. (2012) interview for this history.

cause for concern. Universities are expected to make the student experience more personal, and this is no doubt desirable: but what exactly does it mean? Class contact hours only tell part of the story. 'Half an hour's one-to-one email conversation with a lecturer trumps an hour's lecture in a group of a hundred students,' Simon Gaskell asserts. 'A brief interaction can be priceless. I remember once working very late, and a student emailed me at 2am with a question; so I replied. That student felt that getting an answer in the middle of the night was amazing.'[180]

As this book has demonstrated, official opinion on the function of Higher Education has changed dramatically in the past twenty-seven years, and equally dramatic changes in policy have followed. The present tuition fee system supposes that the benefit of studying for a degree is to the individual, not to society, and consequently moves the burden of payment entirely to the student. This thinking, Simon Gaskell believes, has become entrenched. 'In the last decade, potential students have been told only about the usefulness of a degree in getting a job and earning more money. No-one has told them about the fulfilment, the intellectual challenge, the enjoyment of life, the prospect of becoming better citizens in a democratic society. The question for universities is how to mitigate this, especially for students where there's no family history of higher education, and no-one to tell them it's about more than money.'[181]

At the same time, one consequence of attracting greater numbers into higher education is that the bar for entry into the professions may in future simply be set higher: at Masters rather than first-degree level. By 2015, people may be graduating with debts of £50,000, taking into account living costs as well as fees. Will those from lower-income homes once again be deterred from studying for the higher level qualification they need, by the prospect of even greater debt? Simon Gaskell believes that a new approach will be needed, to ensure that postgraduate education doesn't become the new sole preserve of the rich. Employers, for example, could be encouraged to identify talented graduates and support them

through a further period of study. Despite the instrumentalist approach of the Wilson Review, he believes that many employers in recruiting look beyond specific job training to, for example, analytical skills.

The College in 2012
Faced with the complex changes in funding and potential political pressures, QM has taken some significant steps to reinforce its position. One, announced in March 2012, is joining the Russell Group of twenty-four leading UK universities. Membership is by invitation, and demonstrates a recognition of the College's present status. The Russell Group prides itself on excellence in research, teaching and learning, graduate employability, and links with business and the public sector. Its representatives are frequently heard on radio and television, in discussion of higher education issues. The visibility that membership of the Group offers can only enhance its recruitment of high calibre students and academics. Sir Nicholas Montagu, Chair of Council at QM, reflects:

Queen Mary in 2012 feels like what it is – an already leading university on an upward trajectory. The developments covered in this history have come together in a way that is in the most literal sense coherent. The result is a university which is in the top UK dozen for research, and which at the same time can boast an enviable record on widening participation, in terms both of ethnic mix and of students from non-traditional backgrounds.[182]

In the same month, QM announced a new strategic partnership with the University of Warwick. The aim is to combine resources in teaching, research and recruitment; working together to widen access for students from disadvantaged backgrounds, for example, and building on, amongst other initiatives, QM's long term intervention strategy (detailed in Chapter 19). Post-doctoral research fellowships drawing on expertise in both institutions have already been announced. They include *Ethnicity and Mental Health In Post-War Britain; Discrete Mathematics; Functional*

180. ibid.
181. ibid.

182. Montagu, N. (2012). Written contribution to this history

Molecular Materials, and, intriguingly, *Rewiring the Renaissance*. A joint Book festival will be held at Warwick in 2012; in the following year, Professor Amanda Vickery from QM and Professor Richard Aldrich from Warwick will lead a Literary Festival at Mile End. It seems likely that collaborations of this kind will become increasingly important in the sector.

In April 2012, Barts and The London NHS Trust joined two other Trusts, Newham University Hospital and Whipps Cross University Hospital, to form Barts Health NHS Trust; and shortly before, in October 2011, QM and Barts and The London NHS Trust joined UCL partners (UCLP) – to form the largest Academic Health Science System (AHSS) in the world.

Academic Health Science Systems (AHSS) are clusters of healthcare organisations and academic institutions that align education, research and clinical practice to maximise the health of the populations they serve, and to speed the development of new diagnostics and treatments into clinical practice in both communities and hospitals.

David Fish, Managing Director of UCL Partners added: "This is a tremendously exciting opportunity to deliver step change advances in health and healthcare through this new partnership with major providers of clinical care and academic excellence. Beyond our primary service to the local and national communities it will enable a real powerhouse for global competitiveness supporting the crucial role of London in healthcare innovation and the associated economic benefits."[183]

Links with the federal University of London remain no less important. QM has remained an active member throughout this period, taking a full role in the governance of the University. The importance of the federation has perhaps diminished relatively over the years, as the Colleges grew larger and were given direct financial access to the Higher Education Funding Council for England (HEFCE) and its predecessors. The Colleges are also keen competitors. Nevertheless,

the College continues to draw great benefits from the University, especially in the Humanities where the University Library, at Senate House in Bloomsbury, is much valued, as is the Institute for Advanced Study in areas such as Law, History or English. QM continues to award University of London degrees, though it now has its own degree awarding powers if it wishes to exercise them.

Internally, too, the College continues to adapt. As part of the celebrations for the 125th anniversary of the People's Palace, a new inter-disciplinary centre will be launched in Autumn 2012, to both reflect and update the original vision. The Centre for Public Engagement will build on the College's existing initiatives – the Mile End Group, People's Palace Projects and the Centre of the Cell, for example – spreading best practice and encouraging new ideas for engagement.

QM in the public eye

Turn on *Today*, BBC Radio 4's best-known daily news programme, and it seems you have a good chance of hearing someone from QM: Matt Parker, Maths Outreach Co-ordinator, for instance, on the teaching of Maths in schools (see below). Try the various Radio 3 cultural programmes, and Professors Maria Delgado or Peggy Reynolds may be in conversation with artists and writers. On television in early 2012 you could find Professor Peter Hennessy discussing *Class and Culture* with Melvyn Bragg, Professor Miri Rubin in *Christina: a Medieval Life* with Michael Wood, and Professor Amanda Vickery with Lucy Worsley on *The History of the Home*; in the *Guardian* newspaper, Professor Kairbaan Hodivala-Dilke wrote on the subject of avoiding cancer.

These examples – there are more – not only show that QM has some high-profile academics: public intellectuals, who make their knowledge and their capacity for reflection available to the widest possible audience. They help to create and maintain the 'virtuous circle' by which the College is increasingly recognised for excellent scholarship and a commitment to disseminating often complex ideas.

183. http://www.qmul.ac.uk/media/news/items/smd/57483.html
    Accessed July 2012.

Other, non-broadcast events reinforce the point. The Maths Outreach project aims to encourage young people to study Maths at A-level and beyond. Matt Parker, Maths Outreach Co-ordinator and 'stand-up mathematician,' puts on an interactive maths magic show in schools. In October 2012 Matt won the Joshua Phillips Award for Innovation in Science Engagement, which recognises innovative approaches to engaging the public with science. His performances also include *Your Days Are Numbered: the maths of death.*

Professor Lois Weaver of the Department of Drama delivered her inaugural lecture, *What Tammy Found Out: a front line report from the back porch, the schoolyard and the dinner table*, in March 2012 in the persona of Tammy Whynot. Tammy claims to be a trailer park survivor who gave up a career in country music to become a lesbian performance artist and a university researcher. Tammy is dedicated to the facilitation of public engagement in social and economic justice and experimental forms of democracy. She applies her considerable courage and uncomplicated curiosity to her research project, *What Tammy Needs to Know*… about education and class; high art and popular culture; performance and human rights; feminism and femininity; and most recently, sex and aging. The lecture presented Tammy's findings from her 62 years of research.

Less dramatically, but no less significantly, the Mile End Group has also been in the news. In February 2012, members of the Group were at Downing Street for the launch of the history section of the no.10 website. The Group had had the tempting request to re-write the biographies of eleven Prime Ministers, from Clement Attlee to Gordon Brown: a remarkable accolade, given the inevitable political sensitivities involved. A few weeks later, the Mile End Group hosted Ed Balls MP, who spoke to one of the regular meetings on the perhaps equally sensitive subject of being Shadow Chancellor.

Ambitions

The College is clearly in good shape to face a future that may bring many challenges. The task is to devise strategies for managing the impact and continuing to develop. In his introduction to the 2010–15 Strategic Plan, referred to in chapter 12, Simon Gaskell reasserts the College's core values:

> In developing our strategic imperatives, we are guided by the ideal – unchanged for centuries – of a university as a centre for the development of fundamental ideas and the expansion of the boundaries of knowledge, independent of political and other transient opinions.[184]

Targets to be reached by 2015 include:
- ranking within the top ten broadly based UK universities according to research quality, and within the top twenty according to research power [*quantity*].
- increase of 50 per cent in number of post-doctoral research assistants
- doubling of number of PhD students
- place in top decile of UK universities for student entry qualifications
- doubling of numbers of students from beyond the EU
- 30 per cent increase in students taught on programmes based outside the UK
- 50 per cent increase in students working in local community[185]

These are, Simon Gaskell acknowledges, ambitious; but none the worse for that. They are a statement of the College's faith in its existing capability and its capacity for further improvement. 'When I started here in 2009,' he says, 'academic self-confidence had not yet caught up with the reality of recent achievement. That's changed now. It's not that I think we have to meet a hundred per cent of these targets – if we did, I'd feel we hadn't been ambitious enough. But I expect us to make significant progress on all of them. We're saying, to academics as well as to the wider world, the work of this College is of high enough quality to harbour such ambitions.'[186]

184. Strategic Plan 2010–15 (n.d.) London, QM
185. ibid.
186. Gaskell op.cit.

Appendices

Appendix A: QM Officeholders 1985–2012

Chairmen of Council
1982–1989   Sir Arthur Drew
1989–1995   Martin Harris
1995–2003   Sir Christopher France
2003–2009   Dr Colette Bowe
2009–current Sir Nicholas Montagu

Treasurers
1983–1989   WL Cockburn
1989–2000   Stanley Wright
2000–2010   Charles Perrin
2010–current Simon Linnett

Principals
1976–1986   Sir James Menter
1986–1989   Professor Ian Butterworth
1989–1990   Professor Graham Zellick (*Acting Principal*)
1990–1998   Professor Graham Zellick
1998–2008   Professor Adrian Smith
2008–2009   Professor Philip Ogden (*Acting Principal*)
2009–current Professor Simon Gaskell

Senior Vice Principals
(Senior Pro Principals before 1989)
1987–1990   Professor Trevor Smith
1989–1990   Professor Graham Zellick
1991–1999   Professor Molly Scopes
2005–2011   Professor Philip Ogden

Vice Principals (Pro Principals before 1989)
1978–1986   Professor K W Sykes
1985–1987   Professor Trevor Smith
1987–1989   Professor MA Laughton
1988–1990   Professor J M Charap
1987–1988   Professor Ian Roxburgh
1989–1990   Professor J Chalker
1990–1991   Dr P M Scopes
1992–1998   Professor Ken Young

Wardens of Barts and The London School of Medicine and Dentistry (1995–2011)
Vice Principal (Health) (2011–current)
1995–1996   Professor Sir Colin Berry
1996–2001   Professor AS McNeish
2001–2011   Professor Sir Nicholas Wright
2011–current Professor Richard Trembath

Vice Principals (Science and Engineering)
1997–2002   Professor John Edgington
2002–2005   Professor Malcolm McCallum
2005–2009   Professor Ursula Martin
2009–2010   Professor Ray Playford
        (*Acting Vice Principal*)
2010–current Professor Jeremy Kilburn

Vice Principals
(Humanities and Social Sciences)
1998–2006   Professor Philip Ogden
2006–2010   Professor Trevor Dadson
2010–current Professor Morag Shiach

Vice Principal (Academic Planning and Development 1999–2001)
(Academic Policy 2001–2005)
1999–2005   Professor A D Olver

Vice-Principal (Strategic development)
2001–2005   Professor D M Williams

Vice-Principal (NHS Liaison 2003–05)
(Strategic Alliances 2005–10)
2003–2006   Professor P G Kopelman
2006–2010   Professor Ray Playford

Vice-Principals (Teaching and Learning)
2005–2010   Professor Morag Shiach
2010–current Professor Susan Dilly

Vice Principal
(Research and International Affairs)
2010–current Professor Evelyn Welch

Vice Principal (External Relations and Public Engagement)
2012–current Professor Peter McOwan

Heads of the Administration
1979–1991   Grahame Williams
1991–2004   Keith Aldred
2004–current Dean Curtis

Appendix B:

Student headcount at QM 1985–86; 2001–02 to 2011–12

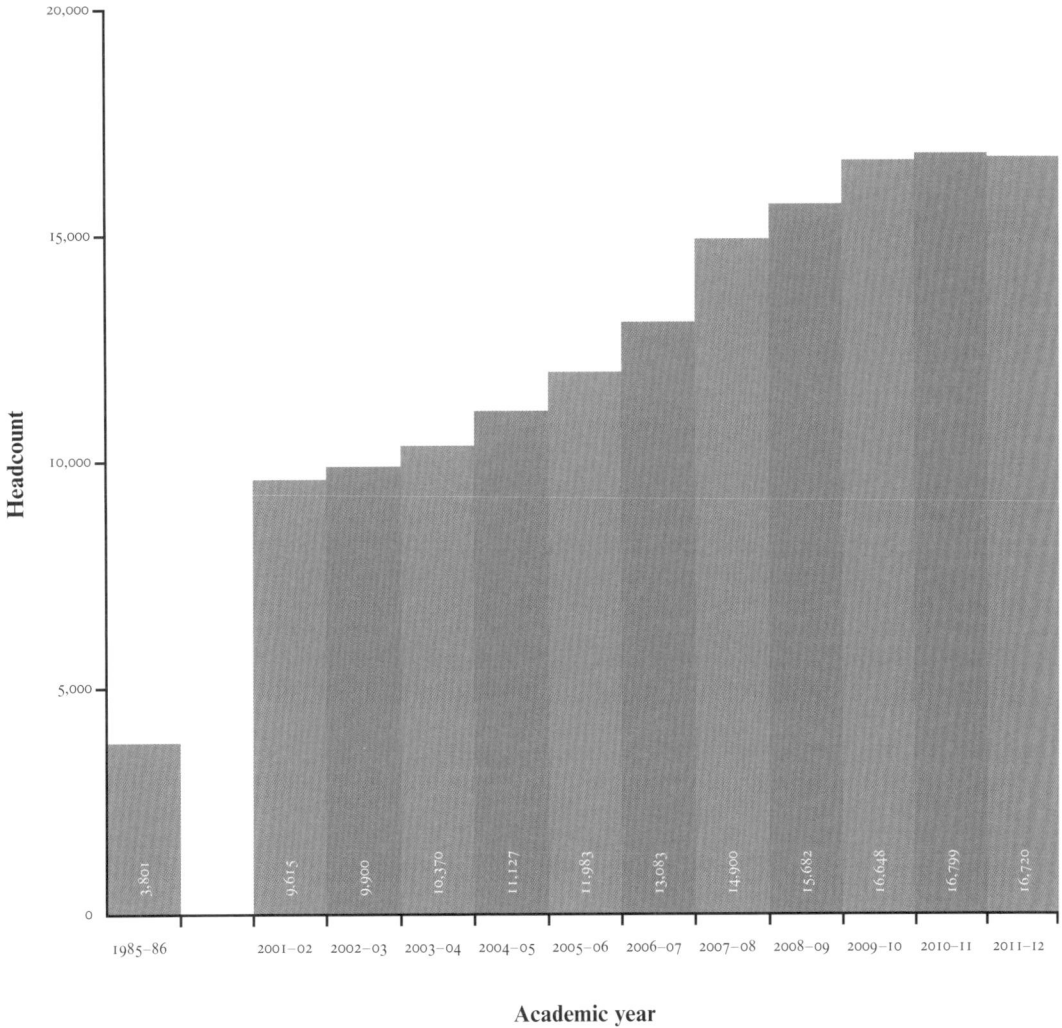

Headcount (y-axis)

1985–86	3,801
2001–02	9,615
2002–03	9,900
2003–04	10,370
2004–05	11,127
2005–06	11,983
2006–07	13,083
2007–08	14,900
2008–09	15,682
2009–10	16,648
2010–11	16,799
2011–12	16,720

Academic year

Figures include BUPT students, but exclude
students who are distance learning outside the UK

189

Appendix C:

Total income QM 1985–86; 2000–01 to 2010–11

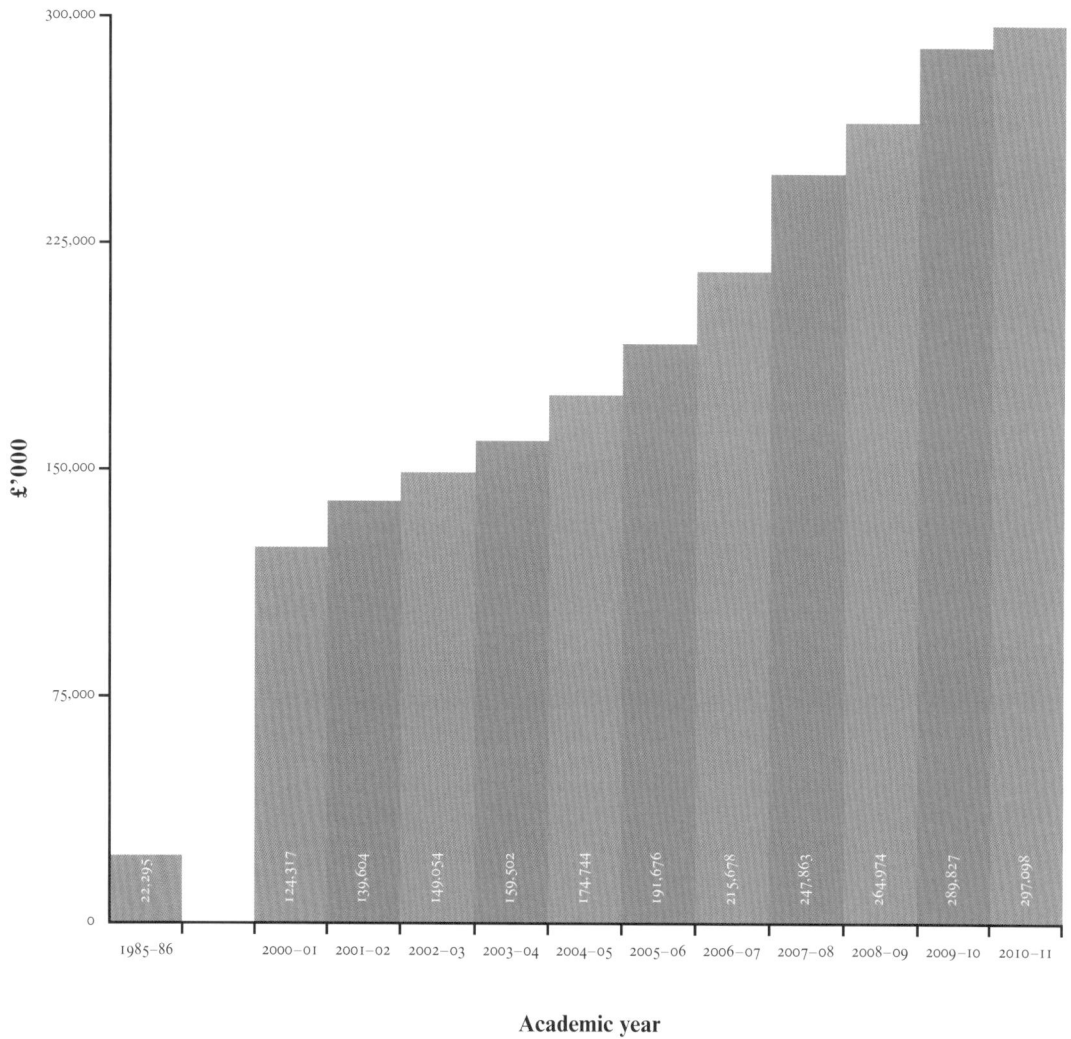

£'000

1985–86	2000–01	2001–02	2002–03	2003–04	2004–05	2005–06	2006–07	2007–08	2008–09	2009–10	2010–11
22,295	124,317	139,604	149,054	159,502	174,744	191,676	215,678	247,863	264,974	289,827	297,098

Academic year

Appendix D:

Research grants and contracts QM 1985–86; 2000–01 to 2010–11

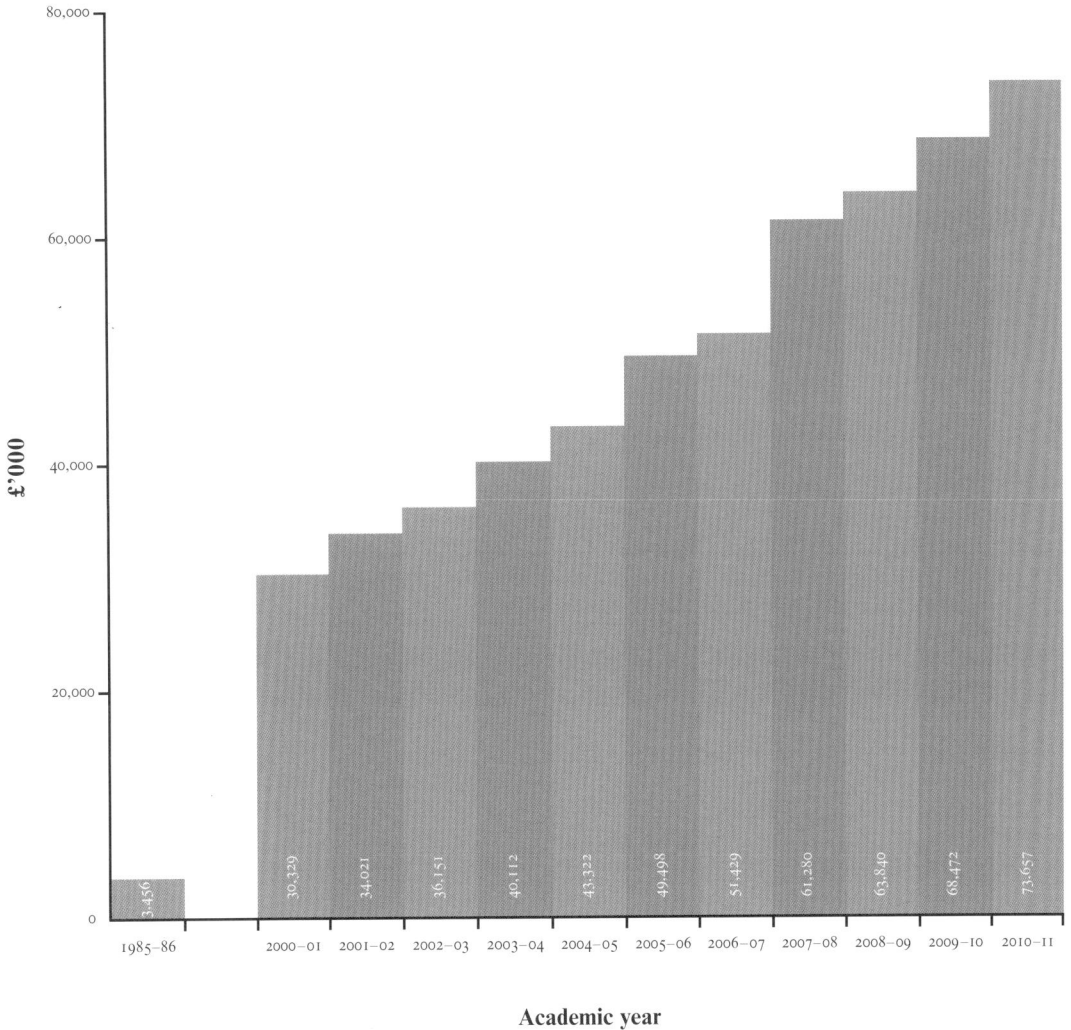

£'000

1985–86	3,456
2000–01	30,329
2001–02	34,021
2002–03	36,151
2003–04	40,112
2004–05	43,322
2005–06	49,498
2006–07	51,429
2007–08	61,280
2008–09	63,840
2009–10	68,472
2010–11	73,657

Academic year

Appendix E:

Queen Mary was placed 13th out of 132 UK institutions by *The Times Higher Education* in its analysis of the Research Assessment Exercise 2008

1	Institute of Cancer Research
2	University of Cambridge
3	London School of Hygiene & Tropical Medicine
4	London School of Economics and Political Science
5	University of Oxford
6	Imperial College London
7	University College London
8	University of Manchester
9	University of Warwick
10	University of York
11	University of Essex
12	University of Edinburgh
13	**Queen Mary, University of London**
14	Durham University
=14	University of St Andrews
=14	University of Sheffield
=14	University of Southampton
=14	University of Leeds
=14	University of Bristol
20	University of Bath

Index

Academic subjects are listed by subject, rather than department, faculty or school